# IN FORMATION

# IN FORMATION

## ONE WOMAN'S RISE THROUGH THE RANKS OF THE U.S. AIR FORCE

### LIEUTENANT COLONEL
# CHERYL DIETRICH USAF (RET.)

YUCCA

Yucca Publishing books may be purchased in bulk at special discounts for
sales promotion, corporate gifts, fund-raising, or educational purposes. Special
editions can also be created to specifications. For details, contact the Special Sales
Department, Yucca Publishing, 307 West 36th Street, 11th Floor, New York, NY
10018 or yucca@skyhorsepublishing.com.

Yucca Publishing® is an imprint of Skyhorse Publishing, Inc.®, a Delaware
corporation.

Visit our website at www.yuccapub.com.

10 9 8 7 6 5 4 3 2 1

Library of Congress Cataloging-in-Publication Data is available on file.

Cover design by Yucca Publishing
Cover photo credit: Michael Mauney

Print ISBN: 978-1-63158-067-3
Ebook ISBN: 978-1-63158-075-8


Printed in the United States of America

3 2 0 1 4   5 3 2 7

# IN FORMATION

# CHAPTER ONE

# "IN THE BEGINNING"

In the flat country of South Texas, dusk turns to night like someone hit a light switch. One moment I had been hurrying after Bronson's stocky figure twenty feet ahead. Then suddenly, she faded into a scrambling shape in the darkness. I slowed and worked my way carefully through the scrub. I could hear her breath coming out in ragged pants, her frantic words, "Got to get out, get out of here, got to get out." She didn't seem to notice me following her. When I reached out and touched her arm, she jumped, then stopped. I could feel her trembling.

"It's okay," I said. "It's just me—OT Duncan. I'm in your squadron." Frantically I tried to remember her first name. Something with an *a* at the end. *Martha, no, Elena, Darla, Linda—Brenda, that's it!* "Brenda, I'm Cheryl. What's going on? Hey, I know we've all had times when we wanted to get out of this place, but there are easier ways, you know."

I was just trying to lighten things up, but she pulled away and started walking, so swiftly I could barely keep up. She mumbled something.

"What?"

"Fence. Can't go out the gate. They'll stop me. Got to get to the fence."

"How will you get out? The fence is high."

"Climb. Got to get out. Can't breathe."

She slowed down as I kept her talking, asking her how she would get over the fence, where she would go. Her replies were mainly a repetition of "got to get out." Gradually I turned our steps so we were walking just outside the perimeter of light that spilled out of the Officer Training School barracks windows. When she realized where we were, she started to shy away.

"It's okay." I said. "We don't have to go inside. I'm tired. Are you tired? Let's go sit over here in the dark."

I led her to a low wall. I kept talking, all the while scanning the driveway leading up to the building, looking for someone to arrive or something to happen. Someone or something to rescue me from what felt like a ton of responsibility. I was not ready for this. What would I do if she made a dart across the dark fields, headed for the fence?

Just fifteen minutes ago I'd gotten a note to go see another officer trainee I worked with. She had Bronson in her barracks room, trying to calm her down. Bronson's eyes darted frantically in every direction. Her hands moved up to pull her hair, then release it. She opened and closed her fists, grabbed at her neck as if to push some blockage out of her throat. She heaved harsh breaths, muttering low, "Got to get out," over and over. We asked her what was wrong but got nothing except, "Got to get out. Can't breathe. Got to get out." Eventually, she settled down a little and stood there panting, looking down at the floor.

My friend looked at Brenda, then at me. She cleared her throat. "I almost forgot. I need to go make that phone call I was telling you about."

"Of course," I said. "Go on. I'll stay here and chat with OT Bronson."

At that moment, Bronson had pushed me aside and took off. She ran down the corridor, through the outside door and into the night, while we stood gaping after her. "Go on," I said. "I'll stay with her, while you get help."

4

So I had no one to blame but myself that I was sitting in the dark with a desperate, frantic woman I didn't even know. I started talking about harmless subjects. I asked her about her family. She talked about her brother. I asked her about her boyfriends, her favorite movies, anything to distract her attention from the despair inside her till she was someplace safe (till I was someplace safe). I didn't hear anything she said. My ears strained to catch the sound of a motor, maybe even a siren. We sat there for perhaps half an hour or perhaps through an eternal night—we are, I'm convinced, still sitting there somewhere in the space-time continuum.

I felt a breeze ruffling my hair, cooling after the heat of the day. I couldn't enjoy it, not with my body so tight with tension, my mind on edge. I was outside, alone with a woman who could turn violent at any minute. Not to mention—*wait! Wind in my hair. Shit, no hat. I'm outside and I'm not wearing a hat.* Just twelve weeks ago that would have meant nothing to me, but now it felt like the worst part of the whole mess. I felt naked. *No hat no hat no hat* pulsed in me like a heartbeat. Just days away from commissioning, and I'd committed one of the cardinal sins of Officer Training School.

An ambulance slid into view, no flashing lights, no siren. It pulled up in front of the building, a car behind it. "We're over here," I yelled. Brenda started. I touched her arm, gently but prepared to grab if she started to run. "It's okay. They're here to help you get out."

A man in medical whites walked toward us, his voice reassuringly calm. "Hey, Brenda. I'm Lou. Let us help you. Okay?"

She was breathing heavily and seemed poised for flight. But he approached her with such quiet confidence, I could feel her body relax. Something inside her melted, and she started to cry.

"You go ahead and cry all you want, honey." He took her arm and led her away.

I felt dizzy and slumped back down on the wall, only to jump up when I realized a captain was standing in front of me. I saluted him and rushed to explain. "I'm sorry I'm not wearing a hat, sir. I had to run out—"

He cut me off with an impatient wave of his hand. "Doesn't matter. Go back in. You all did good work tonight. I'll let your commander know."

"What will happen to OT Bronson?"

"She'll go to the psych ward at Wilford Hall, then we'll see."

Later I lay awake listening to my roommates, one lightly snoring, the other muttering in her sleep, the creaking of iron bedsteads as their bodies shifted. My mind reeled with fragments from the night's events: Brenda's panic, the solitary dark and the light breeze, the overwhelming sense of responsibility, the nakedness of my uncovered head.

I had known the panic and suffocation Brenda felt. But I had experienced them in lonely nights of prayer and tears, kneeling on the floor of a silent apartment, smothering in the demanding confines of faith. So I understood what could make a person just cut and run. But what Brenda ran from, I ran to. The U.S. Air Force as refuge.

A year earlier, I had been kneeling in the narrow alcove that served as my living room. "Help me, O Lord, for my eyes have grown sick of their weeping." I repeated it over and over with the vague sense that I was quoting from a Psalm. An ancient agony sounded in my plea. I was weary. My body longed for sleep, but my spirit starved for . . . what? Relief? Comfort? Maybe just recognition.

I had been an ordained Presbyterian minister for less than a year, but this was not the first midnight to find me here after a particularly bad day at the hospital. A day trying to comfort parents who'd been told there was no more the doctors could do for their little girl. Perhaps crying with the young wife, now widowed mother, whose husband had keeled over from a heart attack, no warnings, no previous signs. Perhaps it was an accident victim or the delivery of a dead baby. Any of a number of cruelties life dishes out, to which I, as a chaplain, was supposed to bring the assurance of a loving God.

It's normal to be angry with God, to have doubts even. But I had never doubted, not even then, not even now. God exists, no question about it in my mind. We can't truly understand the mysteries inside ourselves, much less the mysteries of the universe. And God, by definition, is beyond our knowing, a being we only comprehend through metaphor. The warmest of these is God as parent: divine Father, great Mother.

"Help me, Father." I sat back on my heels, gulping in breaths of air, groping for a tissue. *I should go back to bed*, I thought. *Tomorrow morning comes too early.*

But I continued to sit there, trying to calm myself, stop the tears, steady my breath so the hiccups that threatened would settle down. As I rhythmically inhaled and exhaled, I began to think of my mother. I'd battled a bad sinus infection earlier that spring. Some days it felt like knives jabbing into my head, my cheeks, my teeth. One particularly bad Friday afternoon, I called her. "I want my mommy," I said and laughed to show I was being facetious. Except I wasn't. She heard the need underneath my silly words and told me to come home.

I'd had just enough strength that afternoon to drive the hour from my apartment in Dayton to my mother and stepfather's house in Cincinnati. Mom tucked me into bed, brought me tea, sat and chatted quietly while I dozed off and on. She couldn't make my misery go away but she comforted me, made it possible for me to bear the pain and go back to work on Monday.

So as I sat crying and praying on the floor that night—the last night I would do so—I thought of my mother's love, her acceptance, her open arms. *I want my mommy*. It was as simple as that. My mother would never let me go through torment without at least a word of comfort. The tears that had been flowing steadily for months dried suddenly and a new question occurred to me. Was the God I'd believed in all my life a worse parent than my lovely but flawed mortal mother?

"I know about Jesus dying on the cross for me," I said aloud. "But that was almost two thousand years ago. What have you done for me lately?"

I argued with God that night, rudely, roughly, with a "last chance, bucko" attitude. I threw down angry challenges. I was irreverent, to say the least, surly, poking and prodding at a divinity I wanted to believe in. I stopped my ravings periodically to listen for a whisper of recognition, to look for a sign that God knew I was there, to smell the air for a whiff of ethereal essence blooming in my stale, smoky apartment. But I heard, I saw, I smelled and sensed nothing. Nothing at all.

I did not lose my faith. I discarded it, shed it like a snake does her skin, with pain and out of necessity. It may still linger there in my Dayton apartment. I never stopped believing in God. I just stopped believing that faith mattered. The dream was gone—not to mention the career.

I had a contract to fulfill at the hospital, where they had no problem with an apostate chaplain as long as I showed up for work on time. I used those months to explore my options. It was the late seventies, and the world had cracked wide open for women. I had lots of choices but no idea what I wanted to do—a situation both scary and exhilarating.

In seminary, my friends and I used to joke, "Well, if the ministry doesn't work out, we can always join the Army." Liberal pacifists that we were, we cracked up at the absurdity of the notion. Now the stale old joke kept buzzing around me like an annoying fly that I swatted at absently, as I considered the options open to me.

What did I want? I wanted to travel. I wanted to get out of Ohio, to see the world. I wanted Greek temples and Ayers Rock and herds of zebras running on an African plain. I wanted Carnival in Rio, the accordions of Paris, the beer of Germany. India, Japan, Argentina,

Israel, Lebanon. I pulled out maps of the world and slobbered over them like pornography. I tried to talk a friend into going with me.

"Around the world," I said. "Stopping wherever we want, as long as we want, getting jobs, just enough to pay the way." She refused politely, but her voice hinted that I'd gone mad. I had the dream but not the courage to go by myself.

The fly buzzing around me whispered, "In the military, you could travel."

Just four years, that was the commitment for a commission—time to save a little money and figure out what I really wanted to do. I totted the advantages up: an opportunity to travel, decent pay, medical benefits, an opportunity to travel, no one asking how many words a minute I could type, someone else making decisions for me. Did I mention travel?

Disadvantages: Joining the military-industrial complex. Becoming part of the war machine. Oh, and calisthenics, marching, all that saluting, the uniforms.

The voice of pacifism nagged in my brain, so I cobbled together a rationalization to quiet it. Like it or not, war was a reality, and the military as necessary as the local police force or the security guard at the bank. Who was I to admit the need for defense but disdain the defender? Wasn't it a citizen's duty to shoulder a share of the dirty work? And after all, it would just be for four years. Strains of "You're in the Army Now" began playing in my head.

The Army did not want me. I'd called almost on a lark, daring myself. The first question the recruiter asked was how old I was. When I answered, "Twenty-eight," I was told brusquely I was too old. The same thing happened with the Navy. After that second refusal, I dialed the Air Force right away just so I could say I'd done the rounds. (I never even considered the Marines; I was so obviously not one.)

"Hello, I'm Cheryl Duncan. I'm calling for information about getting a commission."

The Air Force recruiter's first question was, "How old are you?" It was almost a relief to hear it. "Twenty-eight."

"Let's make an appointment for you to come see me."

So a year after my ordination, I was sitting in front of an Air Force recruiter fielding his questions with an ease that built my confidence. I could see a look dawning in his eyes, which I interpreted to mean: *This person is officer material*. He was probably just giving thanks for finding a live one. He handed me a lengthy questionnaire to take home and fill out.

"Make sure," the sergeant warned me, "that you fill it out properly the first time. You can't come back and change answers later. These questions especially." He turned to a page that had to do with drugs. Any illegal drug usage disqualified an officer candidate. "I knew a guy who answered no to all these, then later, at a security clearance interview he admitted he'd smoked pot. They kicked him out for falsifying a government document." He gave me a look I had no trouble translating: *If you have to lie on this form, make sure you're prepared to stick to that lie forever.*

That evening, I lit a cigarette and sat down with the questionnaire. I painstakingly filled out the personal information requested, name, date and place of birth; made my way through a tedious list of every school I'd ever gone to, every job I'd ever had; penciled in some potential references; then came to the page that would disqualify me.

I'd been a teenager in the sixties. I'd never been into drugs but sure, I'd tried pot. Did I want to join an organization that preferred to be lied to? I picked up my pen and marked the block for "Experimenter." In the Remarks section, I wrote, "Anyone who went to college in the late sixties and says they didn't try pot is lying." The Air Force could decide whether I belonged or not.

My application was approved without comment. I received an Officer Training School (OTS) date several months away.

When I told my mother I'd decided to join the Air Force, "Oh, Cheryl," was all she said, though she achieved a strained smile to go with her worried look. I knew what the look meant: *Here's something else for Cheryl to fail at. Why can't she just settle down and do something normal?* Later she handed me a brochure about a school for executive secretaries. "Just thought you might be interested," she said. "You know you can make good money at that level." I set the brochure down without reading it.

My stepfather Bob's reaction was more to the point. He arranged for an Air Force captain, the daughter of one of his coworkers, to come to dinner. Linda was attending law school in Cincinnati at the time. When she and her husband walked into my parents' house, she wore a pregnancy smock and a big grin that drew me to her immediately.

In the thirty years since we met, Linda has barely changed. She still has a ruddy complexion, surrounded by frizzy, dirty-blonde hair fighting to go free, intelligent blue-gray eyes, and a deep dimple set askew in one cheek, which gives her face a rakish imbalance. She looks comfortable and soft, the image of a cozy mother. She takes in strays routinely—I was one of them. But under all that nonthreatening nurturance are a razor-sharp brain charged with energy and integrity, a wicked sense of humor, and a strict adherence to justice. She also tells a great story.

That night at my parents' house, she spun tales of the Air Force like Scheherazade. Comedy was her forte, perhaps as a needed foil for her sober law studies. She talked about the absurdities of a military life and its hardships, the constant niggling trivialities and the big inspiring moments. With her elastic face and lively voice, she called up pompous colonels, demanding drill sergeants, meek officer trainees. My parents' dining room teemed with characters she brought to life. We all leaned into her words, fascinated by the vivid world she described.

She also talked seriously about what life was like for women in the Air Force and how it had changed. She had come up through the ranks in tougher days. Like many enlisted members, she'd gotten her bachelor's degree in night school. She then applied for and was accepted into OTS, then later into the Funded Legal Education Program.

When she'd first entered the Air Force, U.S. law *allowed* the services to discharge pregnant women, but the services had written their regulations to *require* it. If a servicewoman married a military man with children and those children spent more than thirty days a year in their household, *she* had to separate from the Air Force. A military woman could only receive single allowances (for housing, for example) despite her marital status. If her husband was a civilian, he had no entitlement to dependent benefits the laws extended to wives, like medical care.

The repeal of the draft in the seventies and the establishment of the all-volunteer force created a need for more women to fill the rapidly emptying spaces. About that time, Congress and the services coincidentally discovered the gross iniquities in how differently male and female service members were treated, and passed more balanced rules. In five years the climate had changed so dramatically that Linda's tales at the dinner table seemed like distant history to me. But as she spoke, she cupped her hand protectively over the small swelling of her unborn baby.

I didn't learn for many years that Bob had invited Linda to dinner so she could talk me out of going into the Air Force. She had demurred ("After all," she told me later, "the Air Force had been very good to me—they were paying my way through law school!"), but she agreed to tell about the hardships as well as the good times, and not to pull punches.

She likes to talk about that evening and always ends with her dimpled grin and the punch line: "I was supposed to talk her out of it—it's the only thing in my career I ever failed at!"

With my OTS class date just days away, I showed up on a Friday morning at the Military Entrance Processing Station in Cincinnati, suitcases in hand, excited and scared. My processing stalled as soon as I weighed in. An Air Force sergeant (whose rank I still couldn't figure out from counting his stripes) informed me I was nine pounds too heavy. My recruiter had delicately told me months before that I needed to lose a few pounds, and I'd done so. But months of waiting during a cold, rainy winter had done their damage, and I hadn't been monitoring my weight all that carefully. After all, how significant could a few pounds be?

I was in my newly acquired warrior mode, so I refused to let it faze me. I took a deep breath, squared my shoulders, and nodded cheerfully at the sergeant. "Okay. Well, I guess I'll have to work on that. My family gave me a big farewell party." I laughed. "Guess I overdid it."

The sergeant didn't laugh, didn't even smile. He closed the folder in front of him, my folder, with a slap, and set it to the side of his desk. He sounded bored as he explained that I wasn't going anywhere. He couldn't send an overweight candidate to OTS. "Sorry. Next!"

"But wait! The class doesn't start till Tuesday. If I can lose the weight . . . ?"

He shrugged. I decided to hate him. "Sure. If you can lose nine pounds over the weekend, come back Monday morning. Next!"

I lugged my suitcases home, perplexed. I was good officer material. The Air Force wanted me. Would it really reject what I had to offer because I was a few pounds over an arbitrary weight standard? This intrigued me, the notion that there were absolutes in life which neither God nor prophets had imposed. Despite my religious background, I'd had little experience with unchallenged authority, strict rules, or unequivocal standards. Even the Ten Commandments had always seemed reserved for canonization candidates, while the rest of us could expect to sin and be forgiven. The Air Force's insistence on precise conformity with the rules seemed bizarrely rigid but comforting somehow. As long as I knew what the rules were, I'd know where I stood.

What I knew then was I had to lose nine pounds in three days. I called my mother at work to tell her my bad news.

"Are you sure you want to go?"

*Of course not.* I'd never been sure about this decision. It was strictly a leap of faith. Now I had an opportunity to let the whole thing drop, to take the job offer I'd received from a local business office. "Yes," I said. "Yes, I'm sure." It was pure stubbornness that answered.

My mother came home later that day bearing grocery bags and a plan. From now till Monday morning, I would drink nothing but water. I would eat nothing but boneless, skinless chicken breast, egg scrambled without milk, salad dressed only with vinegar. And with every meal, I ate either cucumber or asparagus, both natural diuretics. No salt. It was a disgustingly bland diet. The worst part was the asparagus, a vegetable I'd never encountered before. My mother bought cans of it, thin, slimy sticks I warmed up and choked down. I ate so much my urine turned pale green, but there was a lot of it. I vowed never to touch the yucky stuff again.

Monday morning I went back to the processing station. A nurse weighed me, my file open in her hand. "This can't be right." She frowned and fiddled with the weights on the sliding bar. "Well, it has to be. You lost eleven pounds." She looked at me with admiration.

The same bored sergeant stamped my file without a word. He gave me a folder containing instructions, official orders, shuttle bus voucher, and plane ticket. I called my mother to say goodbye, then walked across the street to a cafe for a late breakfast: waffles with a side order of sausage.

# CHAPTER TWO

# "IN TRAINING"

## 1980: Officer Training School, Medina Annex, Lackland AFB TX

## A. DECENCY AND GOOD ORDER

I woke up at OTS in San Antonio on 11 March 1980. I'd entered a world so linear that even time proceeded methodically, with dates climbing from day to month to year and hours numbering from oh-one-hundred to twenty-four-hundred. In the Air Force everything had its place in an ascending order of hierarchy. Organizations marched from small flights into squadrons up to groups and wings. Line officers progressed from officer trainee to second lieutenant to first lieutenant and on up to general, and nobody got to skip grades.

Like Calvinism, the Air Force valued the prim virtues of decency and good order. So I figured officer training should come naturally to me, who was still Presbyterian in character if not belief. I wasn't prepared, however, for the excess of orderliness exemplified in a humble laundry bag.

"Write it, Miss Duncan!" Officer Trainee Mondrigal said to me. She was a petite blonde, the upper-class OT responsible for the new women. She pulled my laundry bag down from the rail at the foot of my bed and shook it at me. "When are you going to get serious about this?" She threw the laundry bag on the floor, turned on her heel and left.

I opened the rules binder, pulled out the piece of paper with my name on top, and dutifully "wrote it," (that is, recorded another demerit) for failing to have my laundry bag properly pleated. This black binder, OT Operating Instructions, as I thought of it, spelled out the school rules—in tortuous detail when I thought there should be room for interpretation but annoyingly vague when I needed to know precisely what the standards were. I flipped the binder to the section on room maintenance and found the description and diagram of how to hang one's laundry bag. I picked mine up from the floor and compared it once again to the diagram.

The standards for the required laundry bags belonged in the tortuous detail category. They had drawstrings at the top, by which we hung them over our bedrails, and a zipper at the bottom through which dirty laundry could be inserted or removed. Each bag was to be pressed into equal accordion pleats halfway down its length, so that it hung neatly and narrowly at the top and fanned out pleasingly at the bottom. The diagram in the rules binder provided exact measurements for the pleats. It seemed everyone was capable of ironing and hanging a laundry bag properly but me.

OT Mondrigal had made one thing clear: there would be no quarter given for sloppy laundry bags, no tolerance for diversity in thought or execution concerning dirty clothes receptacles. Every evening she inspected our room. Every evening I failed laundry bag. Every evening I pulled out the iron and the diagram and a ruler for, well, good measure, and I worked on that damn bag.

I stared down at it in my hands, this pitiful, wrinkled cloth sack filled with crumpled, dirty underwear, and I felt sorry for it. It didn't belong in the same room as the crisp, neat bags hanging from my two roommates' bedsteads. I tried to work up a good counterbalance of anger and frustration. *Why am I putting myself through this? It isn't important. It's a laundry bag, for God's sake, a stinking laundry bag. So much going on in the world and the Air Force wants me to waste my time over a laundry bag.*

It didn't work. I sat slumped over, the weight of failure bowing my shoulders.

OT Mondrigal popped her head in again. "And another thing—oh." The expression on her face change from irritated to indecipherable. She came in, closed the door behind her, and took the metal chair opposite the one in which I sat crushing my laundry bag in my hands. She grabbed it from me. "Don't do that. It'll just make it harder to press."

Here was my chance to announce that I wasn't going to take part in this charade anymore, to stand up and fling the laundry bag aside, symbolic of the Air Force commission I would be rejecting. But I couldn't capture the righteous indignation I needed for the grand gesture.

"I try and I try and I can't seem to get it right." I struggled to hold back the girly tears that threatened me under stress. "I know it's a mess, but I don't know what else I can do."

"*You* don't have to do it!" Her sigh was long and exasperated, that of a frustrated teacher trying to reach a slow student. "Not by yourself. Get someone who knows how to do it to help you. Trade for something you can do for them. Offer to polish their shoes or something."

"I don't have to do it myself?"

"Hell, no." She leaned toward me as if she were imparting a secret. "The Air Force couldn't care less whether you can iron pleats or not. You just need to learn how to pay attention to details; that's all. So." She got up and set the laundry bag back on the table. "Get someone to do it for you, then we can both move beyond it and I can find something more interesting to write you up for."

She was at the door when I thought of something else. "But how do you keep it looking so neat, when you're shoving dirty clothes in it all the time?"

"Good God! You weren't actually planning to put your laundry in it, were you?" She left, shaking her head at the incredible stupidity of the current crop of OTs.

I swallowed the pride that had preferred failure to asking anyone for help. The first guy I approached was delighted to have me press his uniform while he pleated and hung my laundry bag. I shoved in a few pieces of underwear to fill out the bottom a little, then never touched it again.

So where did my dirty clothes go? Like everyone else, I used my security drawer. The top drawer of our chests had a latch so we could put a combination lock on it. In here we placed money, credit cards and any valuables we'd been foolish enough to bring along. The security drawer also hid anything we didn't want inspected, our dirty laundry, literally and figuratively.

In 1980 OTS was the principal business of Medina Annex, a noncontiguous section of Lackland Air Force Base, where officer trainees were segregated from the enlisted trainees on the main base, as well as from the real Air Force and the real world. New classes began every six weeks with approximately five hundred trainees in each class—the military "baby boom" of the early eighties after the post-Vietnam drawdown in the seventies.

Unlike the other two commissioning sources, the Air Force Academy and Reserve Officer Training Corps, OTS trained officers in twelve weeks, not four years. OTs already had bachelor's degrees—a requirement for commissioning—and instead of eighteen to twenty-two years old, the average OT age was late twenties. "Prior service" trainees, who came from the enlisted ranks, made up almost a third of the school. The rest of us were civilians who had to be taught things as basic as how, when, and whom to salute. We were all looking for a new start.

On day one, I had hauled my suitcases along a bare corridor in the women's wing of the barracks to the room I'd been assigned to. I'd glanced into the communal bathroom and the laundry room with its foreboding number of irons and ironing boards. Not an extraneous decoration anywhere in this bare-bones, no-nonsense building.

I found my two new roommates settling in. They had already laid claim to their territory, including the bottom bunk of one bed and the small single bed. One of them, Laura, had the grace to look abashed and suggested we draw lots for the top bunk. "Or we could switch every four weeks," she suggested. The other woman, Theresa, snorted, shook her head, and said, "I don't think so. You guys go ahead if you want to." I assured Laura the top bunk was fine.

Our room lacked any trace of comfort. A faded shade covered the only window, beneath which stood a table and three chairs. Laura's cot stood against one wall, the bunk bed against another. Three narrow closets and three chests of drawers lined the fourth wall, interrupted only by the door into the hallway. An overhead fixture lit the room with a startling white glare.

Everything was gray and metal, except the three of us. And we were "much of a muchness" ourselves, each with our pale skin and short brown hair. Only in our body types did we differ: short, stocky Theresa; slim, lithe Laura; tall, fleshy me. We finished unpacking and putting away the few items we were authorized, took a last wistful look at our civilian clothes, and deposited our locked bags in the storage room. Then there was only this bleak room and the three of us in our ill-fitting fatigue uniforms.

There were also ten men in our outfit, Flight 2-16. They ranged from a hapless engineer, who seemed even more out of place here than I did, to knowledgeable noncommissioned officers. Our commissioned flight commander was a pleasant-faced captain, with reassuring freckles. Captain Peck was responsible for us the next twelve weeks. He would supervise, train, instruct, lead, assist, order, inspect, test, correct, evaluate, discipline, and eventually commission us. Theresa nicknamed him Daddy Peck, and behind his back, we all began calling him Daddy.

Along with our civilian clothes, OTS had taken away our names. We were to refer to one another formally by our last names with the address Officer Trainee, OT, Mr., or Miss. Even in private, we usually called each other by last name, though I persisted with first names for my two roommates. My own first name disappeared, as if it were locked away inside my suitcase in the storage room. Even casually, I was now just Duncan. Duncan meant "dark warrior." Well, there was a fittingness to that, wasn't there?

Speaking of "fitting," for the first time in my life, everywhere I looked everyone was neat, clean, healthy, and physically fit. I felt like the ugly duckling in such a good-looking group. I'm not being overly modest or self-deprecating when I say that. Captain Peck decided my profile was too generous. He placed me on the OTS Image Program, a special exercise regimen.

"But I'm within standards," I said, clinging to that hard-fought triumph.

"I know. But you just don't look good in uniform." He spoke awkwardly, as embarrassed as any decent man is about commenting negatively on a woman's appearance—to her face, at any rate.

I sucked it up (and in) and started daily treks to the gym for a half hour of weight training. I hated it, not just for the activity itself or for the time it stole from my day, but for the stigma I imagined I was marked with. None of my flightmates ever mentioned it to me, however.

Even though I worked out, the main standard I continually failed was that of appearance, my image never that of a sharp, impeccable officer. The least breeze blew my hair around, or it had a crooked part or too much frizz. My fatigue shirt wilted in the heat. My slacks were lap wrinkled, my black shoes smudged and dusty. When our full uniform sets arrived, I discovered even more opportunities for write-ups. Clothes for me had always been dirt magnets. Keeping the polyester blue uniform slacks and light blue cotton shirt soil free over the course of a busy day was virtually impossible. It seemed most of my spare time was spent around a washing machine and ironing board. Who knew that military life would be so domestic?

The women's blouse was a light blue, boxy shirt that ended at the waist and had a dark blue cloth tab that snapped under the Peter Pan collar at the neck. A pair of baggy slacks or a straight knee-length skirt made up the rest of the outfit. For special occasions, we put on a squared-off dark blue jacket. This comprised the "Class A" or "service dress" uniform. The overall effect was that of a stewardess from the fifties, without the little white gloves or the cute little pillbox hat. We wore a dark blue beret instead—more reminiscent of the Girl Scouts than of the Green Berets. It was round as a puffball mushroom and with no internal design for remaining on one's head. To keep the beret on and straight, we employed long dark bobby pins. Protocol was strict: hats on outside; hats off inside. Officers lurked in doorways to assign demerits to any OT whose hat was off or on a second after exiting or entering. While the men walked blithely into a building, jerking their hats off, we women stood fumbling with our bobby pins. We were always the last in, the last out.

During our first week at OTS, Captain Peck met with each of us for an individual intake interview. I remember only one of the questions from the checklist he used. "If someone attacked you, and you had a gun, would you shoot him?"

I was silent, creating a scenario, trying to imagine the unknown weight of a gun in my hand. Part of me was still trying to make sense of the step I'd taken. For my own sake, I needed to answer as honestly as I was able. Captain Peck repeated the question.

"I don't know," I said. "I don't know if my brain could make my finger pull the trigger."

He set his pen and questionnaire down on the desk. "Nobody knows that, not till it happens and you have to respond." He paused to let me take that in. "But do you have any problems rationally with defending yourself by shooting your attacker?"

I didn't hesitate. "Oh, no, sir. I don't have a problem with that."

He sat back and picked up the questionnaire again. "That's all the Air Force asks of you."

Of course, I knew even then that the Air Force asked more of its members than self-defense or even defense of country. I had clear memories of the Vietnam War and few illusions about our nation's leaders. But the law did not allow the military to select the wars it would fight, nor did it allow military members to pick and choose among missions. Once I agreed to the principle of killing in self-defense, I was in for whatever came.

Still, my response to that question clarified something for me. While I admired Gandhi and King, not to mention Jesus, I'd only been paying lip service to their teachings. I didn't really believe in nonviolence in response to violence. I believed in defense.

After I'd gone public with my apostasy and subsequent decision to join the Air Force, I had waited anxiously to hear from old seminary friends. I was especially concerned about one of my favorite professors, a fervent member of Amnesty International. Finally, I received word from him: "Better a good warrior than a bad pacifist." Very well. Since I obviously wasn't a good pacifist, I'd try to be a good warrior.

As it was, life at OTS was too full to dwell on the philosophical aspects of the step I'd taken. Soon I forgot my qualms about the military in the day-to-day press of a schedule crammed with activity and exhaustion. I just wanted to survive long enough to get a commission and leave with my pride intact.

I handled the academics of OTS with little problem. By nature a perpetual student, I knew how to take notes, how to study, how to research, how to write papers, and most important, how to take multiple-choice tests. The only subject I sweated over was Defense Studies, a dry lecture course on military history, strategy, and weapon systems. It took place in a darkened auditorium, popularly referred to as the "Big Blue Bedroom," because five hundred officer trainees struggled to stay awake in it while grounded pilots droned on and on over dull slide presentations. Officers patrolled the aisles looking for drooping heads, as the instructors recited the specifications of aircraft or the warhead capacity of missiles. I was a complete dunce in those classes and to this day can't distinguish an A-10 from an F-15. But one lesson branded itself on my memory.

A grizzled captain stood dwarfed next to a huge screen hanging down over the stage and with his laser pointer led us through a list of military targets. The list, in neat bullet format, began with property, then continued through transportation routes, enemy aircraft, enemy combatants, war production plants. At the bottom of the list were two words, "collateral damage."

"This is when untargeted civilian populations and property are inadvertently hit," he said. The transparency disappeared and was smoothly replaced with a new one on a different subject. The captain stared at the new slide then called out, "Hey, Airman, put that last slide back up."

He walked in front of the screen and punched the bullet next to the words, "collateral damage." The screen rippled and the words quivered in the air.

"Okay, ladies and gentlemen. Take a good look at these words. You're going to hear them a lot. When you do, remember what they mean: somebody's baby got killed or somebody's mom or grandparents or maybe a whole family was wiped out. Or a schoolhouse full of children or a park bench with a couple of old men sitting on it. Never . . . ever . . ." with each word, he punched the screen again. "Never forget what these words mean."

He took a deep breath. "Okay, next slide."

## B. RUNNING IN PLACE

The run test was the first physical hurdle we had to pass. It would come after our third week of training. Men had to complete a mile and a half in ten and a half minutes; women in twelve—both faster than Air Force regulations required. So it was with OTS: weight, speed, image, all had to be honed to a sharper edge than in what I was learning to think of as the *Real* Air Force.

I usually chose the cool dusk of the San Antonio spring for my daily run. On the oval quarter-mile track, it took six laps to complete the mandatory distance. I didn't try to time myself in my practice runs. It was enough for me to complete the laps in a slow jog, stumbling and close to hyperventilating each time. A senior airman from the base gym worked at the track to monitor and advise us. I dubbed him Airman Running Czar. To me, he always said the same thing. "You have long legs. Stretch them out. You take twice as many steps as you need."

I tried. I would complete maybe half a lap deliberately stretching my legs out. *Think of yourself as a filly with long, strong legs that rejoice in the run, in the speed,* I exhorted myself. But soon, I'd be back to short, squatty steps. Theresa laughed. "Duncan, you waddle like a penguin."

When the day of the run test arrived, we were bused to a different part of the base. This track was a full mile and a half that wound its way through scrubby woodland and even found an uphill slope or two. We ran one flight at a time, a minute between starts.

That is, everyone else ran. I jogged. I trotted. I loped. I . . . well, I waddled. The rest of my flight was way ahead of me after the first quarter mile. Soon I was by myself, struggling to keep going. My breath came hard. I tried stretching out my legs. They resisted. I pulled them in and did my normal penguin stuff. When I reached the half-mile marker, Airman Running Czar yelled out, "Five minutes. Speed it up, ma'am!" I sped up for a while, slowed down, sped up again, slowed down—and stayed slow. At this rate it would take me over fifteen minutes to complete the course. There was no way I could pass the test. I walked the last half mile, head down, steadying my breathing. Runners from the flights that started after mine whizzed past me. I stayed well to the outside, out of their way.

Airman Running Czar found me. He was disgustingly fresh and lively, despite rushing up and down the track, timing runners, checking the course for obstacles. "There you are! Captain Peck sent me back to make sure you were okay, that you hadn't twisted an ankle or something."

"No. I just can't do it." I was panting so hard I could barely get the words out.

"The last turn's coming up. Your flight and your commander are waiting for you up ahead. Come on now. Go in running. Show your commander you're trying."

"What's the point? I've already failed."

"The point is to look like you're trying. Come on. Man up!"

I wasn't a man, and I had stopped trying a mile back. But with the airman nagging at me, I lifted my feet and stretched my legs out and as I passed the turn, my gait could be considered if not a gallop, at least a trot. I jogged maybe twenty yards, then stopped.

I walked the rest of the way in, exhausted and discouraged, humiliated by my flightmates' exchange of looks and Captain Peck's studied silence. But I pulled my head up and pretended not to care. I wasn't the only one in my flight to fail the run test that day, but I was by far the slowest. And I was the only one to saunter in, the only one to fail the perception test.

I had two more chances to complete the run. Determined to redeem myself next time around, I went to work in earnest to build up my speed and stamina—without the help of the Running Czar, who barely managed to restrain himself from a sneer whenever he saw me.

A few days before my second shot at the run test, a light rain broke through the humid heat and left the air soft and fragrant. It was the time of day when the sun turned the sky a pale yellow, an optimistic promise of a gentle night. As I neared the track I felt unusually mellow, happy even, ready for my evening run to begin. A sudden surge of confidence fueled me.

Something was wrong, however. As soon as I stepped out of my warm-up walk and began a slow jog, pain almost sent me tumbling. When my right foot hit the ground, a sensation like an electric shock ran up my leg into my knee. I stopped and walked a few paces. No pain. I began to run again. Left foot, fine. Right foot, shock. Left foot, fine. Right foot, agony. Several times I tried walking a bit, then began running, as if I'd imagined the pain. Each time, the pain was a bit stronger, impossible to tough out and run with, even if I hadn't been afraid of causing more damage. I stopped running and walked off the track.

A few years previously I had dislocated my right knee while hiking. "You can see where it healed crookedly," the doctor at the Medina Annex clinic told me, pointing to a vague shadow on the x-ray. "So, you're probably always going to have problems with it," he said cheerfully (and accurately, as it turned out). "The thing to do now is to figure out how to get you through your run test. They won't commission you without it."

He placed me on a medical waiver—no physical requirements for me. I sat on the bleachers with the rest of the walking wounded, watching the sports, the parades, the runners. The doctor had insisted I use a cane, even though walking wasn't painful for me. I accepted the prop without objection, since it provided concrete evidence of my injury. *Look, Captain. I really do have a bad knee. See my cane? I'm not just faking it.*

Those of us on medical waivers weren't even allowed to march, so we limped or shuffled behind our flight formation on our canes or our crutches or with invisible mystery ailments. We were literally set apart this way, our inadequacy on constant display.

After the inflammation in my knee healed, I began physical therapy at Wilford Hall Air Force Medical Center. At my first appointment, we started with massage, next slow walking on a treadmill. Then the therapist set the timer for twenty minutes and told me to start jogging. "Not fast. Take it easy. Do as much as you can. Stop if your knee starts hurting. Someone will be here to help you off as soon as you've had enough. You probably can't do twenty minutes yet."

I jogged slowly, carefully, taking it easy on my tentative knee. I stared at a poster on the wall, red canyons in a Utah desert, the only distraction I had. Despite ample permission and reason to quit early, I kept going. When the timer went off at twenty minutes, I was as surprised as the therapist. I was stumbling by then, wet with sweat. My legs were jelly. The therapist and an orderly had to hold me up and walk me around the room to cool off. Finally they helped me onto a white metal hospital bed, placed an icepack on my knee and a blanket around me to keep me warm. I drifted into a doze, blissful with accomplishment in my warm cocoon.

I woke when the doctor came in. He looked at my chart. "Good. Good. Okay, you can get dressed and go now. We'll do this again in two days, okay?" He placed his hand on my cheek and said softly, "Good on you, Cheryl."

*Cheryl.* A shock of pleasure surged through me. It was the first time I'd heard my name in weeks. The sound was surprisingly sweet, an affirmation that somewhere inside the rather inept OT, I still existed.

Theresa hadn't participated in any of the run tests yet. After the second week of school she'd complained of a mysterious pain and was placed on a medical waiver that temporarily excused her from physical activities and testing. Sooner or later, she would have to run, but until then she stayed away from the track altogether. Whatever her physical problem was, it didn't keep her off the dance floor on Friday and Saturday nights, when the OT Open Mess brought in live bands. She bragged openly about gaming the system.

On Friday evenings I also dressed in my service dress uniform, complete with the dark blue jacket, as yet bare of ribbons, and went to the open mess to unwind. While she boogied away, I sat over a beer or two or three and glumly turned down invitations to dance.

(With four men for every woman, I was more in demand than I'd ever been before or would be since.)

It gave Theresa another reason to sneer at me. "You're such a tightass, Duncan."

I *was* a tightass. Besides some legitimate concerns that the movements might cause me more trouble, I just didn't think it appropriate to be on a medical waiver and be seen dancing. It was the wrong image. Perception counted. I had learned that lesson finally. So I sat with my cane at my side, radiating disapproval at Theresa.

The bands that played at the OT Open Mess on weekends were indistinguishable from one another. They played loud, lively blends of mainstream rock with an occasional crossover country song thrown in. They all knew the one song to get us going, the highlight of our evening, the unofficial anthem of OTS: "We Gotta Get Out Of This Place." It was an old Animals hit that military members had adopted as their own during Vietnam. It still spoke to us. Its opening bars were invariably greeted with whoops. When the chorus came around we'd turn to one another, clink our glasses together, link arms, sway like Germans at a beer fest and sing along at the top of our lungs.

I have seldom felt so much love as when I sang that song with my flightmates. At those moments, we had a passion for one another that went far beyond sex. OTS was a world in miniature where we shared everything, most significantly the same goal: to get out of this place with gold bars on our shoulders. We understood one another then more clearly than spouses or lovers.

OTS was a pure life, simple, secure, the rules written out, one's place in the hierarchy clear. Punishment, usually in the way of demerits, came fast, standard, and temporary. Meals, lodging, entertainment, and medical care were all provided. We had no bills, no rent, no dogs to walk or in-laws to placate, no children to discipline. No spouse/lover/partner to share ourselves with. After I left OTS, I heard a comment that summed it up for me: "Twelve weeks of hell, and I loved every minute of it." But I only realized it was love in retrospect.

OTS offered an escape hatch, an easy way out: SIE, self-initiated elimination. All it took was telling your commander, "I don't want to be here. I want to leave." And you could. For a prior civilian like me, it would have meant a plane ticket home and a future once again clear and free. The SIE option made it easier for me to stick with OTS. No matter how bad it became, I could drop out any time I wanted. The thought seemed terrifying and extreme, but wonderfully comforting.

Years later when I saw the movie *Private Benjamin*, one scene stood out. Goldie Hawn, playing the hapless, spoiled daughter of privilege, stands rain soaked and miserable in full Army gear. A smirking Eileen Brennan holds out a clipboard, which contains the paperwork that will put a blessed end to Judy Benjamin's Army training, a career move chosen out of desperation and ignorance. All she has to do is sign, then she can leave this hell of a place and go home with the parents who've come to rescue her. She stands there with full knowledge that her freedom is just a scribble away. She stares silently at the clipboard extended toward her. Her face is smeared with tears and rain and mascara, but she looks like the hardest person in the room when she straightens up, faces the captain, and says, "No, thanks. I think I'll stay." She executes the sharpest salute a soldier can make, does an about face and walks out. Her shoulders are square and her look is—finally—determined.

I recognized that look. I'd felt the same way at OTS. Knowing I could leave and flee to the comfort of an undemanding family. It just took a signature. But I squared my shoulders. I was determined to stick with it. Pride would not let me go whining home. *No thanks, I think I'll stay.*

## C. LIFE WITHIN THE CHRYSALIS

After six weeks, we became the new seniors, halfway there. As if we didn't have enough to do, some of us also applied to fill positions in the squadron, which brought with them more headaches and more work. Command was what the truly ambitious OT aimed for, since command, after all, was what being an officer was ultimately about. I, however, had serious doubts about my ability to command. Besides, I still thought like a seminarian: I wanted to serve, not lead. It had been less than a year since I left the church, but apparently, the church had not yet left me.

I became one of the Social Actions program monitors, responsible for advising the commander on matters of human rights and relationships within Squadron Two. We were the watchdogs charged to help maintain an environment of mutual respect and individual freedom. We also became quasi-counselors, helping other squadron members get through the stress of OTS and notifying the commander of any potential mental health problems.

My first challenge lay in my own flight. His name was OT Rabinowitz.

In our first week at OTS, the thirteen members of Flight 2-16 had adopted a fourteenth flightmate: OT Rabinowitz, a klutzy caricature sprung from the imagination of two of the guys. He was invisible, inaudible, and completely inept.

Whenever OT Gerner was late for muster, someone would assure him that OT Rabinowitz hadn't shown up yet either. When OT Jordan racked up five thousand demerits in one inspection, apparently OT Rabinowitz had accumulated six thousand in dirty socks alone. When OT Duncan came out with an asinine remark, you should just hear what OT Rabinowitz said once! He was the slowest, dullest, clumsiest, most clueless OT in the school.

The bright minds who created OT Rabinowitz never described him. They didn't have to. We each had our own image, dredged up from a dark place of cultivated biases.

I was uncomfortable with the jokes and never participated. But I also never objected. I told myself that the boundary between humor and prejudice was narrow and subjective; that I was being too prim, Duncan the tightass; that OT Rabinowitz enhanced flight unity as a harmless, even benevolent mascot; that he filled a needed role as the OT who was the butt of the flight's jokes, a role that might otherwise have devolved onto a real flight member—like me. There was some truth to these thoughts, but underneath I could smell the stink of rationalization.

I was afraid to speak up at first, afraid of attracting their derision to myself. Later it seemed too late to take a stand. So for six weeks, my silence had made me complicit in the flight's casual bigotry. But now I had an official duty to, among other things, "nurture respectful human relations."

With my new responsibility weighing heavily on my shoulders, I stood in the barracks corridor as the flight gathered to march to breakfast. Some of the guys started joking about OT Rabinowitz. My belly grew queasy with nervousness. I knew what the squadron Social Actions officer should do, but I didn't know if Cheryl Duncan could do it. Then someone remarked that we'd have to introduce the new underclassmen to OT Rabinowitz.

*Man up, Cheryl.* I took a deep breath, clutched my cane hard, and said in as steady a voice as I could, "You know, guys, some of our new OTs may be Jewish and might find OT Rabinowitz offensive."

They stared at me as if I'd grown a purple mustache. Theresa whispered loud enough for me to hear, "There goes Duncan showing off again."

Before the silence could dissolve into shrugs and snickers, I swallowed hard and went on. "In fact, even though I'm not Jewish, *I* find OT Rabinowitz offensive."

"Thank you, Miss Duncan." The stares turned away from me toward Mr. Gerner, who'd just walked out of his room. "I *am* Jewish and it offends me too."

His roommate Donelly, our OT flight commander, looked stricken. "God, Gerner. You told me once it bothered you, and I never did anything about it. I'm really sorry."

Silence hovered awkwardly, until Theresa said, "Jeez, Duncan, didn't you even realize *Gerner* was Jewish!"

Everyone began ribbing me good-naturedly. I felt foolish at first, then decided my best response was to join in. I pointed my cane up at tall, coffee-colored OT Jordan. "Next thing I know you're going to tell me Jordan here is *black*!"

We were all laughing when the remaining two members of our flight came rushing up breathlessly, one still buttoning his blue uniform shirt. They apologized for running late but assured us that OT Rabinowitz would arrive any minute. There was a long silence, then Donelly said with quiet authority, "OT Rabinowitz is dead."

Around the same time, Desert One failed. It was a covert joint service mission to rescue the hostages in Iran. Not only wasn't a single hostage rescued, one of the helicopters crashed into the C-130 transport waiting in the desert, resulting in the deaths of eight airmen and marines. We crowded into the squadron dayroom to watch the reports on television. In the middle of the broadcast, I noticed a woman slip out of the room. There was something in the slope of her shoulders that made me get up after a few moments and walk down to her room.

I found her sitting cross-legged on a bottom bunk, leafing through a photo album. "Hey. Are you okay?"

She didn't look up but continued turning the pages. I felt awkward, hesitating in the doorway. "There," she said suddenly. "I felt sure I had a picture." She held the album out to me.

I perched on the edge of the bed and looked at a snapshot of three men. They were in T-shirts and jeans, squinting in the sun, holding beer cans up as if toasting the photographer. They were laughing. She pointed to the one in the middle. "That's my husband. He's a staff sergeant. And this guy," she said, tapping the one on the right, a tall man with an arm draped casually over her husband's shoulder, "was on the rescue team, one of the guys killed in the plane."

I was silent. I didn't know what words to use. But she didn't seem to need me to speak. "He was over at the house just the weekend before I left to come here. He was helping Ray fix our car. He was a great guy."

"I'm sorry."

"Yeah," she said. "Me too."

"Do you need me to stay?" She shook her head. I left her there, staring at the photo.

One weekend, several of us decided to treat ourselves to a decent dinner in the OT Open Mess dining room. We wore our service dress uniforms and posed for Theresa between the club's portico columns. We ordered steak dinners at a large round table covered with a white tablecloth—luxury with crystal wine glasses, salad forks, linen napkins. Some flip remark of Theresa's sent OT Kroehn off on a rant about people on medical waivers. He bitterly excoriated the slackers who gamed the system by making up a medical complaint while the good guys slogged ahead meeting all the requirements.

His disgust released a fury I hadn't even realized I'd been storing. Here I was, one of the good guys slogging ahead, obeying the rules, doing the right things, and then a bum knee opened me up to ridicule and scorn from the likes of Kroehn. Anger rose up in me, hot and bitter as bile: anger at being despised by some of my own flightmates, anger at having to use precious time to attend physical therapy, anger at having to walk behind the flight like a camp follower.

Maybe some of my anger involved that stupid laundry bag and evenly spaced clothes hangers. Maybe it was anger over all the arbitrary rules and the demerits. Anger over sleeping with no blanket, only a thin bathrobe flung over me, so as to save precious time by not having to make the bed in the morning. Anger over being too cold at night, too tired during the day. Anger over the Image Program and having to go to the gym because I didn't look military enough. Anger over the mind-numbing routine, day after day with every moment scheduled, wearing just the right uniform, pinning my beret at just the right angle. Anger over how everything was a test.

So when Kroehn went on his rant in that elegant dining room, calm, steady, nonconfrontational OT Duncan snapped. I jumped up so quickly my chair fell over. I slammed my cane down flat and hard and loud on the white tablecloth, sending crystal glasses tumbling. The dining room fell silent. I had *everyone's* attention. Even the servers paused agape with their water pitchers and plates in hand. I was too mad to care.

"I'm sick of this shit!" I yelled. "Nobody asks for this. I don't want to carry this stupid cane and have to find time I don't have to go to therapy. Why would anyone want that? This could be you, so quit being all superior. I'm tired of the sneers and the cracks. I'm sick and tired of it all."

Sick and tired, angry and frustrated, and now mainly embarrassed. Every person in the room was frozen in position, staring at me. So I did the only thing possible. I picked up my cane and limped away to the sanctuary of the Ladies Lounge.

Locked in a restroom stall, shaking with emotion, I admitted to myself that a lot of my anger was addressed toward Theresa and her ilk. She did precisely what Kroehn complained of. Even more, I was angry at myself for being inadequate in so many ways, for falling short of perfection—a true warrior wouldn't have a bad knee, or at least she would tough it through. I felt sick and tired of everyone and everything, especially my own struggling self. As I cooled off, I realized that maybe I was just plain tired.

Close to the end of training, everyone was tired; tempers were short. We snapped back and forth at one another like sled dogs harnessed together for too long and too hard a drive. At that moment I so heartily wanted it to be over, I was almost ready to walk out the front gate and hitchhike to the airport. But not quite. Those gold second lieutenant bars beckoned, less than two weeks away. *No thanks, I think I'll stay.*

I could only hide in a toilet stall for so long. I had a steak ordered and a bill to pay, even if I didn't eat it. There was nothing for it but to go back to that table with as much dignity as I could muster. I walked back into the dining room with my head high, despite Theresa's audible snort and remark, "Look who's crawling back." I sat down and picked up my napkin.

"I'm sorry, Mr. Kroehn. I shouldn't have taken my frustration out on you. I apologize."

"Apology accepted, Miss Duncan." It wouldn't have killed him to extend an apology as well, but he didn't, just kept on eating.

We all resumed what we'd been doing—eating, chatting, light jokes and casual gossip, Theresa flirting with the guys on both sides of her. I cut into the cold, overcooked steak in front of me and began to eat. Suddenly I was ravenous.

Two weeks before graduation, my orders arrived. A stapled stack of fifty sheets defined my future for at least the next two years. I was disappointed at first. Air Force specialty: Personnel Officer. That I had expected, though I'd harbored a secret hope that I would be delivered to something more exciting. I was being assigned to Carswell Air Force Base in Fort Worth, Texas. I groaned. More Texas! Cowboys and heat and dead armadillos along the roadside and people who treated cactus as a garden plant instead of nature's cruel joke. I was not a Texas kind of girl.

One of my prior service flightmates looked over my shoulder. "Carswell! Ah man, you are so lucky. That's one of my favorite bases!" He'd received Whiteman (Missouri). Others were going to Chanute (Illinois); Wright-Patterson (Ohio); even worse, cold, barren Minot (North Dakota). Fort Worth began to look better.

Before I could go anywhere, I still had to get off waivers and pass the run test. For most of my OTS life, I'd been carving out two hours, three days a week, taking a shuttle to Wilford Hall to run on a treadmill. My third and final chance to pass the run test without being held over into a new class was early next week. I had to pass it. I couldn't hold on much longer. My façade of almost-officer felt on the verge of crumbling around me, leaving OT Duncan lying in rubble at the feet of a naked, scared Cheryl.

By the second lap I was ready to die. We were running on the oval quarter-mile track because there were so few of us left who hadn't passed the test yet. It was a lot harder to run on a dirt track in the morning sun of a South Texas June than on a treadmill in an air-conditioned building with nothing riding on the results. I had just one thing going for me: the knowledge that this was my last chance. Stopping was out of the question.

I'd taken a tip from OT Donelly and held a second lieutenant's gold bar cupped in each of my hands. I pressed them into my palms every time I began to flag. Although I'd ignored Kroehn's suggestion to take the frogs off them, so the metal prongs would press into my skin, the frogs themselves were rough enough to nip me as I squeezed them.

Lap two is dead, I told myself, as I passed the finish line the second time. Airman Running Czar yelled out the time. I was doing okay, but not enough to dare slow down. Theresa was several yards ahead of me. I had no idea how she'd gotten permission to run. As far as I knew she hadn't set foot on a track or a treadmill for weeks. But she kept ahead of me, her squat bulldog figure the target I used to keep myself focused. I sped up a little to keep the same distance between us. I didn't want to fall too far behind.

I spent my time around the track doing confused math in my head. If it took five minutes and forty-nine seconds to complete three laps, how was I doing? How much time did I have left? What time should I expect to hear after the fourth lap? I tried to occupy myself with these clouded calculations instead of thinking of my legs, how weak they felt, the start of a blister on the ball of my right foot, and worse, the shallow hard breaths struggling out of my smoker's lungs. I avoided thinking about my right knee, as if by doing so I would jinx it back into pain. My blue T-shirt stuck to my sweat-covered back. I had to grip the metal bars more tightly to keep them from slipping out of my damp hands. As I began the last lap, I had less than two minutes left to complete the course on time. I inhaled a deep breath, stretched my legs out and ran as fast as I could push myself. I concentrated on Theresa up ahead. *Catch up with her*, I commanded my legs. *Catch up with her.*

Pressing the rough metal into the palms of my hands, pressing my legs back and forth against the wind, pressing the soles of my feet into the dirt, pressing the air in and out of my lungs, I ran. I passed the finish line to the sound of "eleven minutes, fifty-two seconds." Eight seconds to spare. Two flightmates appeared to grab my arms and hold me up as I slowed to a stumble.

Just ahead, Theresa was also being supported by flight members. I could hear her struggling to breathe, just as I was. I also heard the first thing she gasped out. "Duncan—where's Duncan?"

"She came in right behind you."

Theresa turned and saw me. A grin spread across her face, and she pumped her right arm in the air. Now, if I'd come in before her, my first words wouldn't have been "Where's Theresa?" I wouldn't have even thought about her. And if I heard she failed, in my right-eousness I'd probably have thought, *serves her right*. The unexpected generosity of Theresa's spirit humbled me. I returned her grin and raised both arms, Rocky style.

I finished walking the track on trembling, joyful legs, then went up to the gym locker room to shower, change clothes, and puke my guts out.

I saw my mother before she spotted me. She sat in the tiny reception area at the front entrance of the barracks. She turned as the door opened and OTs came piling in. Her eyes slid right over me at first, then jerked back, startled. That told me more than a mirror. The daughter she'd last seen twelve weeks ago had slouched around, pasty, flabby, and sloppy. I have a picture of myself as my mother saw me in San Antonio on 5 June 1980. It shows a tall, slim woman with a tan, alert face, wearing a crisp blue uniform, shoulders thrust proudly back, chin held high. She looks capable and competent. She looks like an Air Force officer.

My mother had brought my grandmother with her. She was looking around with stunned amazement. A mountain woman from the Tennessee Cumberlands, Granny had never flown before. This was almost her first time off the familiar route of Interstate 75 between Tennessee and Ohio. She held on to her purse tightly as she stared at all the commotion in blue uniforms. Later, I took them on a tour of the base and amused myself by pointing out the things I thought would be foreign to her ("Look Granny, flowering cactus"), just for the pleasure of hearing her say, "La! Did you ever!"

That night was the class Dining In at the OT Open Mess. A Dining In by definition is limited to military members, as opposed to a Dining Out, at which civilian guests provide a civilizing influence. A Dining In usually resembles a fraternity party with formal attire and better food, but we'd been warned to keep this one tame. OTs had been known to lose a commission through drunken hijinks at their pre-commissioning Dining In.

We wore the formal uniform, the "mess dress"—a name that can only imply formality in military jargon. The men's version somewhat resembled a tuxedo, cummerbund and all, gaudy with ribbons and braiding but recognizably formal black-and-white gear. The women's mess dress, unfortunately, was designed to mimic the men's, so despite its floor-length, slit skirt, we also looked like we were wearing tuxedoes.

As was typical of everything at OTS, even this party was designed as a lesson: Dining In 101. We were exposed to just enough of the traditions to allow us to function on future, rowdier occasions. A junior officer was appointed master of ceremonies. This was the role for a natural buffoon, someone with no self-consciousness, the class clown. On a dais in front of the room, the table of honor held the wing's most senior officers and the visiting VIPs. The OT wing and vice wing commanders were the only trainees invited to the VIP table. I did not envy them.

What I was most fascinated with was the small table in front of the dais, on which stood a punch bowl of noxious-looking, snuff-colored liquid—the infamous grog bowl filled with a lethal mixture of booze. Anyone guilty of messing up the strict and arbitrary protocol of the Dining In could be sent to the grog bowl, where he (almost always a "he") would fill a punch glass with the putrid stuff, toast the head table, toast the room, chug down the contents, then place the cup upside down on his head to demonstrate he had indeed emptied it. It was a guy thing, a funny kind of honor straight out of the frat house. The men took great delight in proposing one another for the grog bowl for the silliest of reasons. "Sir! OT Blank just split an infinitive!" Great consternation, while the head table conferred before inevitably announcing, "To the grog with him." And OT Blank would stand up, grinning, march with squared corners to the grog bowl and acquit himself like a man. I couldn't see the humor in it myself, at least not after the first ten or twelve.

Mom and Granny were taken care of. Daddy's wife, Judy Peck, had invited all the flight's civilian guests to a pay-as-you-go dinner at a local restaurant. At that time, officers' wives fulfilled much the same function as ministers' wives. I envied them the friendly, female gossip over a cozy meal in comfortable clothes, but I dreaded what they might be talking about. I knew my mother would have worked it so she was sitting right next to Judy. They were probably gossiping away like old friends. My ears burned throughout the meal.

The banquet and its interminable toasts (to which we dutifully responded "Here, here") and the occasional grog bowl excitement eventually wound down. Time for dessert and coffee, announcements and awards, the guest general's speech. Then dismissal. I found Mom and Granny waiting for me in the OT Club front hall.

"Judy told me you made Distinguished Graduate," Mom said. "And that you got the briefing award. She said it would be announced tonight. See, I knew before you did." She smiled a teasing, happy smile. I was right. She and Judy Peck had hit it off like old cronies.

Tonight, life was good. Tomorrow would be the end of security, the beginning of challenges, but for now, nothing could go wrong. I led Mom and Granny into the bar, where a DJ was spinning loud platters of mainstream rock 'n' roll. Granny sat bemused over a cup of coffee, in a bar for the first time in her life, far from her dry Baptist county. She looked around at the goings-on like a tourist who'd stumbled into a nest of quaint but harmless natives.

Mom sipped a Coke and chatted with flight members who dropped by, lighting restlessly on the extra chairs at the table before jumping back up to greet other OTs and their guests. It was festive. Excitement, adrenalin, joy informed everyone who sat and danced and stood and talked—even those who served in the dark bar, correctly anticipating generous tips.

There's nothing like showing off to a mother who had doubted your ability to succeed. Tonight she was glowing with pride and confidence in me. I'd lasted the twelve weeks, achieved the status of Distinguished Graduate, and won one of the few individual awards given out. And on top of it, I seemed to be popular enough to have friends surrounding me, greeting me, chatting up two older versions of me. One flightmate pulled up a chair between Mom and Granny and flirted with them both. Donelly came by to introduce his wife. Theresa waved from the dance floor. My other roommate, Laura, and her husband joined us at the table. Pale, pasty OT Simpson brought his wife by, an elegant black-skinned woman from Kenya. Granny gaped in surprise, then smiled in enchantment. "La, did you ever," she whispered to me.

OT Kroehn stopped by the table too, standing ramrod stiff and unsmiling as usual. Also drunk, but fortunately neither Mom nor Granny seemed aware of it. When he asked me to dance, I could see ecstasy brimming out of my mother's eyes. Not only had I excelled in this environment, I looked better and fitter than I had in years. Now here I was, getting up to dance with a good-looking guy. I could read Mom's mind. I was entering a society chock-full of men—young, healthy, vibrant men. Maybe there was hope for me after all. Maybe I'd finally get someone to marry me. She had a one-track mind where I was concerned.

I leaned over to her and whispered, "Don't even think it." But I smiled.

"You don't know what I'm thinking," she said and smiled back.

Next morning, my last at OTS, I was up and out even earlier than usual. Nothing required it, but in my present generous mood, I had agreed to go with Laura down to the track. We slipped out while Theresa was still snoring.

We didn't go to run ourselves but to cheer a runner on. OT Arba, a beautiful black woman in our squadron, had come down with a disease a few weeks into the course. She had been sent home but recovered enough to return and rejoin the class. She had remained on medical waivers until now, so she'd had no opportunity to run for eight weeks. Her skin, normally glowing smooth and dark, looked gray and mottled in the early dawn light. Her narrow face was lined with worry and pain. This was her only opportunity to graduate with us.

It didn't matter that I didn't know her personally. She was a member of our squadron, our class. There were about twenty of us there that morning, milling about while she went through her warm-up exercises.

"Can we run with her?" one of the guys asked. I held my breath—this I had not counted on. Cheering was one thing; running another.

Fortunately Airman Running Czar was at his most officious. "Absolute not, sir! Running with someone to help pace them is strictly forbidden. No one is allowed on the track except her."

She walked one lap of the quarter-mile track to complete the warm-up. The rest of us spread out around the outside of the track to clap and cheer and yell enthusiasm at her whenever she passed. She began to run. "Atta, girl," we yelled. "Keep it up." "You can do it." "First lap down." Over and over again I clapped and yelled, "You can do it," though by the second lap, she was already beginning to stumble. Even from outside the track I could see the sweat coating her face and arms and legs. Her mouth had a hard set to it, but a quick look at my watch showed me that she was behind already.

People started to yell, "Speed it up." "Faster." "Faster." "Faster." And less convincingly, "You can do it." She tried. She sped up, then stumbled and fell back again. She ran as close to the inside rail as she could get, but by the time she passed the starting line and began her third lap, she was already almost two minutes behind.

Airman Running Czar looked at his stopwatch. "Speed it up, ma'am," he yelled. Then, "Ah, shit! Out of my way, you guys!" He threw his clipboard down and began to run. He ran right outside the track, through gravel and stones. We moved back to let him pass. He reached OT Arba. "Keep up with me," he yelled at her.

I could see her attention narrow to his figure, just ahead of her on the outside of the barrier. She sped up and concentrated on him. That was all. She stayed with him through the remaining four laps. Once she crossed the line for the final time, everyone rushed onto the track. We grabbed her, hugged her—or tried to though she was so covered with sweat she slipped out of our arms. We were all laughing and crying, hearts thumping as if we'd been running. We were, every one of us, OT Arba at that moment.

"Back off, you all. Give her air," the airman yelled. He had barely broken a sweat. "Walk your cool-down lap, OT, then go clean up. You've got a commissioning ceremony this morning." He walked the lap with her, supporting her on one side while a friend took the other.

"That's great," I said to Laura, as we headed back to the barracks. "The whole squadron has made it."

She gave me a curious look but said nothing. I had already forgotten Brenda Bronson.

We were officers before the official parade began. In a small, ceremonial room, just large enough for one flight at a time, we had taken turns stepping to the front, standing before the U.S. and Air Force flags, raising our right hands, and swearing to the commissioning oath. My mother and grandmother watched as I repeated the powerful words after Captain Peck.

"I, Cheryl Lee Duncan, having been appointed a second lieutenant in the United States Air Force, do solemnly swear . . ." We could say "affirm" if we liked, but I had no objection to swearing. In fact I preferred it. "Affirm" sounded hopeful; "swear," glumly determined.

"That I will support and defend the Constitution of the United States against all enemies, foreign and domestic." This was something I could believe in: the Constitution—not the flag, the economy, the way of life, the millions of square miles, the red, white, and blue of a country-western song—just those cold, stern words, solid as stone tablets.

"That I will bear true faith and allegiance to the same; that I take this obligation freely, without any mental reservation or purpose of evasion; and that I will well and faithfully discharge the duties of the office upon which I am about to enter. So help me God." We'd also been instructed we could leave off the last line, but I repeated it. Even though I was no longer sure about God's role in my life, I did believe in keeping my options open.

I brought my right hand up to my forehead in a smooth salute. Captain Peck returned it, then called Mom and Granny up to "pin me" with my new rank. There were no pins involved. They unbuttoned the epaulets on the shoulders of my shirt and unsnapped the stiff, fabric-covered cardboard displaying my OT rank. They slid on new cloth epaulet covers, a deep "flight blue," each embroidered with a single gold bar.

One last time, we gathered in flight formation and marched down to the parade ground. The parade itself was wonderfully uneventful. Nothing untoward happened. The sky maintained a helpful cloudiness, blocking the sun's rays but avoiding any actual rain. No one fainted, and no one—not even me—marched to the beat of a different drummer. A military march well done is a thing of beauty, and we gave it the swing of joy. We again repeated the commissioning oath, this time in unison, five hundred voices swearing and affirming. Then we were dismissed. The women's berets and the flat-brimmed caps of the men flew into the air in a flutter of triumph. Like butterflies bursting through a chrysalis, trainees transformed by the hundreds into lieutenants.

# CHAPTER THREE

# "ON BASE"

## 1980–1982: Carswell AFB TX

## A. THE FLYING CIRCUS

The microphone swung through the air like a lasso, as if Roger Daltrey wanted to capture me. His muscles bulged against his tight T-shirt, and his voice ran the scale from innocence to howling rage. I was in lust, maybe a little drunk. Oh, the power of rock 'n' roll—I wanted to be writhing on the floor with him right then and there in the heat of the crowd, under the lights centered on the stage, amid the noise and smoky haze of Reunion Arena. "Pinball Wizard" trembled through the air, along with heady whiffs of pot. I breathed deeply but made do with my tobacco-filled cigarettes and a huge plastic cup of pale beer, my hands wet from the inevitable sloshing as I passed cups down the row from the cardboard tray at Mary's feet.

There were four of us that night at the Who concert in Dallas, all lieutenants. Mary was my new boss. She had arranged for the tickets, organized the car pool, established the beer-buying roster. Billy, like Mary, was a first lieutenant and married. He'd left baby and wife at home to cut loose tonight. Don and I were second lieutenants. Don smoked thin cigarillos, and his only form of expression seemed to be a single raised eyebrow. I was the most junior by Air Force reckoning, but easily the oldest of the group.

*Sex, drugs, and rock 'n' roll.* I'd never thought of myself as a rock concert kind of person—symphony perhaps, opera definitely, but rock concert, no. "Teenage wasteland . . ." we sang with the band. I was bumping up hard against thirty, but I felt more like a teenager than I had as a sixteen-year-old. I'd just entered the Real Air Force, and I was already starting to rue a youth spent virtuously and soberly. Thank God I had repented my holy ways in time to start enjoying life.

A few days earlier I'd driven past the Fort Worth city limits sign as the radio announced 104 degrees. The wind coming through the open windows brought little relief, just moved the heat past me and out the other side. The uniform I'd ironed so carefully that morning had glued itself to my body in damp wrinkles. I resigned myself to replacing Luigi, my unairconditioned, boxy Fiat 128. *The first of my loved ones to be sacrificed to the military*, I thought dramatically (and inaccurately, having already abandoned my dog with my parents for an indeterminate length of time).

I had lingered over several cups of coffee that morning, reluctant to get on the road. More than reluctant, terrified. My first assignment, me finally an officer—an officer! Who was I kidding? I was a meek civilian girl who should've looked into that secretarial school like Mom wanted. Too late now. No SIE choice anymore.

I arrived at the front gate of Carswell Air Force Base and handed a copy of my orders to the guard. "Welcome to Carswell, Lieutenant," he said. "The Cee-Bo's easy to find. Just go . . ."

I missed his instructions, temporarily panicked by "Cee-Bo." What kind of language was he speaking? Then I realized he was referring to the CBPO, the Consolidated Base Personnel Office, which my orders identified as the organization I was being assigned to. He motioned me through the gate, then saluted. That also rattled me. I stalled the car trying to shift it into gear while returning the salute. I felt my face go even hotter from embarrassment. I was a disgrace to my very bedraggled uniform. *Yes, Luigi, you definitely have to go.*

"Ma'am, Second Lieutenant Duncan reports as ordered!" Fingers pressed tightly against the edge of my glasses, holding my nervous body stiffly at attention, I stood before the desk of First Lieutenant Mary Winston.

A heartbeat of an awkward pause, then she quickly returned my salute. "At ease, Lieutenant. Uh, you don't really have to do that." Chalk up the first difference between OTS and the Real Air Force. "You drove all the way here in your uniform?" she asked, looking me up and down, her forehead wrinkled into a frown.

"I thought I needed to be in uniform to report in."

"No, that's not necessary." Second difference. Apparently I was going to have to forget huge chunks of what OTS had branded into me. The trick was going to be figuring out which chunks. I stood before her while she looked me over, doubt evident in every feature of her face. "Well, have a seat, Cheryl."

"Thank you, ma'am."

"That's not really necessary." Third time—I was making a great impression. "There's what we refer to as a brotherhood of all lieutenants. You can call me Mary."

We sat looking at one another, sisters in the brotherhood. Finally, she said, "A bunch of us are going to the Who concert in Dallas this week. There's an extra ticket. You want it?"

Mary and I were women in the Air Force but we weren't "Women in the Air Force" or WAFs. That designation was long gone and had never actually indicated a separate corps, as the Women's Army Corps, the WACs, had done. We were part of the large motley mainstream called the line: men and women, pilots and navigators, engineers, supply officers, administrative, finance, security police, maintenance officers—all the standard specialties that didn't require years of postgraduate work to achieve a specific degree. Theoretically, as a line officer I could be moved out of Personnel at any time and, given the required training, become a maintenance or finance officer or—way, way theoretically—a pilot, even.

Those first few months at Carswell, Mary was my boss twice over, as chief of the Quality Force Section, within which I was assigned, and as the CBPO's "acting" chief, while we waited for a captain replacement to arrive. The CBPO controlled most of the base-level military personnel actions, processing assignments, promotions, decorations, testing, retirements, separations, and evaluations. We kept military personnel records. We managed the paperwork for ID cards.

Supervising seventy-odd people supporting a wing of almost five thousand military members was a big job for a lieutenant, but Mary was more than up to it. She pulled long hours and suffered no sloppy work. She knew the missions, the planes, the strategies, the inner workings of the Air Force. She could joke with airmen as well as colonels, but no one dared cross her. She had the image: short blonde hair never out of place, thin athletic body, every pleat of her uniform sharp enough to cut paper. Her language was the coarsest of anyone I'd known up to now (though a Baptist chaplain who supervised me in seminary was a close second). Mary was a great role model.

I must have worked some that first week. I remember being escorted around the building and introduced to people. I remember asking, "When do I report to the wing commander?" only to hear Mary say again, "That's not necessary." I remember going through the base's INTRO program. But these memories are insubstantial as dreams, with none of the vivid immediacy of Roger Daltrey twirling his microphone or beer spilling onto my wrist as I passed a fresh one down to Billy. Or Mary's crooked grin and swaying hips, the music so loud we had to scream at one another.

Whatever doubts Mary may have had about me seemed to vanish the first evening. Mary, Don, and I went out for burgers, downed with pitchers of beer. Don flirted with a pretty waitress, implying he was a pilot (somehow Personnel officer doesn't have the cachet it deserves).

"Yep, those BUFFs that fly in so low, rattling the windows all around, that's my bailiwick." She didn't seem impressed enough, so he added, "Now you may be worried about all those nukes you hear about on base, but I can't tell you if we really got them or not, because then I'd have to shoot you." It was an old sally, but enough to make her giggle. He added, "Now I'm not saying there *aren't* any nukes, and I'm not saying there *are*, but—"

I interrupted. "Let's just put it this way. Yesterday he was female. You figure it out."

She walked away still giggling. Don scowled, but Mary gave me a sideways look, her pale blue eyes hooded under guarded eyelids, and said admiringly, "Well, all right, Cheryl!"

We ended that first night at Don's apartment complex, cavorting in the pool—having decided to disregard the posted pool hours and climb over the locked gate. I finally got to bed in the little rattrap motel I was staying at around two a.m. Duty hours started at oh-seven-thirty. I barely managed to drag myself in and stay awake all day.

The next couple of nights were similar, then the Who concert. The following day Mary popped her head into Don's office, where he and I were talking and said, "Rancher Dan's tonight for barbecue? And I've heard of a great place for live music, a hole-in-the-wall called the Blue-bird. You in?"

"Great!"

"Super!" But after she left, I felt a sudden drain, my energy rushing out of me. I pictured myself curled up in bed that night, reading a murder mystery, nibbling on a bag of chips, and except for the ticking of the clock and the turning of the pages, no sound but blissful silence.

"Wow," I said, "Mary has so much energy. I don't think I can keep this pace up. I'm exhausted."

Don removed the cigarillo from his mouth and exhaled slowly. "Don't worry. Mary's husband gets off alert tomorrow. That'll end the partying for this month."

He was right. That night was the last blast for a while. I had three weeks of quiet, restful evenings by myself to replenish my introvert's store of energy. But as soon as her husband, a B-52 crew member, entered his monthly rotation on base in the alert facility, Mary charged like a racehorse out of the gate. This became routine, the rhythm of my life at Carswell: three weeks of quiet, sometimes lonely evenings; one week running with Mary; repeat.

In the Real Air Force, I got my first name back. I had two names now: Cheryl and Lieutenant. They seemed like two different people, at best two sides of me, but all too often as if Cheryl was the real me and Lieutenant an imposter, wearing the uniform as a disguise.

In my first meeting with my noncommissioned officer in charge (NCOIC), a staff sergeant, he had asked me, "So, can I call you Cheryl?"

We'd been warned about this at OTS. It was a test. I mostly felt like quavering, unsure Cheryl at that moment but I thrust her back inside and answered firmly, "I prefer to be called Lieutenant Duncan. I'll be happy to extend the same courtesy and call you Sergeant Janson."

He grinned. "Nah, just call me Harry. And it's Jensen, Lieutenant, not Janson."

There were unwritten rules regarding first names, rules every bit as solid as if they'd been codified in the regulations. Officers of the same rank could call each other by name; to do otherwise in fact was considered affected. "Where do you think you are—the Marines?" was a response I got from a lieutenant I addressed by rank my first week on base.

Officers could also address those they outranked by their first names. Even as a baby lieutenant, I addressed the airmen and NCOs I worked with by name, though I made a point of asking the NCOs what they wanted to be called. A chief master sergeant, though, was always just "Chief."

At one time I would have considered this inequality of naming rights a noxious side effect of hierarchy, but in practice it felt different. In a world of nametags and rank insignia, everyone could identify me as "Lieutenant Duncan," which had the peculiar effect of making me feel anonymous. The use of my first name by a senior officer made me feel more significant, more valued. There was no tag identifying me as "Cheryl"—they had to know me, see me, recognize me as an individual.

I was in charge of the Evaluations Office. It was an NCO's job, a temporary place for me until a section chief position opened up. I didn't mind. I knew little about the Air Force, nothing about Personnel, and had never supervised anyone in my life. I preferred to start "small"—though it didn't feel all that small to me. Every one of the five thousand military members on base was required to receive a formal evaluation at least once a year and they were all processed through our office.

I worked the officer reports by myself. Since these were primary documents used by promotion boards, rating inflation had become the accepted norm. Like Lake Wobegon on steroids, in the Air Force all the officers were in the top one percent, every last one outstanding, ready for immediate promotion and more responsibility. Even me. In my two years at Carswell, I was "exceptional," "the finest in the wing," "100 percent effective," "unsurpassed." After all those years of prayer and meditation and good works, I had finally achieved perfection just by joining the Air Force—from mortal clay to paragon, and with documentation to prove it.

Besides Harry Jensen, I supervised three other people. Ben was an airman, with only one stripe on his sleeve. Greg and Pam were three-stripers who'd only recently put on NCO status and now held the rank of just plain "sergeant." (Confusing Air Force redundancies: We were all airmen but there were also four ranks called "airman"; all NCOs were sergeants, but there was also this rank called "sergeant." For clarification, the rank became informally known as "buck sergeant.")

Eighteen-year-old Ben was just out of high school, still prone to acne, eager, good natured, and dumb as a lump of granite—dangerous-dumb in that he never recognized it, never realized he didn't have the experience or knowledge not to forge ahead on his own.

Greg on the other hand was smart and capable, a tall, good-looking black man. The first thing I heard about him was his radio, a boom box he kept at his desk. People complained that he'd been playing it too loud, so Mary had ordered it off. "He's going to ask you if he can turn it back on and the answer is *no!*" she told me.

Sure enough, my first day, Greg said, "Mind if I turn this on," reaching for the knob.

"Keep it off, Greg," I said. "Lieutenant Winston's orders." He sat back unhappily.

Pam was his opposite, a short, plain white woman. She was eccentric—no, peculiar. Oh, hell, the woman was weird. Most days she spent talking to herself as she worked. It wasn't the kind of muttering one does when concentrating on a task ("Let's see. Can that go here? No, that's wrong. Hmmm, wonder if . . .") Although she spoke too low to be understood most of the time, the pitch and stress of her words indicated an ongoing conversation. It was hard not to think of her as the Gollum of the office, hissing, "Yesss, my preciousss, must have my preciousss," all day.

One Wednesday morning, during the CBPO's weekly in-house training hour, I prepared a list of questions about arcane rules in the Air Force regulation governing evaluation reports. "The point is," I told them, "not to know every detail of the reg, but to know how to find the answers."

They took to it eagerly, like a game, except for Harry, an ex-cop who liked being active and hated anything resembling reading and paperwork. So he bumbled around "helping the other three" while I used the quiet twenty minutes to go see Mary.

"Mary, it's been weeks now. I know I've asked you before but it's time. Greg's been good about the radio. He's learned his lesson. How about we let him turn it back on?"

Mary rubbed her temples. "I know he sent you down here to ask me."

"No, he didn't. I didn't even tell him I was going to ask."

"Well, the answer is still no. Don't let them use you. You know, Cheryl, you've got to take charge, be in control. I know you let Harry Jensen call you 'Cheryl.'"

I was stung. "No, I do not. In fact, he asked if he could and I told him to call me 'Lieutenant' and he does." Mary looked skeptical. "Well, at least to my face," I conceded.

The meeting didn't go well. Mary was cross; I was cranky. I left with the start of a headache. When I got back to the office, I heard music. Greg was at his desk, on the phone with a girlfriend, boom box playing. Ben was drawing airplanes in the margins of the regulation. Pam stood facing the wall, having a lively argument with herself. Harry was nowhere to be seen.

"Greg, off the phone," I snapped and reached over to turn off the radio. "Ben, stop that. Pam, come over here. Where's Sergeant Jensen?"

"Why, here I am." Harry stood behind me, steaming cup of coffee in his hand.

Greg grumbled. "The CBPO's closed to customers right now. I finished the assignment. I figured it was okay to play some music."

"Here's my test," Pam chirped, oblivious to my mood.

"It was too hard for me," Ben said. His paper had two answers, both wrong, and doodles covering the rest of it.

"Grade them now, Lieutenant," Pam said. She must have been the kind of little girl who'd wave her arm excitedly in the air, frantic for the teacher to call on her. (No, wait. That was me.)

"Lieutenant, can I talk to you in private." Harry sounded unusually serious, even stern.

We went into the empty section chief's office next door. He closed the door behind us. "Ma'am, I know you and Lieutenant Winston are buddies and she's also your boss. But you need to learn that you can't just side with her all the time. You've got to stand up for your troops. You need to get Greg his music back."

I was pissed. First Mary, now Harry giving me a lecture. "For your information, I just came from asking Lieutenant Winston to let him turn the radio back on. I tried to persuade her. She said no—again. It was the third time I've asked her. It seems like asking just makes her get stubborn about it. So I'm not going to ask again for awhile. Greg's going to have to keep that radio off, and you, *Sergeant*, need to help me enforce it."

"You already talked to Lieutenant Winston about it?"

"Three times."

"Well, you need to let your troops know that so they know you're standing up for them."

"I don't want to be played as a go-between. You don't need to tell them." Of course, he would—I counted on it. Harry was a genial gossip who never met a secret he wouldn't pass on.

After he left, I sat alone in the quiet office for a few minutes, smoking a cigarette, wallowing in my crankiness, probing my headache to see if it would get worse and feeling contrary enough to want it to. When I stepped out the door, I almost ran into a lieutenant colonel striding down the hall. "You're Lieutenant Duncan." It sounded like an accusation.

I saw his nametag. Stevens. I'd heard about him already. A bad day was rapidly getting worse. Lieutenant Colonel Stevens was a pilot, commander of an elite squadron, a golden boy, promoted early to major and lieutenant colonel, now on the fast track to full-bird colonel. He was sharp as a knife blade and just as cutting. He waved an Officer Evaluation Report I'd sent back to his squadron for correction. He did not agree that it contained an error, he refused to correct it, and he never wanted to have his or his staff's time wasted with my bureaucratic nonsense again. All of which he informed me of in words and tones that tore strips of flesh off my bones. He thrust the uncorrected report at me and strode back down the CBPO hallway. I could have sworn the hall rumbled at each step. And to make it worse, I realized he was right about the error.

Harry peered out the Evaluations Office door. "I see you met Colonel Stevens. Phone call for you, ma'am. It's the DO's secretary."

What now? The civilian woman who worked for the Director of Operations was normally a sweet, gentle woman but not today. Apparently, Ben (with his one stripe) had sent the Operations colonel (with his wings) a stern letter about an overdue report. It was, according to the secretary, handwritten, rife with spelling and grammatical errors, and completely impertinent.

So now I had to deal with Ben. "*You* do not send letters to colonels—ever. You may prepare a draft, send it to Sergeant Jensen to review, and he will send it to me. Understood?"

He looked like a puppy wagging his tail, promising to do better next time, but I'd had too much experience with puppies to trust him. He went back to his desk, cheerful as ever, cheerful as Pam. Where was Pam by the way?

"Harry, you need to keep an eye on that kid."

Harry agreed but added, "You know, ma'am, that showed great initiative on Ben's part. It's better to have an airman you got to rein in, than one you got to prod."

"Put a leash on him, Harry. A tight leash."

"Ma'am!" It was a sergeant from across the hall. "Pam has a long knife in her hand, and she's headed for Lieutenant Winston's office!"

Harry and I jumped up and raced down the hallway. We could see Pam's figure up ahead, could see her turn into the CBPO chief's office, could even see the glint of metal from the blade. When we rushed into the office, we saw Mary watching warily as Pam brandished a long, sharp knife at her. Mary was made of strong stuff. She said, "Pam, put the knife down."

"Okay." Pam set the knife on the edge of Mary's desk. Harry immediately grabbed it. A breeze filled the room from the simultaneous exhalation of our individual breaths.

"What's with the knife, Pam?" Mary asked calmly, though a vein throbbed in her forehead.

Pam looked curiously around the office of tense people. "It's a cake knife. Someone left it in the women's restroom. I thought it wasn't safe there so I brought it to you."

Sure enough, there were chocolate crumbs clinging to the blade. Harry and I looked at one another sheepishly. It occurred to me that perhaps we were the weird ones.

I spent the remainder of the day grumbling over incorrect OERs [Officer Evaluation Reports], fussing about late Letters of Evaluation, in turn being fussed at over the phone by higher head-quarters. I snapped at the staff till they were tiptoeing around me. Late in the afternoon, Harry informed me that someone had left a broom lying on the window ledge outside the office.

I looked out the window behind my desk. Sure enough, there was an old broom. I hauled it in. "Good," I said. "I've been wondering how I was going to get home tonight."

Harry and Greg glanced at each other and burst out laughing. I figured they'd planted the prop, but I at least got to provide the punch line.

There were many days like that, when work was a nag of annoyances and complaints, with normal people acting oddly and the odd people scaling it up to bizarre, days when I felt my nerves rubbing against the inside of my skin. You know what I mean—days when you trip over small inconsequential obstacles, when drips of salad dressing stain your blouse right before an important meeting, and the one person who has information you need right away calls in sick. Everyone who's ever worked in an office has experienced this day, the mundane stuff of real life.

But there were just as many days when the sun shone gold light on everything and my hair curled pertly under my beret and my salutes snapped briskly. On those days, Harry mentioned that the NCOs I talked to at headquarters thought I had a sexy voice; I got a staff paper back with a note, "Good job!" scribbled on it; and I heard Pam talking to other people but not once to herself.

Occasionally, though, there were the weird days, neither good nor bad, just weird. On those days I felt like I'd fallen down a rabbit hole and into a world where everything listed, all slightly askew.

The base loudspeaker marked off our days with blaring music, including the mandatory military trinity: Reveille first thing in the morning; retreat with the National Anthem at five (seventeen-hundred); Taps late in the evening, though I was seldom on base to hear it. At twelve, in lieu of a noon whistle, some musical soul in the command post began half an hour of marches. While it played, every military foot on base automatically adjusted to marching cadence, left . . . right . . . left right left, and every military arm began to swing loosely and rhythmically. The lure of the military march, its beat like a heartbeat, its brass like a soaring spirit—even I couldn't resist it, klutz that I was. As with disco, you can love it or hate it, but your body can't ignore it.

The noontime concert always concluded with the "Air Force Song." The rest of the mix varied daily, ranging from traditional Sousas, like "Stars and Stripes Forever," to arrangements of "Grand Old Flag," or the handclapping "Radetzky March." But every day, somewhere in the mix, sounded the familiar notes of what I have since learned is Sousa's "Liberty Bell March."

First time I heard it over the loudspeaker, Mary and I were walking (marching) to the O'Club for lunch. At first I thought nothing of it, but then its unexpected familiarity stopped me, halted the rhythm of my swinging arms and steady step. "Why, that's—"

"Yeah, the theme from Monty Python." Mary grinned. "This guy plays it every day."

According to Mary, the general and some of the older colonels didn't approve of what they considered the subversive popularity of *Monty Python's Flying Circus*. They had advised their junior officers not to watch it, advice that largely went ignored. The show's cheeky irreverence spoke to the communal self-image of the base's lieutenants and captains so it remained must-see, water-cooler fodder. Whoever the military DJ was, he must have had a revolutionary streak, each day musically flipping the bird to our stodgy bosses.

The general's car approached, the one-star license plate loudly proclaiming his presence in our midst. Mary and I saluted the car as we walked, the shadowy figure inside too distant to identify, too unclear to be real. We were saluting a box of metal and an idea of leadership, marching through the midst of our own flying circus.

Line officers spent two years as a second lieutenant, then were automatically promoted to first lieutenant. After two more years, came promotion to captain. Although a promotion board reviewed all eligible officers' records to determine who was to be promoted, it was virtually noncompetitive. In Mary's words, "You have to be a fucking axe murderer not to make captain."

Mary pinned on captain in the fall. We held a ceremony at the CBPO. Mary exchanged her single silver bars for the double captain's bars. She gave me all her first lieutenant insignia. I wouldn't need them for more than a year and a half, which seemed impossibly far away.

We held a reception in the Quality Force office with chips and salsa, beer and champagne. Gradually, people drifted away until only we officers remained and nothing came out of the last champagne bottle. So we moved the party to Mary's, each of us stopping to grab more beer. Mary's husband wasn't home that evening, having been slated for a night flight. They had a large comfortable house, and we made ourselves right at home there. We smoked and drank beer. We shot pool and drank beer. We watched videos and drank beer.

We watched *The Kids Are All Right* because Mary got a kick out of seeing me drool over a younger Roger Daltrey swinging his mike at Woodstock, his blond hair in curly locks falling over his chest, which was barely covered with a fringed leather vest. "Oh, go on, Cheryl, say it!" Mary urged.

"Fringe!" I yelled at the TV. "Fringe!" It was our code word for my incredible lust. Mary, Billy, and Don fell back on the cushions laughing hysterically. We played loud music—ZZ Top, AC/DC, Led Zeppelin. And we drank beer. Don got up, staggering, and insisted on leaving.

Mary, Billy, and I drank more beer and started another movie. I stretched out on the couch. I heard Mary say, "Man, I'm shit-faced" and stumble into her bedroom. I fell asleep.

"What the hell!" Mary's husband had come home to find beer cans all over the house, ashtrays full and stinking, me struggling awake on one couch, Billy snoring on the other. "Get up. Go home and go to bed. Go. Go."

It was after three. Driving Luigi, I followed Billy for the first couple of miles. I crept along in the empty darkness, giggling each time Billy fell over on his motorcycle, which he did frequently, slowly and gracefully like Arte Johnson falling over on his tricycle on *Laugh-In*. I found it outrageously funny. *That idiot, he's so drunk he can barely see straight.* It didn't occur to me to apply the same thought to myself. Miraculously—God looking out for fools, perhaps—we both made it home safely, though I understand Billy's wife tore him a new one when he came crawling in.

I arrived for work at 7:40 the next day, ten minutes late but still the first officer to make it in. I was in that rotten state of being still somewhat drunk but already hungover. Harry said, "Lieu—I mean, *Captain* Winston called. She'll be a little late. I hear you officers decided to go on a bit of a binge last night." I managed a weak smile and a grunt. Billy trudged by looking green. Don was merely gray.

Around eight thirty, as I sat staring at reports that seemed to be written in Sanskrit, trying to take notes with a shaky hand, Mary came in. "I feel like shit! Let's go get an egg sandwich."

If she had suggested any other kind of food at that moment, I would have felt like throwing up, but an egg sandwich . . . I hadn't eaten one since I was a kid. It suddenly seemed like the best food in the world, the one thing my alcohol-battered system craved.

The two of us went to a grungy little snack bar off base, where we gradually turned human again. We didn't talk, just sipped coffee and ate and thought. Mary's friendship was showing me a side of myself I hadn't been introduced to before. It wasn't that I wanted to drink so much as a rule or go out all the time. I really didn't even want to make it with Roger Daltrey (well, maybe). But I liked knowing I was capable of it. I liked feeling a part of things, no longer a detached outsider.

As my innards stopped quivering and the fog in my brain began to clear, I looked over at Mary, who was nursing her head in her hand. I took another bite of the bland sandwich and chewed, swallowed, ingested. It tasted like contentment.

## B. PESKY CRITTERS

My off-base apartment was infested with the stuff of my nightmares: Texas-sized cockroaches and the three S's—scorpions, spiders, and snakes. Who could spend a cozy evening curled up, reading a good book with all those critters around? Scorpions basked on my bedspread or loomed over me, their shapes magnified in the glass bowl of the overhead light. They skittered across the floor in front of my bare toes and threatened me with stinger and waving claws from inside the bathtub I was stepping into.

I opened my front door once to discover a hamster-sized tarantula on the threshold. I swear it had a leg raised, getting ready to knock. I slammed the door quickly, then nervously stared at the narrow space under the door in case it decided to squeeze its hairy self in uninvited. Add the occasional rattlesnake sunning itself in the parking lot, and no wonder I was jumpy.

One evening, the doorbell rang. I peered out, half expecting to see a gigantic hairy spider. Almost as bad, two strange men stood there. I opened the door but left the chain on. "Yes?"

A burly, red-faced man in sunglasses flipped open a badge at me, then quickly slapped it shut. "Sheriff's department. Got a few questions."

I unhooked the chain and stepped outside. The big man thrust a bunch of letters at me. "You seen this fellow lately?" He spoke in a drawl that heightened his resemblance to a movie stereotype.

Surprised, I looked at the name on the letters. "I don't know him. Don't know who he is."

He raised his eyebrows, pursed his lips. "Really? Well, he used to live here."

"I've lived here for four months now. I've never heard of this guy."

"Right. Well, you see him again, you call the sheriff's department. You hear me?"

"I have no idea what he looks like." Under the sheriff's sunglassed stare, my face grew warm. His disdain almost convinced me I was guilty of whatever he suspected.

He obviously didn't believe my denial. He snorted. "You see him, you call us."

The younger one repeated, "You call us," jabbing his index finger at me with each word. They left, adding to my list of fears an unknown criminal who might show up at any time, who might even have a key to my apartment. Almost as scary was the notion of the sheriff dropping by again. I locked the door carefully, put the chain on, and pulled an easy chair in front of it.

That awful apartment was Texas in a microcosm to me—hot, bare, crawling with hostile critters in an expanse of dust and scrub. Utterly inhospitable. Until one morning when I was driving to work, day unfolded in front of me, a cloudless blue sky rising up out of the gray dawn. In that clear, early light, for the first time I saw the sky as a discrete entity, more than just an absence of landscape. The firmament. "This inverted bowl we call the sky." I could see the soft curve of the bowl overhead. I felt myself within it, covered by its tremendous glory of light and color, blue shimmering with gold streaks, no tree-covered slopes to distract from its magnificence. The sight stunned me, a physical sensation like a sweet shock. I pulled off the road and got out of my car to gape at it, turning in every direction. I didn't feel like a despised creature crawling beneath it but one blessed by the protection of its majesty. I fell in love with the sky and understood Texas better—a place that hunkered close to the earth to give the sky all the space it needed.

I arrived at work, trembling with excitement and possibility. I pulled in next to Mary. It was the first time I'd met her outside in uniform since she put on captain. I saluted her.

She returned the salute but said, "Cheryl, we're friends. You don't have to salute me."

"Sure I do. You outrank me. Besides, how do you think it looks to the airmen walking around if they see a lieutenant not saluting a captain?"

"Yeah. Yeah, you're right." She beamed at me as if I were a slow-witted student who was finally catching on and had just earned a gold star.

Under that bright, open sky all sorts of things were becoming clear to me. Like the connection between rank and respect and how friendship could thrive even in a hierarchy. When I saluted Mary there was joy in the simple gesture.

"So what are you so happy about?" she said.

"I just decided I like Texas. And I've decided to move, find a better place to live in."

I found a small town house I could afford in an attractive, grassy development. If there were critters lurking in my rooms there, they at least had the courtesy to stay hidden. On my first leave, I drove to Cincinnati. When I returned to Fort Worth I brought back my dog Tippy, a scroungy mix of poodle and terrier and God knows what else. I drove a new Fiat, having tearfully traded in my reliable Luigi for an air-conditioned model.

Now I felt settled. I had friends, a home, a dog, and a car named Eric, a Strada.

At work all day, I heard the roar of the planes, bombers primarily, and then I stopped hearing them, the constant engine noise moving naturally into the background of my consciousness. The B-52Ds were large, lumbering planes. Taking off and landing, they rumbled low overhead as I drove back and forth to work or shopped for groceries or went out to eat or for a walk. You could see the underbellies of the huge bombers, which came in vibrating as if they would split apart and cast debris down on the earth and all of us upon it. They never did though, sturdy, reliable workhorses of an airplane, known affectionately as BUFFS—big ugly flying fuckers or fellows, depending on your audience. I loved the BUFFs. I gloried in standing within the shadow of one flying overhead, all other sound blocked out.

With its bombers, Carswell was part of Strategic Air Command (SAC). Its motto, "Peace is Our Profession," we mocked with lewd cartoons and puns. But we believed in it also or wanted to believe. It was the Cold War, and the strategic bombers were one leg of the nation's nuclear triad. Carswell kept aircrews on alert and aircraft engines running 24/7. We preened ourselves on preventing the balance of power from tipping over into outright war. We all had our parts to play.

One night I woke up with the telephone ringing next to my bed. I groaned, looked at the clock. Midnight. I picked up, hoping it was nothing more than an obscene call. It was Captain Rush, the new CBPO chief. "This is a recall. Activate your pyramid alert."

I grabbed my phone list from the nightstand drawer and made calls to other groggy voices. Then I jumped out of bed and into my uniform, no showering, no shampooing, no makeup. I left Tippy sleeping in a pretzel position in the middle of the bed.

The streets were empty until I got to Carswell's front gate, where cars were backed up with airmen reporting for the recall. I drove to the flight line, to a large hangar where the Mobility Processing Unit (MPU) and Mobility Control Center (MCC) were set up. Mary was already there, supervising a shaggy group of NCOs and airmen.

Women with long hair wore it twisted up into the simplest, most pragmatic forms. Men's faces showed stubble that would have earned them a reprimand at normal times, but not tonight. A man who'd stopped to shave would have been as guilty of poor judgment as a woman wearing eyeliner.

In the MCC, phones were already ringing. NCOs and officers bustled with activity. Terse acronyms flew through the air. Someone was making coffee, our life blood. If the Soviets ever managed to kill our coffee supply, the world would be theirs. I looked at the schedule. The first group to deploy, sixty maintenance troops, was due to process through in fifteen minutes. Impossible. We were busted from the beginning.

///EXERCISE EXERCISE EXERCISE/// This was how every piece of paper I looked at that night was marked. Not that I was tempted to believe it was real. If the Cold War should erupt into combat, well, the implications were something no sane person could hold in her mind for long. But we had to prepare for it, pretend we could survive, even win. We exercised our wartime plans frequently, usually unannounced, with no pattern to the alerts and middle-of-the-night wake-ups.

In mobility scenarios, we practiced our capability to deploy hundreds of personnel from Carswell to a designated forward operating location, where they would provide wartime support for our bombers and aircrews. Depending on the plan, we deployed everyone from pilots to maintenance crews, security police, sometimes administrative and other support staff. The CBPO was responsible for out-processing them, hence the MPU.

These exercises were the most important thing I did at Carswell, my first slight taste of what it was to be a warrior. I hated them. I resented the pretend wartime, so messy and inconvenient. I preferred the boredom of checking evaluations for misspelled words to the frantic, contrived urgency of an exercise, with its frenzied atmosphere that bred mistakes, the rapid, half-heard instructions, the criticisms from inspectors, the whines from bleary-eyed airmen slogging through the line.

"Listen up, folks. This exercise is going to be different." The MCC chief had everyone's attention. I stopped perusing the mobility list and swiveled around to face him. "Simulations are out of hand," he said, as if telling us something we didn't already know. "The wing commander has forbidden all but the essential ones. As far as personnel and squadrons go, nobody is exempt from participating in this exercise. No exemptions, at all. Got it?"

There was a chorus of mumbled "Yes, sirs." The MCC chief disappeared back into his office where he did . . . something, I didn't know, worked crosswords maybe, napped, sang show tunes, all in the nervous faith he had to have in his underlings. I stepped out to the MPU to make sure Mary knew.

Mary and Billy took the twelve-hour shifts as MPU chief. The MPU was a human assembly line, where deploying personnel lined up to have, first of all, their presence checked. We had by-name lists of everyone scheduled to deploy—they had to·match the skill, level, and rank required by the particular plan we were using. What sounded on paper like a simple process was complicated by the squadrons' frequent failure to keep their lists up to date. Individuals who weren't on the list to deploy showed up, while others who *were* on the list failed to show.

Even those who showed up that night were ill prepared. Too many required a new ID card or dog tags, which were punched out painstakingly on a device that looked like it could have had something to do with medieval torture—one letter at a time, name, social security number, blood type, religious preference. The medics on the MPU had to do quick blood draws and perform the tests to determine type for those members who'd forgotten and didn't have the sense to make it up to get through the exercise line more quickly. Medical personnel who weren't doing blood tests used the

MPU to check shot records. They were busy tonight, updating everyone's annual flu shot.

We had a lawyer on the line to update wills and powers of attorney. Since this wasn't a real deployment, he sat engrossed in a detective story. A chaplain was available to pray with, baptize, or counsel. He wandered around the line, talking to the deploying personnel, bucking them up, though most looked too sleepy and cranky to appreciate his efforts.

Usually, at least some of the participants were simulated, especially the rated officers, who often weren't required to show up due to crew rest requirements. We loved these dummies. They were like imaginary friends who always did what was required and arrived on time with up-to-date shot records and dog tags. No simulations tonight made processing a real bitch.

From my position as the Personnel representative to the MCC, I sat in the relative sanity of a windowed room overlooking the processing line. My role was to troubleshoot problems and provide reports on how personnel processing was going. Around oh-five-hundred, one of the flying squadrons didn't even show up to out-process, the one commanded by the dread Lieutenant Colonel Stevens. I'd had no dealings with him since he flung that evaluation report at me in the halls of the CBPO, and I'd hoped to keep it that way. But with the words "no exemptions at all" in my brain, I dialed the squadron number with a trembling finger. A friendly major answered. He sounded surprised that they were supposed to take part but promised he'd get right on it.

"As soon as you can, sir," I urged. "Your squadron's already late."

Twenty minutes later, the pilots still hadn't shown up. I called back. The same major told me his boss said not to do it. "You see, we have an automatic exemption. It doesn't apply to us."

"Sir, I have a literal mind. And to me, 'no exemptions at all' means no exemptions."

"Okay, well, I'll tell the colonel," he said, a trace of reluctant messenger in his voice.

A few minutes later, I felt a cold draft hit me, like a dead spot in a haunted house. I turned to find him looming over me—not the pleasant major, but the decidedly unpleasant lieutenant colonel. I pulled myself up out of the chair. "Sir?"

"Stop harassing my squadron, Lieutenant. We have an automatic exemption. We've had it ever since I've been here. I negotiated it with the DO and wing commander myself. So I don't want you calling my squadron again. Understand me?"

"Yes, sir." I was barely capable of whispering. I cleared my throat and said louder, "Yes, sir. Uh, the problem is, sir, this exercise, the wing commander said no exemptions. At all. Sir."

"That doesn't apply to us! Are you too stupid to understand what 'automatic' means?"

"No, sir. I understand." I gulped down a frightened air bubble trying to escape. "But I was told that for this exercise, *every* squadron would play."

"But we're automa—oh!" He stopped and exhaled a long, loud breath that froze in midair, pointed like an icicle and aimed at me. "You are the worst excuse for an officer I have ever known. There's no point in arguing with an idiot. Where's your boss?"

I would have loved to pass him on to the MCC chief, but he'd gone to a meeting. I told Stevens this, then, spurred by duty, squeaked out, "Sir, your squadron's already an hour late."

"Okay, that's it! I'm going to the DO. But Lieutenant, you haven't heard the end of this."

After he left, I sank trembling back into my chair, checking my psyche for wounds. The room had gotten quiet during my public flaying, but now the other reps turned back to their papers and phones. The sergeant sitting next to me refilled my cup of coffee; another passed me the exercise message file. They treated me gently, like one who's received a mortal hit.

Mary burst in. "I saw Stevens leave. When are they coming?"

"I don't know. He's fighting it, going to the DO."

She muttered something that sounded like, "What an asshole," and returned to the line, leaving a ripple of nervous laughter in the MCC.

I sat miserably hunched over the message file, thinking that when the wing commander said "No exemptions" what he meant was, "No exemptions—except of course for Colonel Stevens's squadron, which has an automatic exemption so it's not even worth mentioning."

Nothing dreadful would happen to me, except I'd be revealed as the stupid, inept pseudo-officer Lieutenant Colonel Stevens saw and which I often suspected I was. *He's right. I am a wretched excuse for an officer.*

Twenty minutes later the squadron still hadn't shown up, but a pleasant-looking major was pulling up a chair next to me. He introduced himself as Stevens's deputy, the one I'd spoken to on the phone. He said, "The DO confirmed that yes, we do have to play this time, and he told us to get our butts down here to out-process ASAP! He was—umh—let's just say unhappy."

The major had questions about what they needed to do. Later I saw their squadron coming into the MPU, Stevens first, looking— let's just say unhappy.

Though Carswell wasn't a large base, I seldom ran into the flying squadron commanders. So I was surprised to see Stevens in the CBPO two days later, the exercise over. He was stepping out of Captain Rush's office and was heading in my direction. My gut twisted itself into a tangled knot. Yes, I'd won last time we met, but it wasn't always healthy for the mouse to trump the lion.

When he reached me, however, he smiled. The man actually knew how to smile, and what a lovely, warm smile it was. "Afternoon, Cheryl. How are you today?"

Cheryl. He knew my name. I stammered out, "Fine, thank you, sir. And you?"

"Doing great, thanks."

He walked on down the hallway. I watched him, stunned. Cute butt. He was actually pretty sexy—fantasy fodder. Who would have guessed? I turned into Rush's office. "What did Colonel Stevens want? I mean, hello, sir. What did Colonel Stevens want?"

Rush looked up at me, a hint of a smile lurking on his thin lips. "He thinks *you* are shit hot. In fact, he wants to steal you away from us. He wants you to run his orderly room."

"What!" My stress threshold couldn't handle a daily dose of him, fantasy fodder or not.

"I told him, not just no, but hell, no." He grinned. "Don't get cocky. Go back to work."

So I had faced down the lion, defeated him in combat, lived to tell about it, *and* he thought I was shit hot. I strutted all the way back to my office.

## C. BECOMING AN OFFICER

Reassignments came rushing in. Billy achieved his dream of going to flight school, so Mary became the new Personnel Utilization Section chief. I was moved from my cozy slot in Evaluations to take her place as Quality Force chief. When Don was reassigned and two new junior officers arrived, I came face to face with one of the harsher realities of military life: how quickly the people you learned to care about came and went. I wondered when Mary would be reassigned.

Stability was supposedly provided by the civilian force that served also, but I couldn't see it in our one civilian section chief, a pursed-lipped, balding man who ran the Records and ID card programs among other things. Mr. G had ruled his little kingdom for more than twenty years. He despised lieutenants. He delighted in putting me down in the middle of staff meetings, with Captain Rush, the other officers, and most of the senior NCOs there as audience.

"Actually, Lieutenant," he would say with a tiny cough, "I believe the regulation requires you to . . . [fill in one of the many things I was doing wrong]."

He yelled at me one day because some visiting Pakistani officers I was responsible for hadn't come to his section for ID card applications. He brandished a message in front of me from the Air Force-level ID card policy office. "This says IDs for foreign officers *must* be provided within the first week." He was almost foaming at the mouth.

"Let me see that." I glanced over the message. The official who sent it was a civilian with a first name of Lynn. "She's talking about those foreign officers who are *entitled* to an ID card."

Mr. G sneered. "That 'Lynn' is not a she, but a he and he's *the* Air Force expert on IDs. And we *always* give foreign officers ID cards."

I handed him the message back. "Without coming through me? According to the Foreign Officer reg, the only ones who get ID cards are those whose orders specifically authorize it."

I found the page in the regulation and flourished it. *Ha! My reg against your message!*

He grabbed it from me and read the part I pointed out to him. His face turned pale. I said, "I hope you haven't been giving ID cards to all the foreign officers visiting General Dynamics. None of the orders I've seen have authorized it." I got just the right mix of concern, professionalism, and malice into my tone.

Captain Rush blanched. "We've been issuing IDs without authorization?"

"Unh. Unh." Mr. G couldn't seem able to come out with anything more. That was the last time he messed with me. Fortunately, we had the two new lieutenants for him to torment.

With my new job and new responsibilities, I also had more people working for me. A chief master sergeant joined me as my section NCOIC. In looks he reminded me of a ferret, wiry, sleek, and pale gray all over, including a thatch of hair turning from steel to white and intelligent bright eyes. I was wary of him at first, a smart, savvy man at the highest level of NCO rank assigned to work for a second lieutenant. Surely he would resent it. Fortunately, the chief seemed to enjoy guiding a lieutenant to higher levels, playing Yoda to my Luke Skywalker.

SAC ran on checklists. Once a quarter, I was required to pull them out and quiz my NCOICs on their programs. "Do you file each report within thirty days?" "Yes." Check.

"Do you personally counsel separating airmen about loss of benefits?" "Yes." Check.

"Do you provide all retirees with a copy of the Family Assistance brochure?" "No."

"What!" My rhythm broken, my pencil hovered uncertainly over the checklist.

"SAC hasn't sent us any of those in a year. I don't think they make them anymore."

"But, but, do you know that? Have you asked?"

"Nah. They'd send them to us if they had them." I froze. My poor career, ruined from the start for lack of some glossy brochures. "Just mark NA, Lieutenant. Next question's yes."

When SAC announced it was sending inspectors to Carswell, it wasn't good enough just to ask the questions (it never really was). The chief advised me, "Demand to see stuff, poke in the files, pull out the records." Mary said, "Get your hands dirty, Cheryl."

Out of all my NCOs, only Hank, who was in charge of the large Separations office, dug his heels in. Normally a cheerful, easygoing guy, he surprised me with his belligerent refusal. "No way, Lieutenant. We just did a self-inspection last month. There's no point in going over that damn checklist again so soon. You may have time to waste but I don't. And I'm not going to pull my troops away from their work to go over this shit one more time."

His ruddy face was even more flushed than usual, his lips pressed into firm defiance. The chief looked at me anxiously but said nothing. It was time for me to show my officer chops, to let Hank know who was in charge, go *mano a mano* in a power struggle, order him to obey.

*Never let them see your weakness,* I'd always heard. *You've got to stay strong and in charge.* But I never had much faith in my ability to cover up my weaknesses, and I hated confrontation. I suspected that if I pulled the order card I would be working with a hostile sergeant from then on out. Besides, what if in his flushed stubbornness Hank still refused? It would be insubordination. I would have to start some kind of disciplinary action.

I decided to rely on my old standby. I begged.

"Look, Hank. This is my first inspection. Ever since I've been here I've heard horror stories about the inspectors. I got to tell you, I'm a nervous wreck. I'm scared. I need to do everything possible to get ready. So please, just humor me." He looked at me thoughtfully. "Please?"

His mouth relaxed into a smile. He nodded. "Yes, ma'am, we'll do the checklists again. Let me know when you're ready."

What struck me about this exchange, the reason it lodged in my memory, was how easy it was to get cooperation when I made the lieutenant shut up and let Cheryl speak. The inspection came and went without drama. We didn't blow the top off anything but we passed. Good enough.

A new tech sergeant arrived to take over evaluations. Like Harry Jensen, Kyle Harney had been released from Security Police due to some physical ailment. In contrast to Harry's laidback amiability, Kyle was an eager, intense hard-charger, determined to maintain our "Best in SAC" rating, even though he was brand new to Personnel.

"No one expects you to do that right away," I told him, then realized I was repeating the words my predecessor had said to me, words meant to reassure but that had instead dared me. I could tell by the stubborn look on Kyle's face that he too had no intention of taking the offered pass. He worked hard, long hours. He deserved to succeed, but too often he didn't. The chief and I performed cursory reviews of finalized reports. We confessed to one another that we hated to find errors—which we did too frequently, mostly minor, like typos and misspellings in those days before word processing and spell-checker. Kyle winced over each error we pointed out and spent more and more time in the office.

"Don't work so hard," I told him. "Slow down. Get some rest. Don't take it personally."

I knew he would do well eventually, as long as he didn't run himself into the ground at the beginning. The chief tried to take over some of the administrative burdens from him, but Kyle insisted on doing everything himself. I watched him get paler and quieter as if he were losing sap and turning brittle. I worried about him—mainly, in honesty, the office he was running—but had too many other responsibilities now to focus on his problems.

One day Captain Rush walked into the office, frowning. "Afternoon, Cheryl. Chief. We have an appointment at five thirty in the wing commander's office. Hope you don't have any other plans, Cheryl. If you do, cancel them. You're invited to attend too, Chief."

"What's it about, sir?"

"Something to do with an OER on Major Sotero."

"Oh?" Major Sotero was an up and comer, a pilot and executive officer for the Director of Operations. I'd seen his OER just that morning. I glanced at the chief and saw his forehead crease into wrinkles.

"Apparently the DO's secretary sent his OER to us several weeks ago. The wing commander's secretary has been expecting it. The two ladies finally got together, each accusing the other. 'Where's that report?' Looks like it's somewhere in the bowels of the CBPO. So we have an appointment this evening." He grimaced. "Find the report and bring it with you. I've got another meeting now, so I'll have to meet you there."

As soon as he left, I closed the door and turned to the chief. "Didn't I see that report?"

"It was in the Eighth Air Force package this morning."

"I don't understand. Let's hope that package hasn't gone out. Get Kyle and the OER."

Normally OERs had three evaluators, first the supervisor—in this case, the DO—then on up the chain of command. Next would be the wing commander, and in this case, the two-star general who was the Numbered Air Force commander at Eighth Air Force in Louisiana. I could have sworn that the report I'd seen on Sotero already had the wing commander's signature.

The chief brought me the sealed envelope containing the reports to be mailed off base to Eighth Air Force. Kyle was with him, looking paler than ever. I opened the envelope and found Sotero's OER. I was right. "I don't understand. The wing secretary's been looking for this report. How did it get past her?" I saw the truth in Kyle's desperate eyes. "You forged it?"

He winced at the word "forged." The chief bit his lip—I could tell he'd gotten there way before me. Kyle was too broken to try to lie. The story came out, how hard he'd been working, but he just kept getting further and further behind. He was used to excelling. He couldn't face the flak of this important report being so late. "So I typed in the suggested remarks the rater provided—you know they seldom change them—and then I copied the wing commander's signature off another OER. And well, there it is."

"And have you done this with other OERs?"

"Oh, no, ma'am, no." He looked straight at me, the wide-eyed look of the innocent. I wanted to believe him, so I did.

"Why haven't you come to us for help? We've offered to help you a lot."

"I wanted to do it myself." He sounded like a stricken kid.

"Okay. We've got a meeting at the wing in a bit. Don't leave until we get back." Not that he ever did leave that early, but he had the look of a man who needed several stiff drinks. Later, as we headed to the meeting, I saw Kyle at his desk, staring into space.

"What are you going to say, Lieutenant?" the chief asked.

"I have no idea." And I didn't. I wished I'd had a chance to talk to Mary first, but she was on leave that week. I was on my own.

We were on time but they were all already there, waiting for us. It felt like an inquisition, even Captain Rush sitting stiffly in the circle of chairs set up around the wing exec's desk. Major Sotero himself was there, looking embarrassed; also the two secretaries, looking furious; the DO, ditto. The wing exec, a lieutenant colonel, looked harried. He waved us into the two empty chairs. The secretaries immediately started talking.

"I sent it to the CBPO . . ." "Never got it . . ." "Plenty of time . . ." "Boss is asking . . ."

The DO weighed in with his memory of completing the OER weeks ago. As they talked, they stared at me accusingly. Finally, the wing exec raised his hand to stop the barrage. "So where *is* the report?"

The chief had it, tucked into a folder, but before he could do anything, I blurted out, "I'm sorry, sir, but I couldn't bring it. It's ruined. The NCO who works OERs accidentally knocked his cup over and spilled coffee all over it."

"What!" This came from everyone but the chief, who had the presence of mind not to react.

I nodded. "I'm really sorry. This shouldn't have happened, and we'll make sure it doesn't again. At any rate, the sergeant felt responsible to type up a new, clean version and get it back to the DO—for your signature first, sir." I nodded to the colonel. "But frankly, he's been overwhelmed with work lately, and this got pushed to the back burner. I've told him to get it done tonight, and he'll hand-carry a clean copy to you tomorrow morning, sir."

There was some grumbling, but the drama had gone out of the meeting. A coffee accident, everyone could understand one of those in this caffeine-addicted society. The only thing equally likely was destruction in a desk fire caused by the base-wide nicotine habit.

The chief and I walked back to the CBPO alone in the quiet dusk. "You lied, Lieutenant." He spoke almost in a whisper, a strange note in his voice. I couldn't see his expression, but I realized I'd gone out on a limb. I'd created a cover up. The chief, a model of integrity, would be complicit unless he ratted me out.

There was nothing I could do about it now, so I simply agreed. "Yes."

"You lied to protect your troop, ma'am." Now I recognized the tone. It rang with respect, almost awe. I had done something great in his eyes, something beyond what he'd expected of me, beyond what I'd expected of myself. For an NCO, protecting the troops was one of the highest qualities of a good leader. I'd finally demonstrated it. Maybe I hadn't tried hard enough to save Greg's boom box, but I'd stepped forward when it counted and saved Kyle's career.

"Look, Chief, Kyle's been overwhelmed and—" but he knew all the reasons for my lie as well as I did, probably better. I started over. "When we get back, I don't want to see him. You fill him in. Tell him I expect to see a clean new copy on my desk tomorrow morning, ready to return to Ops for signature. And I don't care what he says, I'd like you to go in and work with him till the work gets caught up—and teach him the Personnel business while you're at it."

"Yes, ma'am!"

I don't know if the end ever justifies the means. I don't know if my lie bought time for a bright, capable NCO to find his footing and reach his higher potential in the Air Force. Or if it protected a weak liar, whose dishonesty would play out over and over again in his career. However, I do know that lie was the first time I acted on my own in the Air Force, unadvised and without guidance from regulations or checklists, without Mary's example or the chief's advice. It was my first independent decision, for good or bad. An officer's decision.

The day came when Mary entered my office, sat down, handed me a message announcing her assignment to Blytheville Air Force Base in Arkansas. I had known it was coming, but it was hard having it finalized, the date four months out. Such a short time.

"CBPO chief," I said. "That's great. A good career move."

"Yeah, but, hell—Arkansas!"

"You'll have fun, Mary. You always do. It'll be a good job for you." I felt lonely already.

Those beautiful spring months we spent a lot of time hanging out, usually just the two of us now. We went to museums, the Water Gardens, to the mall occasionally for what we called power shopping. We went to movies, everything from *The Big Chill* to Ingmar Bergman's version of *The Magic Flute*. We went to the ballet, which Mary was as passionate about as rock music. We went to rock concerts—Fleetwood Mac, the Kinks, Rod Stewart. I converted her to Bruce Springsteen, which I figured made us even for the Roger Daltrey thing. After Springsteen song titles, I sometimes called her, "Mary, Queen of Arkansas," and she would respond, "Hey, hey, hey, Sherry Darlin'."

On Sundays, we often walked our dogs in the Botanic Garden, letting them loose to play while we sat under a tree talking. Long-limbed, elegant Kelly, Mary's Irish setter, galumphed around, immediately obedient to Mary's call, while my stubby-legged Tippy darted all over. The day always ended with me having to chase her down while Mary laughed hysterically.

Then overnight, it seemed, Mary and Kelly were gone. Mary and I were never assigned together again, but our friendship has survived, strong and flavored with the spice of a shared youth. I measure the time in dogs. Four elegant Irish setters on her part compared to two scruffy but long-lived mutts on mine. Around the time I finished writing about the Who, about Mary's promotion, about "Fringe!" and egg sandwiches, I received an email from her:

*I've been feeling a bit of melancholy for those times* [at Carswell] *recently. . . . In August, I saw a TV special about a concert dedicated to the Who, with a bunch of various musicians coming out and doing their songs and then at the end, what's left of the Who coming out and still blowing everyone away. I immediately was taken back to our Who concert experience which as I recall was during the first week you were at Carswell. And then all of our multiple viewings of "The Kids Are All Right" (Fringe!!). God those were good times, and I missed you all the more for seeing that show and not being able to share it with you!*

It made me think that invisible strands must connect individuals to one another. That we all sit on the threads of a large, intricate web and when we tweak one end, it vibrates through a winding maze and arouses a response at the other. One of those mysteries I have always associated with God.

# CHAPTER FOUR

# "AT THE CENTER"

### 1982–1986: AF Manpower and Personnel Center, Randolph AFB TX

## A. A SHADOW

The desk across from mine was still empty. Its inhabitant had been gone on a combination of leave and temporary duty the whole two weeks I'd been there. He was due back today, and I was curious to meet him. I bent over my desk, trying to read the dull regulations I was supposed to be boning up on. My head jerked up each time someone entered through the space in the partitions that served as the office doorway. But it was always someone I already knew, wandering sluggishly in to start work.

Major Hallemart arrived and headed directly to the coffee pot. "Hey," he yelled, "Who took the last cup and didn't make another pot?" I heard a muffled "Oops. Sorry, sir," then Hallemart laughing, in a good-natured mood today. Thank goodness. If it had been his Mr. Hyde day, he would have exploded all over the office.

Seven thirty passed. Everyone else was in and busily at work, but the empty desk remained empty. Seven thirty-five. Seven forty. It was seven forty-five before he strode in, a tall, middle-aged man in a blue suit, with the snow white hair of someone who'd gone gray prematurely. He threw his briefcase on his desk and announced to everyone in earshot, "That's it! Divorce is final. And I'm *never* getting married *again*." There was a pattering of hand claps.

Then he spotted me—the newbie watching bemused. A streak of red glowed in his tan cheeks. "You must be our new officer. I'm Lynn."

"Cheryl Duncan." We shook hands.

"Good to have you here. Sorry about the dramatic entrance, but . . . well . . ."

"It's okay," I said. "I gather congratulations are in order."

So this was the great man, the civilian with the transgendered name, who, as Mr. G had once told me, was "*the* Air Force expert on ID cards." At Carswell I'd seen his name on tons of messages, including an announcement that he was the Air Force's Civilian Personnel Manager of the Year. He seemed like a celebrity to me. I'd been thrilled to discover I'd be working in the same office, his fame reflecting on me like glamour off a movie star.

There are people whose mere presence affects the workings of the cosmos around them, and Lynn was one of these. He was the hub of the office. With his arrival everything seemed livelier, with more laughter, more activity, more production. The civilian women openly adored him, buzzing around him like anxious handmaids. The men joked with him and sought his advice. Major Hallemart barely took a step without consulting him.

Lynn was the chief of the DEERS and ID Card Policy Section. DEERS (the Defense Enrollment Eligibility Reporting System) was a new Department of Defense computer database, designed to track and control the military members, dependents, and retirees who claimed military benefits and medical care. It saved millions of tax dollars. All those people affected, all that money—DEERS was the happening place to be, the exciting program in our branch. Too bad I wasn't part of it. But even though I was in the smaller section, the prosaic Records Management, I found having Lynn around made the difference between a dull workday and one infused with possibility.

Randolph Air Force Base in San Antonio glistened like a jewel in the Air Force's crown. Originally built for training the Army's burgeoning cadre of pilots, the so-called "West Point of the Air" wore its aging beauty gracefully. Randolph mimicked its host city's Spanish-style architecture, with buildings on the National Historic Register. VIPs gathered within them for confabs. From the main gate a broad avenue led through the lush lawns of senior officer housing to the base's most recognizable landmark, a white tower called the Taj Mahal. Its beauty earned it the name, though it bore no resemblance to the Indian mausoleum.

In 1982 Randolph was home to a training wing and several higher-level headquarters, including the Air Force Manpower and Personnel Center. This was known so familiarly throughout the Air Force as MPC that when the manpower part dropped out, the Air Force renamed it the Military Personnel Center so as to keep the initials. But for those of us assigned there it was simply the Center, as if the Air Force rotated around it.

It reminded me of an intricate Russian nesting doll stuffed with directorates and divisions and branches and sections, all with dull, elaborate titles and arcane connections with one another.   Lost among them all was the tiniest, almost invisible doll, the chief of Military Records Management Procedures. That highfalutin designation was mine.

The branch I was in was relegated to D-wing, the new, utilitarian section of a beautiful old building, as far as you could get from the sweeping entrance and the commander's office, far from the areas with the new furniture and potted plants and soft carpets. We had concrete floors and glaring overhead neon lights. We shared space with other wallflowers in a huge windowless, airless box of a room and pretended our partitions were walls.

Nevertheless, our branch held one unique distinction: we made policy that was implemented Air Force-wide; we wrote USAF-level regulations. The Personnel staff at the Pentagon liked to say that all policy originated there, but it was really only the sexy stuff they dealt with, things like promotions and assignments and recruiting and separations. The dull work of records and ID cards was happily handed over to us. We were the only policy-making office at MPC. As a brand-new first lieutenant, I may have been the most junior officer in the Air Force to be writing regulations that affected all active duty members. I didn't have a clue what I was doing.

It was common knowledge in 1982 that buying a house was the most solid investment one could make, that housing prices always went up. I'd always thought owning your own home was something reserved for married couples, but now I was eligible for a VA loan—100 percent, no down payment. And MPC, like most higher headquarters, was a four-year assignment; I'd have time to recoup my investment before moving on. So . . .

"You bought your own place?" Lynn asked, surprise and a tinge of respect in his voice. I preened myself on his tone, on the instant status home ownership conveyed.

"Oh yes. It seemed so much smarter than paying rent for four years. That's just pouring money down a rat hole." I'd heard my stepfather Bob say this frequently.

We were standing under the stairwell next to the D-wing exit out to the sidewalk. Large metal ashtrays stood there for us smokers to take advantage of. At the Center, there were only two places where smoking was forbidden, both because of equipment (there was no concern for human health at the time): the large computer room, where a monstrous mainframe managed the Air Force's Personnel Data System, and the Micrographics Branch. We worked next to Micrographics, and as the doorways weren't sealed, we couldn't smoke in our office. So the stairwell smoking corner was set up. Nonsmokers coming and going from the parking lot were expected to pass through the haze without whining. Lynn, though officially a nonsmoker, occasionally joined me here. Never an extremist in his positions, he wasn't above bumming cigarettes.

I lit another, offered Lynn one, and the two of us stood there smoking companionably and quietly. He looked thoughtful. He stubbed out his cigarette—he never smoked them more than half-way, unlike me, who almost burned my fingers getting every puff down to the filter.

"Do you have any plants?"

I had a washer and dryer and sleeper sofa and bed and kitchen table and pots and pans. What else did a person need? "Plants? No. At least, not yet." I threw that last in to be polite, as he obviously thought plants were important.

"I have lots. I'll give you some cuttings if you want."

"Well, sure." It wasn't the sort of offer one could turn down, though my previous experiences with plants had led to their premature death due to my reluctance to water them.

"Great. Why don't you come over Saturday morning? I'll give you directions."

It was the only invitation I'd received in my first month at Randolph. Every evening after work, I went home and watched Tippy run around the backyard. Every weekend, I slept, I shopped, I read, I cleaned, and sank deeper into loneliness. For Mary, Lynn's invitation wouldn't have sounded like a lot of fun, but for me, it was the most exciting thing that had happened here.

First I had to get through the workweek, and it wasn't a pretty one. I'd graduated from reading regs to handling queries, complaints, and suggestions about the programs I managed. That week it was all complaints, complicated things that required coordination from other offices all over the headquarters. I was the last one in the office every evening (not that I stayed all that long—at headquarters, most people were out the door at four thirty). By Thursday evening I felt drained. I looked at the clock. It was close to five but I figured I had enough time to get off base before retreat sounded.

Retreat, when the base flag was lowered for the day, came at five o'clock. Protocol was strict. Military members who were outside stopped whatever they were doing when the first notes of

"The Star Spangled Banner" sounded from the base loudspeaker. If you were driving, you were supposed to pull over and stop the car. If you were walking or talking, you stopped and turned in the direction of the flag, even if you couldn't see it. You snapped to attention, saluted and held the salute till that lingering note of the "braaaaaave" had vanished. Then you could continue on your way.

If you were *inside*, however, no matter how clearly the notes sounded through an open window, you could ignore them. You could continue your phone conversation, your review of reports, your reprimand or recognition of a subordinate, your end-of-work beer with a coworker. Or you could be waiting just inside the door, ready to spring out as soon as retreat was over.

I walked out that evening with five minutes to spare to get off base. I found my car, the fickle Eric, with a flat tire. Cursing and slamming, I pulled out my jack and wrench and knelt down on the concrete. I was struggling to loosen a lug nut when I heard the introductory drum roll. I was tired, I was cranky, and I just wanted to go home. I figured it wouldn't be a stretch if someone saw me to assume I was too involved in this messy task to hear the sound of retreat.

So I stayed on the ground, hunched over my tire. Not for long though. Shiny black shoes topped with perfectly creased blue trousers appeared next to me. A pleasant but firm voice said, "Suppose we stop and pay our respects to the flag. Then I'll help you with that."

I scrambled to my feet, hoping my posture and expression adequately expressed the confusion and surprise of someone so focused on the task at hand she hadn't heard the music blaring out. The officer, a lieutenant colonel I'd never seen before, didn't look at me. He stood proudly at attention, hand held steady in a salute to a flag he couldn't see through the massive headquarters building in front of us. Abashed and disheveled, I followed his lead. When the last note ended, the officer dropped his salute, picked up the wrench and replaced my tire without a word of rebuke. He wished me a pleasant evening and walked away, ignoring my stammering thanks. I watched him leave with the eerie feeling of *who was that masked man?* (I looked for him curiously in the Center's hallways for weeks afterward but never saw him again.)

Friday afternoon—finally. We had a Commander's Call at the Officers Open Mess. Officers were required to attend, to hear our two-star general make announcements, lay out new policies, talk about the state of the headquarters, pin decorations on individuals, and do whatever else he felt like. Duty hours were over by the time he released us. While some officers planned to stay at the club for happy hour, most were ready to go home for the weekend. I was one of them. The club foyer was packed. I had to squeeze my way through the crowd to reach the door. Then I heard those unmistakable notes in the distance and realized why so many people were hanging around. It was gray and chilly outside. I was junior to everyone I saw, so I would be justified if I followed their example and lingered in the hallway.

But as I looked at the blue uniforms gathered around the doorway and the gleam of gold and silver rank on their shoulders, a word sprang into my head. It had nothing to do with patriotism or respect. *Unseemly. This is unseemly.* My sense of propriety was offended. Perhaps I felt I owed something to the anonymous lieutenant colonel of the afternoon before.

"Excuse me. Excuse me." I pushed my way through the captains and majors and colonels blocking the door. Outside I put on my hat, stationed myself on the walkway—the only person there— and sprang to attention. I brought my hand up to a salute and held it, while the music continued to play. The wind blustered, and drizzle coated my glasses. From the corner of my eye I could tell people were gaping out at me through the warm club's glass doors. Suddenly it didn't feel quite so grand to act in a seemly manner. I began to feel foolish, green, I, but I was stuck with what I was doing. There was no way out till the music ended, and it seemed exceptionally slow tonight. Were they playing two verses?

Actually, I couldn't have been standing there long when I heard the door open and a man's firm footsteps come out. He positioned himself next to me. In my peripheral vision I could see a blue sleeve move up into a salute, but that was the most I could tell about my partner in retreat. So now there were two of us saps on the walkway.

When the music ended, I dropped my salute and turned to leave. Then I saw who was standing next to me. I was so startled I almost forgot to salute him. Almost but not quite. My hand knew its business and shot up on its own. "G-good evening, General."

He grunted, returned the salute, and strode away to his waiting car and driver.

The doors to the club opened behind me. People began to slip out, slowly and cautiously. I wondered how they had viewed the scene, but to me it was a vignette straight out of Norman Rockwell: the dignified general and the idealistic lieutenant in a gray drizzle, proudly saluting the flag while other officers gawked through the O'Club windows.

By morning the cold front had passed. Saturday was the best kind of Texas fall day—clear and dry with just a hint of crispness. Lynn moved from plant to plant, energetic in his enthusiasm.

"You want some of this?" he asked me and mentioned some name I'd never heard of and forgot immediately. He didn't wait for an answer but began to dig with a small trowel, careful to bring up the plant with its roots intact. "You'll like this. It'll grow great on your patio—you've got a patio, right? Okay, screened-in. Even better." He gave me instructions for caring for it as he positioned it in a pot for me, his dirt-stained hands packing down the soil mix I'd watched him make up.

I'd thought the office was Lynn's demesne, where he reigned in button-down shirts and ties. But here in his backyard, impossibly lush with thriving plants, he was in his true kingdom. He knelt in the dirt in blue jeans and a faded T-shirt ("Fiesta '79" it said, with a toppling tower of sombreros decorating the back). The almost invisible gray stubble on his square face revealed a man who hated to shave. His love was here, in the bushes and flower beds, in the comfort of the cozy home he shared with his mother and teenage daughter. The latter, a petite, sixteen-year-old blonde, made a brief, sleepy appearance around noon, then disappeared with friends. A small matted poodle trotted behind Lynn for awhile, then flung himself panting under a bush.

"What do you think? Is that enough?" Lynn asked finally as I surveyed a daunting collection of potted plants. Like human tykes demanding food and play time, the plants scared me, but I said nothing, so grateful for Lynn's kindness, for this gift of a Saturday morning. I assured him I had plenty, but he was off again. "Pachysandra. I forgot it. You've got to have some."

After four more plants, Lynn wound down. I had a jungle now to fill my house, my yard, my screened porch—to make my life fuller, though looking down at all these green things arrayed before me had the opposite effect. Returning home felt like returning to loneliness. But I'd been here long enough; I figured my allotment of Lynn's time was used up.

"Hey, thanks. I really appreciate it. I guess I'd better load these up and get going."

He looked disappointed. "Do you have to? Why don't you stay for lunch? Some other friends of mine are coming by this afternoon. I think you'd enjoy them."

I stayed for lunch and met Lynn's shy, tiny mother. I spent the afternoon hanging out, laughing with Lynn's friends, Annie and George, and playing with their three children. Lynn's daughter Cathy came home. We drank Pearl beer on the patio, then frozen margaritas. Lynn made fajitas on the grill while we all pitched in to help. It was dark when I got home with a hatchback full of plants (all of which were doomed to death under my careless stewardship). Tippy greeted me indignantly, sniffed the evidence of poodle on my jeans, eyed the plants suspiciously. When my mother called later to chat, I told her about spending the day at Lynn's.

"Oh, Cheryl, he sounds *wonderful*. You ought to set your sights on him." Where did she get these expressions?

"Mom, he's too old. He's around your age."

"Oh." I could hear the disappointment in her voice, but it didn't bother me not to have found a boyfriend that day. Lynn had become special to me not because I saw him as a potential mate or partner or even date, but because he said, "I want you to meet some *other* friends of mine." He had welcomed me into his community of friends, and that was what I needed.

Lynn had first come to San Antonio in his twenties to attend Air Force basic training. His first wife was from here, born and buried here. His roots were more firmly planted in Texas than in the small German community he was from in Ohio.

He loved every inch of San Antonio and showed it off at every opportunity. He organized groups of friends—of whom I was now one—to attend Fiesta and Rodeo and NIOSA and Folk-life Festival, big events in the ongoing party the city prided itself on. We toured through all the old Spanish missions, not just the Alamo. We wandered the River Walk and the sidewalks of "Sauerkraut Bend," the old German settlement of the King William district. He knew the theaters and the clubs and the parks. He showed me where the old house he'd lived in as a newlywed had stood, the same house where Ike Eisenhower and Mamie Doud met and courted. We went for drinks in the bar of the Menger Hotel, where Teddy Roosevelt recruited Rough Riders.

The San Antonio he showed me was a beautiful, vibrant city, and Lynn had the energetic spirit to enjoy all of it. I could barely keep up with him. He was smart, easygoing, fun, an attractive man with shrewd eyes that changed from blue to green to gray depending on his mood. I could see why the middle-aged women in the Center flocked to him. Not that it did them any good. Lynn didn't want to get involved with anyone for fear of where it might lead.

His first wife had died suddenly when their daughter was a baby. His second marriage ended bitterly and painfully after six years. He had no interest in getting hurt again. His decision seemed reasonable to me given his age—fifty, long past the time for courtship, in my opinion.

My least favorite responsibility at work was managing the official photograph program. All officers were required to have an up-to-date photograph in their promotion selection records. The rationale was that it personalized the record by helping boards see the officer as a flesh-and-blood person, not just a collection of evaluations, assignments, and decorations. The photograph, as piously stated in the reg, "humanized" the promotion process. Being photo-phobic myself, I saw it as another manifestation of the Air Force's obsession with image. The pictures identified flab, plainness, imperfection, the crooked part, the squint, the zit that popped up like a forgotten relative the morning of the shoot, all frozen and spotlighted by the unforgiving lens. I needed a crusade. Armed with studies from the files, I approached Major Hallemart. He interrupted me as soon as I started.

"I need to give you my 'but, sir' speech. This is something my boss told me when I was a lieutenant: You get three 'but-sirs.' When I say no to something you want to do or tell you to do something you don't want to do, you can say—in fact, you're expected to say—'But, sir.' Then you tell me why I'm wrong and you're right. If I continue to tell you no, then you say, 'But, sir,' and you give me another reason. But if you haven't changed my mind after your third 'but, sir,' that's when you salute smartly and do what I've told you. So what did you want to talk about?"

It was not a propitious beginning, but I put forth my best effort to sell him on a plan to eliminate official photos altogether. He gave me my three "but-sirs," but ultimately said, "Absolutely not. Timing is bad right now. Your reasons are good but the program is entrenched. You'll just be wasting your time." I was disappointed but not surprised.

"Okay, change of subject," he said brusquely, then hesitated. He began hemming and hawing, unusual for a man normally so forceful. "Is there any chance you might fail a weigh-in?"

"No, sir," I assured him truthfully, but I immediately felt the low burn of shame creep through me. I had stayed on the right side of the weight standard, but I was aware of every bit of extra flesh, the roundness of me so un-officer-like.

"Good. I'm putting you in for Junior Officer of the Quarter. Just wanted to make sure."

"Thank you, sir." Not that I had a chance of winning, me a lowly lieutenant against a bunch of captains. But it was a nice gesture on his part.

Unlikely as it seemed though, I won, and a few weeks later I stood on the tarmac watching a small plane being fueled. Besides receiving a certificate and a plaque, I also got to shadow the Center commander for a day. He was the same two-star who'd stood outside the O'Club and saluted the flag with me. I wondered if he'd recognize me, what words of wisdom he'd pass on, if he'd sense my capabilities and move me up to his staff.

This was a day he was flying to Maxwell Air Force Base in Alabama. "You're lucky," the general's executive officer had said. "This will be different, not the routine stuff. Just stay close to him and follow him around." He instructed me on the protocols, like getting into the small T-38.

"You're the lowest ranking, so you get in first and squeeze into one of the narrow seats in the back of the plane. There are a few other officers hopping a lift on the general's plane. They'll get on next. The general gets on last and gets the best seat." *Well, of course!*

When they opened the hatch I duly took my place first in the plane that morning. After a couple of majors and two colonels, the general boarded. I said brightly, "Good morning, sir." He grunted, fastened his seat belt, opened his briefcase, and reviewed paperwork for the whole flight. The colonels started to whisper at one point but shut up when he glared at them. It was a silent ride except for the steady engine noise.

First on, last off, I crouched to get out of the narrow door. As soon as I stepped out onto the tarmac, I shoved my hat on (no longer the flyaway beret but the solid, stylish "bucket hat," complete with visor). The general was up ahead with a colonel who'd come out to meet him.

"Take that hat off immediately!" A captain in a flight suit appeared at my side and jerked my hat off. "You don't wear a hat on a runway. Jeez!" He thrust it at me and strode away.

The general's exec had neglected to tell me what should have been obvious to anyone who wasn't a complete idiot, which I apparently was: no one wears a hat on the flight line because of the danger of jet engines sucking them in. Hat in hand, I scurried after the general. He was just stepping into a car. The colonel held the door open for him, while the driver affixed a two-star plate to the front bumper. The colonel noticed me and said something to the general.

"Oh yes, you," the general said. "Just, uh, go off with these guys. They'll take care of you." He waved toward a couple of senior NCOs, who'd been part of the welcoming committee. They glanced at one another, their consternation obvious.

I watched the car pull away, unsure whether I should salute or not on the flight line with no hat. Better safe than sorry. I saluted. No one saw me; neither the general nor the colonel returned the salute. I lowered my hand and stood forlorn on the runway, invisible and insignificant. Insubstantial as a shadow. Why would anyone ever notice me?

## B. LOVE AND DEATH

The phone rang. It was Lynn, wanting to chat, not the call I'd been expecting—no, too strong a word—*hoping* for, dreaming about. I told him I had company, a blatant lie but I was shameless in those days. I remained next to the phone after he hung up. I tried to read, every now and then checking to make sure I'd replaced the earpiece all the way back in its cradle. I sat up late, but my lover didn't call that night.

The affair had started a few weeks after the flight to Alabama. I'd gone on a three-day temporary duty, TDY in military parlance (think business trip) to attend a conference in another city. A lieutenant colonel who chaired a committee I served on had arranged for me to attend. I was to stay quietly in the background, listen, learn, and occasionally hand him a file—all of which I excelled at.

The evening we arrived, we checked into our hotel then went out looking for dinner, a normal, innocent thing to do, dinner between two coworkers. The fact that we were male and female meant nothing. Not until he leaned close to me and sniffed, his light breath tickling the skin below my ear. "Ummm. What a lovely perfume."

He smelled my neck again. I felt a tingle that didn't stop there but traveled leisurely down my body. Then he leaned away and smiled at me. We were on a sidewalk in twilight surrounded by other pedestrians. There was nothing guilty in the smile he gave me. But I swayed dizzily from what felt like a moment of intimacy flaunted in the public eye.

After dinner we stopped for a nightcap in the hotel bar. It was dark and virtually deserted. This time when he leaned into my space, his dark eyes hooded with sleepy desire, I whispered, "Don't." Even to my own ears it sounded less like a prohibition than a come-on.

"What happens TDY stays TDY" is the military version of an expression usually associated with Las Vegas. I told myself this was a harmless fling, far from home and over as soon as we arrived back in San Antonio. On our return flight, I said, "I hope you don't plan to confess to your wife. For her sake. It can only hurt her, and there's no reason for that."

He took my hand and held it hidden under the newspaper he was reading. "You're making me fall for you." He squeezed my hand tightly. "I've never done this before, never been . . ." He seemed to struggle to say the ugly word but couldn't. I believed him. What did he have to gain from lying? Sex? He'd already gotten it without really trying.

I gently disentangled my hand and turned toward the window, studying the ground rushing at us from below, San Antonio coming into focus. He spoke so softly I could barely hear him. "I'm not ready to let you go."

Adultery is a crime in the military, punishable under the Uniformed Code of Military Justice. It is widely practiced and politely ignored when it can be. When pressed—usually by angry spouses—commanders punish it severely, potentially to the point of court-martial or involuntary separation. It rends the fabric of trust and loyalty military units depend on.

Adultery is also a crime in God's eyes, with a commandment all to itself, a ban whose trespass is punishable by eternal damnation. The Air Force is a merciful master compared to the God of the Old Testament. Fortunately, I no longer worried about that aspect of things.

Adultery is also, I still believe (though not so righteously), a crime against the family, against society, against the self. It weakens the ties that hold us together. My father, with his twin demons of adultery and gambling, abandoning his wife and children—his sins sent repercussions through two and three generations. I had always sworn never to have an affair with a married man. It's easy to be virtuous when you're not tempted.

I didn't think of myself as an adulterer. I'd made no promises or commitments to anyone. I couldn't think of him as one either, except in the most technical sense. The attraction had to be extremely powerful to pull an otherwise honorable man to me, a passion he couldn't resist. Adultery may have been a crime and a sin, but it was so flattering, it was also a turn-on.

In truth there was something erotic in the convoluted arrangements we had to make to spend time together in San Antonio, where it seemed all eyes were potential accusers. Our meetings were fraught with the thrill of the illicit, the clandestine, the furtive, the sordid—the very words of infidelity slide seductively over the tongue.

He surprised me one night with a present. "Open it." If he'd been a little boy, he would have had his hands behind his back, his eyes on the floor, and his feet scuffing back and forth.

It was a negligee, but with nothing about it you could call satiny, silky, or elegant. It was, in fact, downright whorish. None of my old boyfriends would have given me such a thing. They'd all been too busy admiring my mind and respecting my character. I held it up, struggling among feelings of amusement, alarm, and titillation. Titillation won.

"Go on. Put it on," he urged.

It was a complicated garment, long and gauzy, white but so thin its color could better be described as clear, as see-through as a window. It hung on the body, shapeless except for a thick braided cord, which was apparently meant to be wrapped around the body and tightened to emphasize breasts and waist and hips. The overall effect created the look of a dryad fleeing a lascivious satyr—but not too fast and only so he could get a look at her luscious fanny.

That I believed was the theory, but its execution was beyond me, a plain pajama girl. "It's pretty complicated. You're going to have to help. Didn't this thing come with—"

"Operating instructions?"

"Actually, I was going to say an owner's manual."

"An owner's manual. I like that." He began pulling the cords around and under my breasts, but we never did get the "contraption," as I thought of it, all the way on.

We didn't have many opportunities to be together in San Antonio. He was so cautious, so careful not to get caught that sometimes I chafed at it. I offered him alibis, excuses I made up like so many fairy tales. I strewed his path with temptation.

One evening while his wife worked late, we managed to get together for dinner, tucked away in a small Italian restaurant where it was unlikely anyone we knew would see us. If they did, it would be easily explainable as a brainstorming session. We had files open on the table, decoys. I had no idea what was in them.

"You sure you can't stop by my place tonight? For a quickie?" I arched my eyebrows. "We could forgo dessert." I leaned toward him and said softly, "I could be dessert."

He smiled but shook his head. I couldn't move him on this and already knew it, but I couldn't resist teasing. The waiter came to remove our salads and replace them with pasta smothered with tomato sauce and olives. He had ordered for both of us. Puttanesca.

We ate in silence. I wondered if he was angry because I pressed him to come home with me or if he thought I was angry. I put my fork down. "I'm sorry to tease you. I really do understand. Neither of us wants to hurt your wife. It's good you're so careful to protect her."

He looked surprised. "You don't get it, do you? You're the one I'm trying to protect."

I didn't know what to say to that. I picked up my fork and knife to cut the long strands of linguini. He twirled his against the bowl of his spoon. I admired his dexterity, the neat little bundle of pasta and sauce he made, then I realized he was concentrating on twirling the pasta just so, loosening it, picking up new strands on his fork, but never actually raising the food to his lips.

Finally, he set his utensils down, sighed, reached for his water glass, put it down without drinking from it. He didn't look at me as he spoke. "You should know that I'm in love with you."

"Oh" was all I could think of to say at first. I was defenseless against the bare truth. "I'm in love with you too." A bleak, fearful confession.

It was only six, still light out, people passing on the pavement. A red splotch of sauce sat at the edge of his mouth. I reached over with my napkin to wipe it off, but he stopped me with a quick look around the room.

No longer just adultery, but love. Once I got over the fear, once I realized *this is real, this is truly love,* I was happier than I had ever been in my life, ecstatically, energetically filled with joy. The world had become a wonder, a background for him and his love to exist in. In our committee meetings, I basked in the feeling of his love radiating out to me. We were usually very professional but sometimes the mask slipped. He was more often the one to make some incautious teasing remark or to look at me too intimately. I would quell him with a frown, bringing us back into line. But I rejoiced every time he took that little chance. I saw his inability to hold his love in all the way, all the time, as a sign of how strong it was.

In those early days of the affair, passion charged everything I did, energized me even at work. Around that time, Major Hallemart left, appointing me acting branch chief ("acting" in this sense meant temporary, but it definitely felt make-believe). Lynn, the highest ranking civilian in the office, a GS-12 with years of experience, would have been the natural choice to be left in charge, but Hallemart thought the increased level of responsibility would do more for my career—a questionable opinion since I wouldn't even pin on captain for several months.

All the other women in our branch were civilians. After I stepped up to "acting chief," the office secretary approached me quietly. She was from East Texas, friendly, competent, and at the moment, nervous. "Cheryl—ma'am—Lieutenant, the other women and I have been talking. We realized that we've always called you by your first name, but we call male officers by their ranks. We don't mean to show you less respect than we do the men. Would you rather we call you 'Lieutenant'? We can do that." She looked at me anxiously.

I'd never even noticed how they addressed me. "It's okay," I said. "Cheryl's fine." I glowed in those days—I felt far more Cheryl than I did Lieutenant.

One afternoon my lover's car was with the mechanic, so I gave him a lift home. He invited me in. His wife wasn't home from work yet, and they had no kids, so we were alone. I asked to see the house. I wanted to stroke the fabric on the easy chair where he sat when he watched TV. I wanted to lean over the bathroom sink and stare into the mirror where he shaved. I wanted to check out the books in his—their—bookcases and see what sat on his bedside table.

He took me on a tour of the house as impersonally as if he were a realtor and I a potential buyer. It was a spacious two-story, a reflection more of his rank and income than of his and his wife's needs. It was neat, nothing out of place, but bland, the furnishings all beige and other neutrals. Like most military homes, souvenirs from the occupants' previous assignments were the only hints of personal history—an intricately carved chest from Korea, a display of German steins. Except for these, all I saw was his wife. Her taste, her needlepoint cushions, a Hummel collection.

I'm a practical person. I was able to gaze on the bed they shared with only a spasm of emotion that came and went too quickly to identify. He opened up the wide walk-in closet for me, where I viewed their clothes hanging across from one another with no reaction but admiration for the neatness, the perfectly spaced hangers.

It was the bathroom that got to me, more specifically the toothbrushes, nestling against one another in a ceramic cup. This was intimacy, husband and wife standing side by side at the double sinks, brushing their teeth together, every morning, every night.

I took a deep breath. "I'd better get going."

"Yes, I suppose. She'll be home any minute." I hadn't been lost to the fact that he'd kept his ear attuned to the sounds of the house, listening for his wife's entrance.

We went back down to the cozy den. "It's a lovely house," I said. "Thank you." *Thank you for giving me a glimpse of your real life, for reminding me of how peripheral I am, how—in the scheme of the day-to-day stuff—I am less significant than your toothbrush, your chair, the tchotchkes you and your wife have chosen together over the years. Thank you for allowing me in and letting me remain here, a speck in your life.* "I should be going."

"Wait. Let me kiss you, just once. I want my home to be full of your kiss."

We kissed, gently, sweetly. I would have liked to press hard sucking kisses on his mouth, the kind that could lead us to throw off all our caution and our clothes. I felt like an invader, and I wanted to conquer with full-out force. He resisted, however, and kept the temperature mild, all the time listening for the sound of the garage door. When he suddenly thrust me away, I knew why.

He patted his short Air Force hair down and looked me over quickly. "Anyway, thanks so much for bringing me home. Can I offer you a drink or something?"

His wife walked in, a small woman with short hair hovering between blonde and brown, everything about her trim and neat. Like the house, a woman of neutral tones. He greeted her with a peck on the lips, as natural as a husband could be. "The car's stuck in the garage till tomorrow. Cheryl was kind enough to bring me home. I've been showing her the house."

She smiled graciously and shook hands with me. "Nice to meet you, Cheryl. Thanks for your help. Can you stop for awhile? Join us in a glass of wine?"

I turned her down politely. Back home, I put on MTV just to fill the house with voices.

I never suggested he leave his wife. He was the one who began hinting at it, with remarks like, "Perhaps it doesn't have to be this way," the one who first mentioned the word divorce.

"You know I will love you anyway. You have me already. I'm yours," I told him, but I thrilled to the idea, to the daydreams forming in my head.

"It's for me," he said. "I want more. This isn't enough. I just don't know yet *how* to do it." He looked thoughtful, like a man trying to solve a puzzle, difficult but not impossible.

I leaned against him. We were sitting up in bed. I kissed his back and stroked it. His skin felt soft to me over the taut muscles. "Whoa. You're beating a dead horse. I'm an old man, remember?" He was just eight years older than me, but it was a pretense we had that I was a child compared to him. The gap between our ranks added to it.

"I just like feeling your skin. It's so soft. That's all I want." I continued to run my hand up and down his back, stroking him like I was patting Tippy (who lay sulking in a corner of the room, displaced from her spot on the bed).

"Well, it's not enough for me. I want more." He pulled me down on top of him.

I felt loved. I felt fulfilled. I felt powerful.

As it was, I spent less time alone with him than with Lynn. Lynn and I had lunch together at least once a week. One day he asked my opinion about an invitation. A friend of his, a widow, was going on an Alaskan cruise. "She invited me to go along—at her expense." He shifted in his seat.

"And?"

"Well, I'd like to go to Alaska. I've never been there. And I can't afford it myself."

"So what's the problem?" I knew exactly what the problem was.

He hesitated. "I'm afraid I might be setting up false expectations."

"So? You like her, right? Neither of you is married. Why not see where this path leads?"

He grimaced. "Into territory I have no wish to explore. Oh well, I guess I won't be going to Alaska any time soon." He took a bite of salad. "Ow!" He probed his tooth with his tongue, then pulled a small white chip out of his salad greens. "I just broke my tooth."

"On lettuce?" I started giggling.

"Yeah." His tone was rueful. He inspected the chip of tooth. He seemed more interested in that than in his lost travel opportunity.

I didn't confide in Lynn about my affair. He was such a straight arrow I figured he would be shocked. I pictured the revulsion on his face. I didn't want to lose his friendship.

From the tremendous high I'd been on, the laws of nature and of the heart demanded an equal balance of down. The affair ran the usual course, times of ecstasy and passion alternating with depression and dissatisfaction. Times when he didn't (couldn't?) call; when the hours we snatched seemed too short, the loneliness that followed too long; when secrecy lost its eroticism. I began confiding in Mary and other long-distance friends, who must have learned to dread my calls. I spent one weekend in Oklahoma sobbing on a friend's couch—probably terrifying her poor little boys. She sat with me for awhile trying to talk, to sympathize, to soothe, but finally placed a box of tissues on my lap and left me there to cry while she went about her business.

Early in December our directorate threw its annual Christmas party. For an officer it was as mandatory as it could be without an actual command. I tried to talk Lynn into attending so I wouldn't have to go alone, but he laughed when I asked him.

"Nope, I'm a civilian. I don't have to go. And I can think of a lot better things to do."

Official parties at Carswell, with its contingent of lusty young air crews, had tended to be rowdy, with local prostitutes waiting at the bar. But at MPC, with its high-level paper pushers and proto-techies, the parties were staid and boring. People clumped into murmuring circles, holding cocktails and exchanging chitchat while Muzak played in the background. Later we would sit at assigned tables, eat rubber chicken, and listen to senior officers deliver long, boring speeches.

Still I started out eagerly. Another chance to be around the man I loved. True, his wife would be there, but perhaps we could manage a moment, a seemingly casual kiss on the cheeks beneath the mistletoe, better yet, a quick tussle in the cloakroom. At least, a look from him, something that connected me with him and made our secret love the realest thing in the room.

I made myself up carefully. My hair was usually impossible, thin and lank, but that night I managed an insouciant flip. I put on my favorite dress, a rich, close-fitting burgundy. I wore my highest heels. I was tall anyway, and these would make me tower like a victor over my lover's pleasant wife. My height was one of the few things I liked about myself. I put an extra treat in Tippy's bowl when I left. I sang Christmas carols in the car.

The party was every bit as dull as expected. I did my awkward best to mingle, chatting briefly with acquaintances before moving restlessly to another group, my eyes constantly drifting toward the entrance. I saw him as soon as he arrived, his wife on his arm. He had a jaunty piece of holly stuck in his buttonhole, and I had a fantasy of his discreetly passing it on to me, of me holding it hidden, its prickly leaves in my palm a constant reminder of our love—sharp and hurtful, yes, but real, undeniably real. I made myself wait ten minutes before mingling my way over to him. His wife greeted me first and pulled me politely into their circle. "How festive you look tonight," she said.

They were in conversation with another couple I knew. I chatted with them awhile, talk so small it dissipated into particles and drifted away in the air long before it reached anyone's mind or memory. We all spoke polite trivialities about the decorations in the club and upcoming holiday plans. Nothing from him but a sense of bored requirement—another evening of mandatory fun. I felt my smile freeze till the corners of my mouth ached. I began to calculate how soon I could murmur my apologies, slip away, and let the interest I'd forced into my eyes fade into dullness.

When I eventually left them, I hoped he'd at least take the opportunity to give me a casual hug, maybe a holiday peck on the cheek. But he just wished me a merry Christmas and started telling the other couple a funny story. I felt my heart deflate and the smile vanish for good that evening. It was rather a relief not to have to carry it around anymore. Well, what had I expected? He was being cautious and rightly so. *Grow up, Cheryl. Handle it like a woman, handle it like that ice sculpture there. Be a cold angel of ice.* I got through the next part of the evening by not feeling anything. I figured I could get through the rest of life the same way if I had to.

At the break before the speeches, I went to the bar for a refill. I gave the bartender my order and stood there frozen, not even trying to chat with anyone around me.

The bartender, a nice-looking young guy, handed me a generous glass of red wine. He said, "I hope you don't mind my saying so, but that dress looks great on you. It suits you."

He moved on to another customer. His compliment touched me. I thought he had sensed my unhappiness and done the only thing he could to assuage it. That was all it took to melt the ice shield. I could taste my heart now, tears salty but sweet; better to have this than nothing at all.

One night his wife was going to be tied up at a work function. He'd begged off from escorting her, pleading boredom. We would have a full four hours together at my house. I prepared one of his favorite dishes, a steaming spanakopita, its crust golden and crisp.

He'd told his wife he was going to hang out at the mall, eat in the food court and rummage through the bookstore. On his instructions, I'd bought a book for him on my lunch hour, smudging the time on the receipt while leaving the date intact. I'd checked to make sure he didn't already have the book but would be likely to buy it: *Andersonville* by MacKinlay Kantor. It waited innocently for him in its Walden bag.

We always coordinated arrival times carefully. I glanced at my watch—six o'clock. I opened the kitchen door to the garage and punched the button. The garage door slowly rose. It stood open less than a minute before his car pulled into the empty bay I'd so carefully cleaned out for him. As soon as he was in, I lowered the garage door.

I was excited. We had time tonight, that precious rarity. Time to eat and drink and talk and still make love at least twice before he would have to shower with the Lifebuoy soap I kept for him, in the scent they used at his house. His wife, he said, had a keen sense of smell.

As soon as we finished our first embrace, he looked up and saw the table set for dinner, candles glowing, wine glasses sparkling, linen napkins purchased for this occasion folded pristinely on the antique plates my grandmother had given me. He bit his lip and turned to me. "Cheryl."

For a moment he said nothing else, just repeated, "Cheryl." I felt uneasy at his tone, his look. "This is so wonderful. What a lovely evening you've planned. But . . ." He stopped for a moment searching for words. I felt a tremendous hurt well up inside me and struggled in vain to pull a door down over it, like hiding his car inside my garage. The ache inside me spread, as he told me his wife had agreed about how boring the evening promised to be. She planned to steal away before dessert, before the speeches. "I can only stay an hour."

Ordinarily, with a door carefully enclosing my pain, I would have smiled regretfully and said something like, "Well, let's not waste any precious moments then." But now I couldn't. My anticipation had been too great. I turned away. "I don't think I can do this anymore."

I said it with no intention except to express what I was feeling, but he took it as an ending, perhaps with a little relief even. Perhaps a lot of relief. I hadn't been the most lively, cheerful mistress lately. I'd become moody (not helped by my going on the pill at the same time I was trying to quit smoking). Maybe he considered it an ultimatum, pressure to come through with the divorce he hinted at. I wondered about it later, after he'd left, after we'd spent that precious hour talking sadly and soberly about breaking up. An hour not eating the dinner I'd prepared, an hour not making love. We didn't kiss goodbye. He took his book and left.

This should be where the story ends, poignant heartache at the end of an affair, so simple.

We couldn't quite let go. We never again indulged in the easy, exuberant passionate affair we'd known, but we did begin to meet again. Mainly to talk. He hinted at a change. I heard his tone telling me to hold on, to keep holding on. So I did. My hopes began to rise. My hormones adjusted. I started smoking again, to everyone's relief.

He received orders for a new assignment far away. I should have been downcast but the closer it got to his departure date, the closer we seemed to be getting again. In his new job, there were already plans for him to go TDY to New Orleans in a couple of months. He urged me to take leave and meet him there. For a week we could be lovers with only the slightest degree of discretion needed. Excited anticipation crowded out every other emotion.

After he'd been gone a month, he called me. "There's a job here that's perfect for you." He launched into an enthusiastic description of it and how his boss could pull strings to get me out of the Center early. I wasn't paying close attention, so busy celebrating inside. *He wants me. He wants me with him. He loves me. He loves me. He loves me.*

Then he said, "Now, you do understand that this is just about a job, nothing else."

I had that feeling like when something you can't quite identify seems to run past the corner of your eye and the hairs on the back of your neck bristle. "What do you mean?"

"Just don't read anything more into this than a job offer."

How was I not to read more into it? "What did you mean 'nothing more than a job'?"

"Exactly what I said. What else would it be?"

I couldn't tell him what I'd thought, about that five minutes of happy-ever-after euphoria brought crashing down. "It's just . . . has something happened? Is something wrong?"

He evaded my questions. I hated talking on the phone anyway and couldn't imagine a worse way to have a worse conversation. "Look," I said. "Let's talk about this next month. Whatever the problem is that'll give us a chance to work it out."

"What do you mean 'next month'?"

"New Orleans. Your TDY."

"I don't know what you're talking about."

"New Orleans! We were going to meet there." It had been his idea in the first place—I was certain of that. Now he denied all knowledge of the plan and had no interest in it.

"I don't understand." I struggled to hold my tears back.

"Look, I have no interest in you anymore," he said, nothing in his voice but brute indifference. "Sorry if that hurts, but that's your problem."

In writing this, I have had to recreate dialogue, to capture as accurately as possible the conversations, the intentions, the feelings from almost thirty years ago. But there are a couple of statements from this man which are seared word for exact word in my memory. This was one of them: *Sorry if that hurts, but that's your problem.*

Here's another good place for the story to end: me nursing my heartache, sadder but wiser, grieving but eventually getting over the lover who discarded me like a plastic toy.

I made it to work every day, but I performed my duties on autopilot. My main concern was just to keep it together till I could go home and lock myself away from everyone else. I even made excuses not to have lunch with Lynn.

He found me brooding in the smokers' corner one day. He bummed a cigarette and leaned against the wall. He began chatting about blessedly inconsequential stuff, harmless office gossip. I listened with half an ear, responding "uh huh" and "really" at the pauses, until he said, "Get this. I was waiting outside the colonel's office yesterday. He was on the phone and I heard him say, 'But sir, she's always like that lately, hair a mess, uniform looks like she'd slept in it. What do you expect me to do?' Who could he have been talking about?"

My face felt warm; tears threatened to spill over. I managed a weak smile. "Me. He was talking about me. He called me on the carpet about it this morning." I burned with humiliation, remembering the colonel's frank discussion of my looks, my lack of the sharp Air Force image that was the ideal, the image that I'd worked so hard at OTS to achieve.

"Oh!" Lynn's face turned scarlet. He struggled to find something else to say.

I excused myself to go to the restroom. After a brief cry inside a stall, I emerged to take a good look in the mirror. I saw what the colonel saw. No longer neat and trim and proud, I looked bloated and messy. My hair was ragged and had grown out of regulation length. My uniform shirts and slacks hung limp and creased. Everything seemed to require too much energy those days, including keeping myself neat and clean.

The love I'd believed in with more faith than I'd ever given to God was a scam. I thought of the man's caution—the soap, the synchronized opening of the garage door so he could pull right in, the carefully bought book with its smudged receipt. How could I not have seen these for what they were, a repertoire of tricks picked up from previous infidelities? I tried to work up a good head of angry steam to fuel my recovery through heartache and out the other end. But I couldn't.

This is the problem with faith: it keeps believing against all evidence. None of the things I told myself seemed as real as the memory of ardent looks he'd given me; his touch—gentle, rough, impatient, teasing, hot as flames all over me; his words of love confessed as though reluctantly, sadly even, in out-of-the-way places. Love, that persistent little monster, whispered to me. *Something's wrong. He's hurt in some way. He needs space. He needs time. You love him. You have to understand. You have to have faith in him and in your love. Give him time.*

I splashed water into my reddened eyes and straightened up, lengthened and stiffened my spine. A puny sort of love it would be that couldn't sustain itself through a bad spell. I would give him six weeks, I decided, without contacting him. For now I would let go of the heartache and embrace my work. It was time to get a haircut, a perm, new uniforms, new attitude. Time to let the lieutenant take over and give Cheryl—who had turned into a soggy, soppy, sobby thing—a rest.

I wrote the date in my organizer, even scheduled a time to call. That helped me feel I had some control. I had six weeks in which to buttress an injured heart with hope. I was cheerful and productive during that time, missing him, longing for him, but no more unhappy than a woman whose lover had gone on an Arctic expedition and was expected back soon. Optimism felt better than certainty; procrastination better than action. I felt so good I put off my scheduled phone call a day, a week, two weeks. Eventually though I called.

"Cheryl," was all he said at first, like that last night. Then again, "Cheryl." He couldn't have faked the relief, the joy in his tone. "Hang on a sec." I heard a slight click in the background, then he was back on the line. "I just wanted to close the door." Is any sentence more romantic?

My heart leapt. I was back in a secret place, where I was happy to be. *To hell with public recognition and affection. Let me be the secret he holds closest to his heart. I'll hide my discontent better.* "Just wanted to call, see how you're doing. See if things are . . . better."

"It's so great to hear you, so wonderful that you called. I was afraid—" He stopped for a moment. I started to say something but he broke in. "No wait, listen. Things are, well, happening right now. Things are changing. Everything's going to be fine. Going to be great. Trust me, please just trust me, okay?"

"Of course. I've always trusted you."

"Then give me a month. I'll call you by then. No, say two months, but that's the most. I'll explain everything then. Trust me on this. Another month and everything will work out."

The Air Force is basically a large gossipy village, so I soon heard that he and his wife were divorcing. It made sense now, even his brusque indifference earlier. He'd been protecting me, making sure my name stayed out of the proceedings and no suspicion lurked around me.

I was promoted to captain. By pinning the rank on, I would add two years to my Air Force commitment, but what the hell—I hadn't come up with anything better to do. As the colonel swore me in, I kept thinking, *Captain, that's me, Captain Duncan. Wow, that sounds cool!*

I threw a promotion party at my home after work. I was surprised at the number of people who showed up. I attributed it at first to free alcohol. But it was more than that. In the military, promotions call for a big celebration. As in the business world, promotion means more money and power, but a military promotion also means stepping into a new life-phase, putting on a new identity. Taking a new name.

Everyone made a point of calling me "Captain" that evening. My living room was crowded and the noise loud, everyone chattering above a background of bouzouki recordings. I held court near the open patio door. When a military couple I knew arrived, they made their way over to me, winding their way around the sofa and coffee table. Even on the outmoded shag carpet the husband, a captain, looked like he was marching, swinging his arms, his back stiff. When he stopped in front of me, I could almost hear his heels clicking together.

"Congratulations, *Captain* Duncan," he said, pumping my hand. Then he leaned in to say, "Now you can call me Jerry."

He was obviously presenting me with a prize I was expected to feel honored by. I resisted an urge to giggle. "Thank you, Jerry. I'm so glad you could come."

His wife, a first lieutenant I knew well, beamed at me. "Congratulations, Cheryl!"

He frowned at her. *"Captain!* She's *Captain Duncan* to you now, Lieutenant."

"But—" She stopped at the look he gave her.

Like an outsider undermining a parent's attempt to instill good manners in his child, I leaned toward her and stage-whispered, "It's okay. You can still call me Cheryl."

She glanced at her husband, smiled at me, and said simply, "What a lovely party." Henceforth, until she put on captain herself, I would be nameless to her. Now that I thought about it, I'd never heard her refer to her husband by name.

Lynn appeared behind them. "There's plenty of champagne and beer over there."

The captain marched off, the lieutenant drifting behind him. Lynn muttered to me, "Oooh, you get to call him Jerry."

"Yeah. But what do you think? You suppose she has to call him 'Captain' in bed?"

"Now there's an image."

The open house had been scheduled from five to eight o'clock, timed to catch people for a drink as they got off work. Most people came and went. At eight, there were just five stalwarts left: Lynn, the friends Annie and George he'd introduced me to, a major I knew and his wife, Sallie.

"The invitation says till eight. Do we need to leave now?" Sallie asked.

"Hell, no. We've still got champagne." Cheap stuff I'd bought for the party.

I'd already had a private celebration after the announcement of the promotion. On the basis of the substantial raise I'd be getting, I'd splurged on Perrier-Jouet and a couple of ounces of beluga caviar. I'd invited Lynn to share; he was the only person I knew who would also appreciate those luxuries. Tonight, however, he seemed equally happy drinking André and eating Doritos. Me too. I opened a new bag and settled in to chat with Sallie.

I'd met her a number of times before we became friends, but we didn't really get to know one another till we sat side by side in a smoking cessation class. Ultimately, neither my one-pack-a-day nor Sallie's three-pack habit succumbed to the program, perhaps because we'd spent most of the sessions whispering and giggling in the back row.

Sallie took another gulp of champagne and put her arm around me, tears in her eyes. "I'm so glad we became friends. Before you, I never got to know any military women, not really know them, not like friends. I didn't like you, them, I mean."

This surprised me, coming from a military wife. "Really? Why not?"

"I always figured you—they—only joined to get at the men, even the married ones."

I was indignant, my affair forgotten for the moment. Besides that hadn't been *why* I'd joined the Air Force, just a by-product. "That's ridiculous. We don't want your husbands."

"I know that now."

Weepily, we swore eternal friendship. The others wandered over to join in the pledges to good friends. More champagne, more beer, more chips. Lynn drifted to the couch, stretched out, and soon light snores joined the murmur of our gradually slowing conversation, the stretching and yawning, the preludes to departure.

"Shall we wake him up?" Annie said.

"No, don't disturb him. I'll throw a blanket over him."

I woke the next morning earlier than usual. My first thought was of Lynn asleep on the sofa. I hoped he was still there. It would be nice to share a quiet breakfast with him. I could scramble eggs, fry bacon. I tiptoed out to the darkened living room, but he had already gone.

Our branch was a minor player in a directorate whose main business centered around the Personnel Data System. The massive mainframe loomed like an imprisoned monster in a climate-controlled chamber. It ran an Air Force-wide data system, considered the most advanced of any of the services at that time. We were at the peak of early eighties computer technology.

Okay, maybe not "we." I personally represented the nadir of technology, barely comfortable with my electric typewriter. I didn't want to know anything about computers; in fact I considered an interest in them slightly vulgar. When the director selected me to be his executive officer, I was flattered, but I didn't want to get in over my head. "You see, sir, I don't know anything about computers. I don't know how they work or the lingo or any of that stuff."

The colonel grinned. "That's why I picked you. We get a lot of complaints that the paperwork coming out of this office is unintelligible. So don't try to learn our language. I want you to insist that everything that comes through you is written so *you* can understand it. I want English, not computer-speak."

"So I'm being hired for my ignorance?"

"Right. Try not to lose it."

I entered the position with a combination of cockiness (*I'm so good, I get to be exec!*) and whimpering terror. This was a big job for any new captain. As the colonel's executive officer, I sat directly outside his door and managed the flow of people and paperwork in and out. Since our directorate was the largest at MPC, there was a lot of both. Twelve-hour days were my norm, but I still usually left before the colonel. No one had instructed me that it was customary for the exec to stay as long as the boss was there. Every evening I would pop my head into his office. "You need anything else from me, sir? If not, I'll be off. See you tomorrow." He never objected, so for over a year I innocently broke a cardinal rule of exec-ing, with, as far as I know, no terrible results. I still see no reason not to leave a capable, grown man to do his own work in peace.

I hadn't expected to hear from my erstwhile lover within a month or even two—these things always take longer than projected. Three months passed, and he still hadn't called. I heard his divorce was final. I told myself that he wouldn't rush to contact me right away. He would need some closure. It didn't bother me. I had enough to do getting to know my new job anyway. Hope kept me happy, buoyant even. Four months and still nothing, except the rumors that paired him with another woman, someone I knew, someone not me. Five months. Armed with bitter resolution, I called him.

He was cold and distant this time and seemed surprised to hear from me. I'd given up hope, maybe even desire of becoming lovers again—or was I just fooling myself? But I needed not to be so insignificant that he could just toss me away like garbage. "We meant a lot to each other," I said. "And it seems a crime to waste that. Can't we find a way to be friends at least?"

This is the other quote seared into my memory: "There's no room for you in my life in any capacity. Now you may think I'm a son of a bitch—"

"Yes, you are a son of a bitch." I stated it simply, a fact I was just now acknowledging. "And I never want to see you again or hear from you again or speak to you again." I hung up; I didn't bother to slam the phone down. I had no passion in me, not even for anger. I felt like an ice creature again, all heat drained out of me, a frozen shield hardening over my wounds.

I gathered everything of his I had (it was precious little) and everything that reminded me of him. I made a pile of the negligee contraption, a few trinkets, every photo he was in, even the damn Lifebuoy. I thought of lighting a fire in the fireplace and feeding each piece to it, chanting, "Here's another piece of the heart you destroyed, you faithless son of a bitch." But I didn't have the passion for a dramatic ending. Besides I had my doubts as to how reliably the synthetic fabric of the contraption would act in the flames, not to mention the soap. So I bundled everything up in a plastic bag and drove it out to a dumpster. Woman triumphant, ready to move on with her life.

That night, however, the ice inside me crumbled. I collapsed on the floor and lay there crying hot, heavy tears into the rough shag. I was drowning, suffocating in my pain. Depression pulled me in so deeply I was trapped inside it. For weeks it seems—but it may have been mere days or many months—I stumbled through work and returned home to do nothing more than lie on the floor and weep. I was in so much pain I felt locked inside one of those fictitious rooms where the walls move slowly in and there's no way out. For the first time in years, I prayed. I cried out to God to take my misery away. There was no answer, except . . .

I think most people at some time or another have thoughts of suicide. In the past, when I'd been unhappy, I wondered sometimes what would happen if I just killed myself, but more out of curiosity than anything else. I'd even drafted elaborate suicide notes in my head. But I'd never before experienced this trap of constant, suffocating pain. My mind was so incapable of thought, the idea of suicide didn't occur to me for a long time. But when it did, it felt like an epiphany of the same nature as the one I'd experienced that night five years ago in Dayton. Then I'd discarded faith; now I would discard pain, and with it, life.

I considered various methods, went down a veritable checklist. I had no firearms and couldn't trust myself to pull the trigger anyway. A sharp razor in the bathtub? I didn't know if I could do that either. I had no sleeping pills. I could probably get them, but it seemed to involve too much effort for a spirit already drained of energy for anything but feeling its own pain.

I had my car and a long weekend, a full tank of gas, blankets for the bottoms of the garage doors. I worked it all out. I worried about Tippy. I was afraid she could starve in the house before someone found me. I wasn't thinking straight enough to consider putting her in the kennel to keep her safe. I decided to take her with me. She loved being in the car anyway. We would just fall asleep together one last time. I thought of writing a suicide note, but I had no interest in explaining, blaming, or leaving instructions. I just wanted the pain to end.

Once I had it all figured out to the detail, once I knew I could do it and exactly how, I stopped feeling trapped. I'd discovered a way out in case I needed it. I could breathe now. I got up off the floor and put Gloria Gaynor on the stereo. "I Will Survive" blasted my whimpering to smithereens. I pulled out the Yellow Pages and found a therapist.

## C. A TEUTONIC RELATIONSHIP

"I will survive," I told myself constantly, playing the song at top volume every night over and over. I worked with a marriage and grief counselor. I scribbled angry letters I never mailed. I wrote a dreadful but satisfying story in which I sent poisoned chocolate to him and imagined him dying of agony. Eventually, I worked my way through to indifference with a healthy splash of embarrassment that I'd been so crazy over a man the most casual observer could have told me was a conniving, egotistical son of a bitch—not that I'm judgmental or anything.

I realized I was truly over him, when I found myself getting interested in other men. Most didn't even notice me, but a captain I used to chat with at work asked me out one evening. I didn't know him well, but at least he was single. We were to go to a place he knew with live music. "A hole-in-the-wall," he described it, "but with decent food and cold beer and great bands."

It was on his side of town. Would I mind meeting him at his house, and we'd drive over from there? I could hear my mother gasp in horror, but I said, "Sure." I was a liberated woman, an Air Force officer. I didn't need to be picked up at my doorstep.

When I showed up that Friday night, he invited me in and motioned me to a seat in a sparsely furnished living room. A layer of dust covered everything. He asked if I'd like something to drink. I figured a beer would be easy, but he looked dubious when I said it.

"Let me see what I got." He disappeared and a few minutes later returned carrying a noxious brand of orange soda. "This is all I have."

"Never mind. I'll get something at the bar. Shall we get going?"

"It's a bit early yet. Nothing'll be happening." He placed the orange soda down on his coffee table, setting off alarm signals in my head about condensation rings. I so wanted to grab a coaster for him, but there was none in sight. (Mom had somehow managed to slip in on this date with me.) After a minute of silence, he jumped up. "You want to see the rest of the house?"

It was like a cruel parody of that other house tour I'd taken. This was a small townhouse with little evidence of comfort or home life. Only the kitchen seemed clean, mainly I suspected due to lack of use. The dining room was empty except for piles of boxes. Up a flight of stairs we went to a small bedroom that had been turned into a messy office, another that held junk and more boxes, and finally the master bedroom. It was the only room that was fully furnished. He had a large stereo set with speakers in four corners and wanted to show it off.

"Sit right here." He perched me on the edge of the bed. "This is where you can really hear it well." He put on Blue Oyster Cult, hiked up the volume, and came to sit beside me. He slipped his arm around me. "Hey, here's an idea. Why don't we just stay here to listen to music?"

I was out the door in a flash and driving away. *See, Mom, there's something to be said for having your own car.* I wondered if I'd seemed desperate and horny. Did he think I'd be grateful for a chance to get laid? Did he know about the affair and figure that made me easy? These thoughts tormented me as I lay in bed that night with no one but Tippy for company. But underneath them all and the anger and shame they inspired, I recognized a bitter truth. He could have had me with a little more effort. If we'd spent a couple of hours in the bar listening to the band. If he'd invested in a six-pack of beer and a bag of chips. If he'd at least bothered to dust.

The next evening, eight full-sized adults crowded into Annie and George's minivan. Anthony Quinn was in town in the musical "Zorba." Lynn had pulled together a group of friends that wanted to see it, including two middle-aged single ladies who had the hots for him. Everyone was chatting and laughing. What with the noise and heat and discomfort of sitting hip to hip with two other women in the third seat, I was starting to wish I'd stayed home.

A long row of seats awaited us at the Majestic Theatre. I started to slide in first, to the seat furthest down the row, but Lynn grabbed my elbow. "Wait." We let everyone else get seated, then he whispered, "How about a glass of wine?"

We slipped back up the aisle like two kids playing hooky. At the bar, we ordered drinks and watched the crowd flood in. "Thank God," Lynn said. "Talk about herding cats. I thought I'd never get everyone rounded up."

Latecomers jostled around us, anxious for a drink before the show began. The tension and negative thoughts began to drain out of me. At least for tonight, I could relax and forget the self-examination, the self-recrimination. No brooding, just enjoying life. *Zorba, teach me to dance.*

"Hey, how'd your date go last night?" Lynn asked.

"Fine. All ten minutes of it." I told him about it, exaggerating the leer in the captain's eyes as he settled me on the edge of the bed. Telling Lynn about the episode took the sting out of it, and soon we were both laughing.

Exec-ing is difficult, challenging, and fun even, but dull as canned corn to describe. Execs experience few personal triumphs on the job; success is measured simply in how smoothly the boss's day goes. I spent my time juggling, trying to catch the ball that was about to smash on the floor, while keeping all the others in the air. Most of my time I puzzled over abstruse technical writing, feeling stupid and incompetent. At least I hadn't lost my pristine ignorance.

One day I got a call from a woman whose father had died. She was trying to get hold of a list of his medals to put in the funeral program and obituary. "I called the Decorations Department and Retirements, but they told me they couldn't help me, they didn't have the records. So I called Records, and they said *they* don't have them. Someone suggested I call you. You're probably not the right person either, but I don't know where else to go. We need it today."

Ah, the ever-popular, bureaucratic, hot potato game. *My turn to pass it on—quick before I get stuck with it!* "I'm sorry. We don't keep records on retirees here. They'd be at the National Personnel Records Center in St. Louis."

She sighed. I heard another voice in the background and her response, "I'm trying, Mother. I'm trying." Then back to me, sounding weary but resigned—she must have known the game too—"I see. Can you give me the phone number there?"

I flipped through my rolodex for NPRC's number. I'd been there once for an orientation tour. It was a seven-story building covering a city block. They would require her to fill out a form, which would then go into a queue with all the other forms they received. It would take her weeks to get the information she wanted. Of course, in the scheme of things it wasn't really as important as the project I was struggling through, which was due to the commander before close of business and needed work. *Cheryl, you idiot! When are you going to get your priorities straight?* I grabbed the hot potato back. "Look, you have enough on your plate today. I'll see if I can get it for you."

As it turned out, I got the information with no trouble. The civilian in charge of Air Force records at NPRC was in her office and sympathetic. The grieving daughter began to sob when I called her that afternoon and read off her father's decorations. For five minutes, I let myself bask in the glow of self-satisfaction. *Finally, something I know how to do!* Then I forgot all about it.

A few weeks later, the Center commander received a letter from the woman who'd called me, expressing appreciation for the help I'd provided her and her family. He sent it to me with a handwritten note: "Good work! This is what I like to see in my officers!" *Good work good work good work.* I felt as happy as Tippy wagging her stub of a tail to my "Good girl. Who's a good girl?" I'd finally impressed the general.

"My father was always proud of his Air Force service," the woman's letter concluded. "The Air Force has a reputation for treating its members better than any other military branch. I know now this is true. Captain Duncan is an officer who helps make the Air Force the proud service it is." Her signature block ended with "Major, U.S. Marine Corps." Wow, I'd even impressed a marine. I couldn't resist. I picked up the phone and called Lynn to brag.

The work went on and the days went on, exhausting but soothing in their sameness. I got into a routine. I came home. I put Tippy out, brought her in, fed her, put myself on the couch for a nap. Sometimes I didn't wake up till midnight, hungry. So I'd snack while reading or watching a movie on cable till three or so. Then I'd be up again by six so I could get to work at seven.

One evening I'd started drifting into a pleasant after-work doze. Tippy finished her dinner and jumped up next to me. She pushed at my side as she curled her warm body into a doughnut. I reached down to pat her coarse hair. She snuffled against my hand—she never licked; she snuffled, as if trying to imitate a human kiss. At that moment, I wanted nothing more than a comfortable couch, a warm dog, and the drowsy start of a nap.

But when the phone rang, I pushed Tippy off and pulled myself up. I was incapable of ignoring a ringing telephone. It was Dick, a lieutenant who spent his off-duty hours at a nearby bar he owned. Inwardly I groaned. Dick wasn't someone to disturb a nap for.

"Hey, there's a guy here with two tickets for the show at the Majestic tonight. He can't use them, wants to give them away. I thought you might like them."

Tonight I liked a nap. "Gee, Dick, thanks but—"

"Guy says they're really good seats. Something called *Jerry's Girls*. Carol Channing."

I turned him down firmly, got him off the phone and myself back onto the couch, resetting into nap mode. Tippy had abandoned me for the ragged blanket she claimed as her bed when she wasn't claiming mine. I closed my eyes. The phone rang again. This time it was Lynn.

"Hey, Cheryl. Haven't talked to you for awhile. Just thought I'd call and say hi."

I yawned, kissed my nap goodbye. "Not much going on at this end. I just got off the phone with Dick." I told him about the call.

"Carol Channing! You took the tickets, right?"

"Nah, it's after seven already. Show starts at eight. Besides, I'm exhausted."

His voice was firm and commanding, a man taking charge. "Call Dick now. Tell him you'll take the tickets. I'll go get them, then swing by and pick you up in, oh, half an hour."

"But—"

"Get yourself ready." He hung up.

I was waiting at the door when Lynn arrived. He didn't even have time to shut off the motor before I was in the car, fastening the lap belt over my sequins. I was awake now, beginning to feel pumped by the prospect of an evening out. Obviously, without Mary's influence, I'd slipped back into my old humdrum ways. Going out to the theater on a work night seemed like something a wild woman would do, life on the edge. "You get the tickets?"

Lynn grinned and patted his pocket. Then he handed me two plastic cups and began pouring a cold clear liquid into them.

"What is it?"

"Martinis. Wait." He pulled a plastic baggie out of his pocket. In it were two little spears of olives which he dropped into the glasses. "For the drive. To the evening. Cheers."

We got to the theater just in time. The seats were indeed wonderful, five rows from the stage. *Jerry's Girls* turned out to be a revue of numbers from Jerry Herman musicals, with Leslie Uggams and Andrea McArdle and that spotlight-hogging, scene-stealing Carol Channing coming down a grand staircase singing "Hello, Dolly."

We were exhilarated and hungry when the show was over, so we went for a late dinner. We talked about music. Lynn had a passion for it, almost all types. His living room was dominated by a parlor grand piano that had been his first wife's.

"Do you play?" I asked him.

"No. I tried to take lessons once, but I'm too old." He flexed his fingers. "They don't obey me all that well anymore."

"You're not so old."

He smiled and a slight blush worked its way up his cheeks. "I made Cathy take lessons when she was younger. I hoped she'd like it, but she didn't. She prefers dance. Do you play?"

"*My* parents made *me* take piano lessons for years. I hated it. My sympathies are with Cathy. If I could dance, that's what I'd choose too. As it is I can't do either one."

I felt relaxed, as content as I'd been stretched out on the couch with Tippy. More than content. Something like happiness was humming around in my head along with the show tunes.

On my doorstep that night, Lynn kissed me for the first time.

Lynn seduced me with food. We were sitting on the floor in his living room, sipping wine, alone for a change. His mother was in Ohio for the summer, his daughter spending the night with a friend. "Will you stay with me tonight?" he asked. "I'll make you eggs Benedict in the morning." I loved the way he added the lure of food, as if he thought he needed to sweeten the pot. He didn't realize I'd have gone to bed with him for less than a can of orange soda.

When I woke in his bed the next morning, Lynn was gone. I found him bustling around in the kitchen. I perched on a stool behind the counter. "What you doing?"

He handed me a cup of coffee and leaned in to kiss me. I felt comfortable here with him, my feet bare, my body snuggled inside one of his robes. No morning-after awkwardness.

"Getting ready to make eggs Benedict."

"Really? You're really going to make them for me?"

He looked surprised. "Of course. I said I would, didn't I?"

"Yes, but—" I leaned over the counter and grabbed his arm as he was turning toward the refrigerator. "You do know this isn't the reason I stayed, don't you?"

He smiled and went to work. I'd never had eggs Benedict before. Lynn even made the hollandaise from scratch. I'd once thought the office was his natural element, then his garden. Wrong both times. It was the kitchen.

Weeks later, he was making dinner while I tried to keep up with the dirty dishes he generated. He chopped quickly, washed herbs almost lovingly, placed every ingredient in its own bowl. I mentally counted the dishes that remained to be washed and wondered why he couldn't let the onion and garlic and celery share one bowl since they were going to get cooked together anyway.

"When I get reassigned, will you write me?" The question was purely hypothetical. I didn't expect to get hit with a new assignment for over a year.

He stopped chopping, set the knife aside, and picked up his wine. "I'm not very good at that sort of thing. When people leave I usually don't stay in touch with them."

I was shocked at his response. It seemed a crime to let distance swallow a relationship so casually. "But *I'm* good at keeping in touch. If I wrote, wouldn't you at least write back?"

He looked pained, like someone having to pass on bad news. "Probably not." He set down his glass and went on with his chopping. I turned back to the sink, my mind blank. Lynn began sautéing vegetables. I collected the bowls as he emptied them and dropped them into the sink.

"So, guess who I talked to today?" he said, then mentioned my ex-lover's name.

"Oh?" I began drying dishes, carefully wiping under the lip of the bowls. The affair had ended a year ago. I'd never told him about it, choosing to follow the standard Dear Abby advice: "Be honest, but you don't have to tell him everything about your past."

His back turned to me, Lynn said, "He's coming here TDY next week for that conference I told you about. He wanted some information." He poured homemade broth on top of the vegetables and turned around. "Have you gotten over him yet?"

I dropped the stainless steel bowl in my hands. It clattered on the floor. I bent to pick it up. When I straightened up, I said, "What do you mean?"

"Are you over him?"

"Yes. Yes, I am." I dried my hands and lit a cigarette. "How did you know?"

He shrugged. "I'm not stupid. You were kind of . . . crazy acting."

I didn't know what to say to that but repeat, "Yes, I'm over it, completely over it." I said "it" as if he had been a disease, not a person. Lynn turned the burner on low, and we sat down on the floor in front of the cold fireplace. I told him everything about the affair, the facts, the feelings, the death of it. It was a relief not having a secret from him.

Lynn picked up my hand and kissed my palm. "It's in the past. Shall we finish dinner?"

I couldn't pretend though that the affair hadn't left a scar. "I'd prefer not to be around when he comes in for the conference next Friday. I'm not afraid that seeing him will arouse any emotions, except possibly the desire to slip arsenic into his coffee. I just don't want to see him. It's like, ugh, seeing some disgusting bug that can't hurt you but you don't want it near you. I think I'll take leave that day and drive up to Oklahoma to visit my friend Carla for the weekend."

"All the way to Oklahoma by yourself?" Lynn looked worried.

"It's just seven, maybe eight hours." (The first sign you're turning into a Texan is a casual disregard for driving distances.) "Besides I won't be alone. I'll take Tippy. She loves it."

"How long will you stay?"

"Just Friday and Saturday. I'll drive back on Sunday. Too bad you have to go to the conference or you could come too. You'd like Carla and Richard—he knows a lot about wine."

"I could fly up on Saturday and then drive back with you on Sunday."

He would do that? To me, a one-way ticket was an extravagant gesture, something I would never have expected from practical Lynn. We agreed that's what we'd do, though I was left wondering what this relationship was turning into. I felt that I couldn't examine it too hard, too soon. That it was something fragile that might crumble under my rough handling.

Carla came right to the point Friday evening, after I'd played with the two little boys for awhile, then accepted a glass of wine from oenophile Richard. "So how serious is this?"

I shrugged. "I'm not sure. I'm really fond of him. But I don't know if it's serious or not."

"Let me get this straight. He's flying all the way up here from San Antonio tomorrow just for the pleasure of a seven-hour drive back with you the next day. But you don't know if it's serious or not?" She began to laugh. I felt my cheeks growing warm.

In October I took leave to visit my parents in Florida, where they'd retired. Lynn joined me. We hit the road in my hatchback, stretching the drive out over three days. The second day, just beyond Pensacola, the car started shaking, the ride became bumpy. Lynn pulled over. The tire was flat. All we had was one of those temporary spares like a big floppy doughnut. It was a Sunday.

We drove carefully back to Pensacola, found a phone booth, and kept calling till we got what seemed to be the one and only garage open in the entire city. A long three hours later, we had a new tire and were on the road again. I felt guilty. After all, Eric was my car, so the flat had to be my fault. I kept waiting for Lynn to get cranky and take it out on me in little snips, to let it be known in sharp, subtle ways that I had ruined this perfect sunny day.

But it didn't happen. Not once did Lynn lose his good temper, or even seem to strain at keeping it. He remained perfectly cheerful, unruffled by inconvenience. *What a remarkable man, not to get bent out of shape over little things. I could fall in love with a man like this.*

It was a good thing Lynn was so composed and even-tempered. When we got to Fort Myers, we found not just my parents but my brother Joe and his wife, who lived nearby. My grandmother was also there, plus one of my stepsisters and her toddler son. Mom said smoothly, "Granny wanted to come visit, so Barb brought her down."

Lynn accepted it all with smiling equanimity. He sat chatting comfortably with everyone on the lanai. Two-year-old David Michael played horsey on his knee. Granny snoozed in an easy chair. Mom and I went out to the kitchen to put together a tray of snacks.

"He seems nice. So tell me, tell me." She stopped struggling with a jar and turned to face me with her "you can't fool your mother" look.

I responded with my wide-open-eyes, honest look. "Nothing to tell."

"We all figured you came to announce your engagement."

"No." I spoke firmly. I figured sooner or later I was going to get hurt (I was just praying for a clean wound, a bittersweet memory), but I didn't want Mom to hurt for me. "It's not going to happen. Don't get your hopes up."

I took the jar from her and opened it. Her hands were weak, shriveled, and contorted into claws by rheumatoid arthritis. Just fifty-five now, she seemed like an old woman, aged by disease, her life centering on pain management. "How are *you* doing, Mom?"

"Pretty good now. We're trying a new medication; it's working well." The problem was they all eventually stopped working, defeated by the disease. But she was grateful for the good times. She began to enthuse about the trip she and Bob had taken over Labor Day weekend.

"Wait!" I said. "*Myrtle Beach! You* were in Myrtle Beach then? So were we!"

In one of those weird coincidences that only real life gets by with, Mom and Bob were not only in Myrtle Beach when Lynn and I were, but the four of us had been wandering around the same store at the same time. The Waccamaw Pottery was a vast warehouse of a building. Like many "potteries," it got its name from its stock of earthenware planters but contained so much more, every type of decorative item one could want—vases, silk flowers, pillows, glassware, figurines. Lynn and I had spent Sunday afternoon wandering through it leisurely, touching, examining, picking things off the shelf, putting things back on the shelf. And as we were making our way down one aisle, they were strolling through another, always working toward and across the wide intersecting central aisle where all the others spilled out. For an hour we must have crossed aisles, passed around one corner as my parents passed around another, crisscrossed, backtracked, lingered, loitered—and never run into each another.

Mom laughed over the coincidence and called out to the lanai, "Hey, guys, guess what!" But it felt ominous to me that with timing and proximity strongly encouraging a surprise meeting in Myrtle Beach, we had somehow missed one another. Perhaps a sign that God, the universe, whatever, did not intend my parents to meet Lynn. That he and I were not intended to be.

If God hadn't intended Lynn to meet my family, you sure couldn't tell it that week. With his easygoing friendliness, he charmed them all. Little David Michael adored him and clung to his side. I watched them together one day. We were at Wiggins Pass, my parent's favorite beach, quiet and clean, picnic tables nestled up in the shade of a pine grove. Lynn was teaching David how to feed the seagulls out of his hand, how to hold out pieces of bread so the gulls would come take it from him. Every time a gull approached, David shrieked, dropped the bread, then chortled, his Huggies slumping down to his chubby knees. Lynn laughed and held out a piece himself. The birds came to him, took bread from his fingers, trust on both sides.

My Air Force future was rushing toward reassignment. I began talking to Lynn about my assignment choices for the following year. He said little, other than "I don't want you to go." Tentatively, I brought up the idea of getting out of the Air Force, finding a job in San Antonio. "Oh, you don't want to do that," he said. I felt frustrated, trying to make a decision in the dark.

The Saturday after Thanksgiving, Lynn and I sat on my couch, listening to Christmas carols on the stereo. The assignment issue had nagged at me all evening, nibbling at the edges of my enjoyment. Once the assignment gurus dropped orders on me, it would be too late. I couldn't afford to wait and see what they'd come up with unaided.

"What Child Is This" played softly in the background. Its soft minor key filled me with melancholy. I felt that I held my future in my hands as I began to talk. "I want a voice in where I go next. If you want me to stay I can see about getting an assignment to somewhere else in San Antonio." (Randolph was one of four Air Force bases in the city.) "But I don't know if I can make it work. Besides, sooner or later, I *will* have to leave, and it'll be harder later." I took a deep breath. *Here I go again, wanting too much, destroying the little I'm meant to have.* "I guess what I'm trying to say is if you want me to stay, I need more of a commitment."

There, I'd used the treacherous word. Lynn didn't say anything. I had screwed it all up, killed a good thing. *Can't you ever learn to keep your mouth shut, Cheryl?*

Finally he set his glass down and turned to me. I steeled myself for rejection. He took my hand. "Cheryl, I love you. Will you marry me?" He spoke clearly, almost formally.

I'd anticipated one of those modern discussions: *Well, maybe we should move in together for awhile. See how it goes. What do you think?* Something tentative and hesitating, a sense of negotiating, holding something in reserve, self-protective. But Lynn honored me with a straightforward proposal. He placed his heart on the table and trusted me with it.

I responded in kind. "I love you too, Lynn. Yes, I'll marry you." It seemed at once the most natural thing in the world—and the scariest.

Our engagement buzzed all over MPC, because Lynn had worked there since its inception and knew so many people. One day, I ran into a civilian secretary I knew from another directorate, a woman who kept her eye on all the happenings at the Center. She said, "Congratulations. I heard about you and Lynn Dietrich getting married."

"Thank you."

"It came as such a surprise to everyone. No one even knew you were dating."

"Well, we were friends a long time, good friends. Then one thing led to another."

Nodding sagely, she said, "I understand. You had a Teutonic relationship."

I managed to choke back a spurt of laughter. But as I thought of Lynn, his temperament, his background, his last name, the phrase seemed to fit. "Yes, that's exactly right."

# CHAPTER FIVE

# "IN SECURITY"

## 1986–1988: HQ Electronic Security Command, Kelly AFB TX

## A. WEIGHT, WEIGHT, DON'T TELL ME

"Join the Air Force and see Texas." That should be the Air Force's motto, I decided. So much for all that traveling I'd thought the military would provide. Not that I objected to this assignment to Headquarters, Electronic Security Command (ESC). It had been a wedding present of sorts, from an assignments NCO and a colonel Lynn and I knew at MPC. I was grateful for the extra two years in San Antonio while Lynn and I figured out how to be married to one another. *Lynn will never leave San Antonio* thrust itself into my head, the kind/smug warning I'd heard from so many of his friends.

I'd left the house at six that morning and made the unfamiliar drive across town in the dark, anxious to make a good first impression. Oh-six-forty and I was already cooling my heels in an antechamber off the guardroom. I wore a badge that said "Visitor." I would wear it till I was found worthy to be let in on the mysteries cultivated here.

ESC thrived on secrecy like vampires on blood. Like all Air Force members I'd undergone a National Agency Check and received a Secret clearance, but to work at ESC, everyone had

128

to have a Top Secret clearance, and what's more, one for Special Compartmentalized Information. Until my upgrade came through, I wasn't authorized to know most of what went on here. I'd have to be escorted every time I left my office.

ESC's motto was "Peace through Vigilance." It listened and watched. That was its whole purpose, to collect communications from foreign countries needed to fight the commies. The electronic spies of the airwaves. A worldwide net of antennas and radio operators, Morse code experts, and linguists gathered information and fed it to the National Security Agency.

A tiny cough interrupted my thoughts. "You must be our new officer."

I sprang to my feet. A lieutenant colonel stood before me, a middle-aged man with thinning gray hair, glasses, and shrewd eyes. I felt he summed me up in the time it took to introduce ourselves and shake hands. But what his judgment was I couldn't tell; his expression gave nothing away.

After a few hours in the office, my every movement watched, I was relieved to be escorted out of the building and set loose on my own to complete in-processing. I took my time, wandering around the annex nicknamed "Security Hill," drinking in the free air. Security Hill was a base in miniature, a geographically separated branch of Kelly Air Force Base. It existed only to support the military and civilian population working inside the headquarters. I wandered over to check out the tiny Base Exchange, a sort of military mini-mart selling cigarettes, milk, shoe polish, and rank insignia. Next to it was the gym, complete with basketball court, weight machines, and exercise rooms. I wandered on down the tree-lined street to the low frame building housing our squadron orderly room. The only one there was an airman sitting behind a messy desk, working a hidden word puzzle. I coughed lightly. "I'm here to in-process."

I handed him my orders and the sealed files I'd brought from the MPC orderly room. He yawned, motioned me to a desk, and handed me more forms to fill out. He went back to his puzzle while I bent over the paperwork. As soon as I finished, he led me over to a shiny white scale. I removed my shoes and stepped on. With one hand he fiddled with the weights, while the other moved the height bar. I looked down just as the airman brought the bar up to the crown of my head. He mumbled, "Five-seven. One hundred fifty-nine."

"What?" I jerked my head up, striking the metal bar. "Ouch! That can't be right."

He shrugged. "You're ten pounds overweight, ma'am. You'll have to meet with the commander when she gets back from her leave."

"But I can't be. I mean, I'm five-nine. I was looking down. We need to redo this."

He yawned. "You'll have to take it up with the major."

"This is ridiculous," I started, but changed my mind. What was ridiculous was arguing with a bored airman. When the commander returned I would just ask her to redo the weigh-in.

I fumed as I strode back to the headquarters building. The height thing really pissed me off. Five-seven! I hadn't been that short since seventh grade. How dare some peewee airman call me five-seven! I was mindful though, that even at five-nine I would still be over my weight standard. My indignation was tinged with uneasiness. An Air Force officer was meant to be razor sharp and angular, ideally built along the lines of a fighter jet. I was built more like a big-bellied cargo plane.

The commander wouldn't be back for a week. I had seven days to lose weight. Lynn was on temporary duty in Washington, DC, for a month, so I was on my own. It was just as well. My mouth watered at the sudden thought of Lynn's fajitas and margaritas and spinach soufflés and scalloped potatoes. Wistfully, I said goodbye to all good things, at least for awhile.

That evening I thought back to my mother's fast weight-loss formula of six years ago, the one that got me to OTS. I broiled an unseasoned, boneless, skinless chicken breast and choked it down with cucumbers and steamed asparagus—thank goodness, Lynn had introduced me to the fresh version. When he called that night to see how my first day at ESC went, I chatted about the headquarters, my new boss, the people who'd be working for me. I lay on the bed with Tippy (normally exiled to the floor nowadays) curled up next to me, her head on my growling tummy. Lynn and I talked for half an hour. I never mentioned the weigh-in.

A week later, I stood in front of the commander's door, my uniform pressed to its sharpest creases, my hair cut and styled, my lipstick freshly applied. Image counted big-time today. The first sergeant told me to report in, a formal practice used primarily with general officers, board interviews—and when facing disciplinary action. I felt like I'd been sucker-punched, but I had no time to react. He motioned me toward the door. I gave it two sharp raps.

"Enter," came the response, and I entered, stepping as firmly as possible to the desk. I stopped at attention and raised my right hand to the tip of my glasses.

"Ma'am. Captain Duncan reports as ordered." My hand shook, despite my efforts to hold it as still as possible. My voice quavered and stumbled on the word "reports."

The commander returned my salute. "Have a seat, Captain."

Since ESC was a major command, our operational commander was a general, too high ranking to handle the people programs. These were delegated to what was called a headquarters squadron commander, in this case a major. She had no authority to tell us what to do on the job but was responsible to ensure we met administrative and personnel requirements. She could even impose punitive and disciplinary action on the enlisted members and junior officers like me.

I was relieved to see she wasn't whippet-thin but inclined to a comfortable roundness herself. She smiled at me. "Now, you reported in as 'Captain Duncan' but your nametag and records say 'Dietrich.' What gives?" She looked at me pleasantly, quizzically.

Hope resurrected itself. "I've just been married two months, ma'am. Still not used to the new name." I pasted on a blushing bride look. Who wouldn't grant leniency to a newlywed?

"I thought as much. Congratulations." She beamed at me. I beamed back. She opened the folder on her desk and whipped out a form. "I need you to sign here and initial here and here."

I stared at it in disbelief. She was putting me on the Weight Management Program (WMP), a program disarmingly described as rehabilitative, not punitive—though it was potentially a career killer, even grounds for discharge. She hadn't even discussed it with me or double-checked the airman's findings. No explanation, no re-dos. So much for leniency. I bent over the paper, signing, initialing slowly, deliberately, giving myself time to push the tears back inside.

She did have me remeasured and reweighed but only to determine what level of the WMP to place me on. The fact that I seemed to have grown two inches since last week faze her, nor did the fact that fact that I'd already lost the offending pounds thanks to asparagus and a jazzercise class at the base gym. I tried not to blame her. Air Force regulations were clear and tight on weight control. Commanders had no options to consider, no judgment to employ. If I'd stolen a carton of cigarettes from the base exchange or been caught in, say, an adulterous relationship, she could have examined the circumstances and determined what she thought the best punishment. Not so with my unauthorized fat. Decision logic tables—if this, then that—spelled out every action she was to take.

Phase I of the WMP put a hold on certain personnel actions—for example, promotions, assignments, professional military education, deployments—until the member established a pattern of satisfactory weight loss. Fortunately, having already lost the offending pounds, I got to skip the draconian part of the program and go directly into Phase II. This entailed a three-month exercise program, along with six months of mandatory monthly weigh-ins. After that I would enter the third phase, a year of monitoring with random weigh-ins. For the sake of a few extra pounds, which I no longer carried, my record would be flagged for a minimum of eighteen months. From a professional point of view, this could be disaster.

I was concerned for my career and angry at the Air Force with its inexorable regulations. But I barely noticed those feelings, so acutely aware of my own guilt, the Calvinist in me having a field day. I'd known the rules, the risk. Shame oozed through me like a nasty, yellow slime.

After a thorough medical evaluation, which cleared me of any significant physical problem, I returned to the clinic for a mandatory series of fitness counseling, a group program called "Lifestyle Changes." I resigned myself to several sessions of simplistic lectures on substituting carrots for French fries and parking at the far end of the lot to get some extra steps in. A narrow young civilian greeted me at the door with a smirk that kept escaping from the corner of her narrow lips. She pointed me to a narrow wooden school desk and handed me a questionnaire.

It was multiple choice. The first question asked: "How long have you been obese?" Number two: "How many other members of your family are obese?"

I stared at the word in shock. I wanted to jump up and say, "I'm in the wrong room. I'm looking for the 'slightly overweight' group."

In the past that was how I'd referred to myself, also full-bodied, heavyset, large, and once in a moment of inspired humor, Junoesque. But never obese. Yet here was this questionnaire screaming at me, "Why are you such a fat cow?"

I wanted to leap through my shame and out the door, but I picked up the number two pencil and started to fill in the lozenge next to the first answer. I chose the "less than a year" option, though I didn't know what the real answer was. I concentrated on filling it in evenly, blackly, staying within the lines.

For three months I had to participate in an exercise program. I asked the squadron WMP monitor, a hearty, self-important master sergeant if I could count the jazzercise class I was already taking at the base gym. It met right after work, so I could do it on my own time, not the Air Force's. My office wouldn't be penalized by my absences during the work day—nor, though I didn't say this, would my boss receive a reminder three times a week of my failure to meet standards. Not that he had ever expressed disapproval, just looked at me intently and grunted when I told him about my weigh-in.

But the WMP monitor preferred the letter of the law to its spirit. Instead of the group session I'd been attending with a trained instructor, he required me to take his "class." For three months, three times a week I signed in at the gym and picked up the official WMP Jane Fonda aerobics video. I exercised in front of a TV unsupervised for an hour, along with a bored airman who spent most of her time napping on her exercise mat. I told myself that a good officer would encourage her to get up and do the mandatory exercises, would scold her, would threaten her, would order her. A good officer would do her part to enforce Air Force standards and WMP rules with this lackadaisical young airman. But screw it, I didn't feel like a good officer in this bare room with its concrete floors and thin gray mats, with Jane Fonda's voice ringing out. So I said nothing to my listless companion, just concentrated on the exercises, on my own body.

Occasionally, the WMP monitor peeked in, yelled at the airman, and nodded at me. It was pitiful how pleased I was at that hint of approval, like a beaten dog extending her head for a pat. It was years before the irony of the burly sergeant's blind faith in "Hanoi Jane" hit me.

Lynn came home from DC and pulled out the old Weight Watchers cookbooks his second wife had left behind. "We could both manage to lose a little weight," he said. He began fixing salads instead of soufflés, broiling liver instead of grilling steaks. Tonic water instead of martinis. He did it all well, but I was not in the best of moods those days. I missed the luxurious feeling of being spoiled with his richest concoctions. They'd tasted like love to me. I began to feel that the Air Force, specifically ESC, was getting in the way of the things that made me happy—Lynn and Tippy and home and good food and wine. I started coming home cranky.

"Cryptolinguists are the pilots of the enlisted force," I groused one night, picking my way around Brussels sprouts. The vinegar that dressed them seemed the perfect accompaniment to my mood. "They're spoiled and pampered. They think they're the smartest people in the Air Force and expect to be treated like little royalty."

They *were* smart, handpicked for their intelligence and provided with expensive, intensive language training. But their job was mind-numbingly tedious, sitting in a bunker or in a specially outfitted plane with earphones on, listening for hours, transcribing anything potentially meaningful. Then every few years they were shipped back to the States to perform mindless work, guaranteed to bore them silly. I could see their frustration in the Personnel directorate at ESC, bright young NCOs running around the building doing jobs out of their primary skill sets, frequently administrative, and often mere gofers pouring coffee for the colonels. Most of them eventually figured out they could use this opportunity to work on completing bachelor's or master's degrees, even occasionally PhDs.

The Air Force had the best educated enlisted force in the world, and ESC the best educated in the Air Force. All of which seemed to feed their sense of entitlement. They were given extra allowances, special bonuses, anything to keep them happy and in the Air Force. They were too valuable a resource to lose. Most of my job centered around finding ways not to lose them, ways to soothe them with special attention, stroke their giant egos. Despite this, our office received constant complaints. And nowadays I was too hungry and cranky to put up with it.

"Sure they're bright," I went on. "But so are some of the rest of us. They insist on being treated so damned special. I am sick and tired of linguists!"

Lynn set his fork down. "Did you know I used to be one?" *Oops.*

I knew that in his twenties, he'd spent a four-year enlistment in the Air Force, reaching the grade of sergeant before he got out. "I thought you were in Personnel."

"I was. But not at first."

In Basic Training tests, Lynn had scored high enough to be accepted into the cryptolinguist career field. In the fifties, all new linguists started out with a four-week course in Russian at Lackland Air Force Base. Only the top of the class would be sent on to study Russian as their specialty, while the rest would be farmed out to easier languages. Lynn eagerly wanted to be selected for Russian, picturing himself stationed in Germany after training, the Fatherland calling to him through his genes. So he worked his ass off to be top of that four-week class. He made it, then got one of those shocks of disillusionment the military is so good at delivering. He'd done too well. He was pulled out of Russian to study a more difficult language: Chinese.

In those days the services contracted with Yale to provide training in Chinese. Lynn spent a year in New Haven, listening to professors who talked while they ate potato chips or sipped coffee ("because that's what we'd be listening to, you know—people mumbling and background noise"). But Lynn felt he wasn't catching on to it.

"The characters, yes. I loved studying Chinese characters." His voice caressed the words, so I could almost see the characters forming in front of me in graceful black ink strokes. "My professors begged me to stay, but there was no guarantee I could get placed in one of the few positions that called for reading. Besides I'd found out where I was likely to be assigned."

A group of New Haven town girls clustered around the language school to pick up the boys in each new class—something about a man in uniform, I suppose. They got to know all sorts of classified stuff that they gossiped about freely, including what they heard from previous boyfriends complaining about their situations.

"I found out the Chinese linguists were almost all stationed on tiny isolated islands way out in the Pacific. So I self-eliminated."

His dream of wandering the streets of West Berlin might have shifted into a not unpleasant notion of Hong Kong or Macao. But a rock in the Pacific—no way! So he'd dropped out of the program. He'd spent the rest of his enlistment working in the orderly room on Security Hill.

I eyed him tentatively after hearing his story. "Well, okay. At least, you're not a prima donna. So I forgive you for your past sins. Now, say something in Chinese."

I'd hoped for something like, "I adore every inch of your gorgeous body," but the twangy sounds that came out meant "Let's eat." Still I had to smile.

"What's so funny?"

"I just realized I married a Yale man. Won't my mom be pleased!"

We fell off the diet wagon soon after that. I got into a routine: three weeks of eating and drinking normally; then a week before my weigh-in, we'd go back to bland chicken, cucumbers, and asparagus. It was stressful but not as depressing as Brussels sprouts or broccoli every day. Lynn tried to be discreet when he sneaked ice cream out of the freezer.

Each weigh-in I approached with dread. Every ounce was important. I presented myself at the scales as soon as the orderly room opened, to take full advantage of the lighter, early morning weight—also because I allowed myself no coffee, or even water, until I'd weighed in. I emptied my bladder and blew my nose right beforehand (okay, I'm kidding about the nose blowing part). I wore my thinnest socks and a short-sleeve shirt, but no sweater, no earrings, no watch, and no belt. Sometimes I squeaked through so narrowly, it frightened me, and I promised myself, "never again." But I'd go home to steak that night, and next month would be the same.

I lost any interest in doing more than surviving the exercise routine and squeaking through the weight checks. Air Force policies had narrowed my objectives to just meeting the minimum standard. They tapped into what I figured was a pretty common human dynamic. If all you got credit for was a C, why would you work for a B, much less an A?

One day I submitted what I considered an inspired idea through the Air Force Suggestion Program. As an incentive to do more than hold steady at the maximum weight allowed, I suggested commanders receive authority to remove members from the WMP early if they reached a weight 10 percent below their max and maintained it for three months. I received a cold, bureaucratic response, basically saying "Quit your bitching and get with the program."

When I was almost through Phase II of the Weight Management Program, the Air Force changed its weight standards based on new, more reliable medical studies. For my height, the maximum allowable weight was raised to 163 pounds. I returned to the commander and pointed out that by the Air Force's own reckoning, I'd never actually been overweight at all. You might think she'd have taken me off the program immediately with an apology on behalf of the Air Force, but if so, you'd be a civilian. It didn't matter. I'd gone on the WMP based on the standards at the time. She had no authority to remove me even after they'd been shown to be flawed.

I quit trying to impose common sense on Air Force regulations. I quit my bitching and got with the program.

That fall a series of articles appeared in the *Air Force Times*, a weekly newspaper covering Air Force issues but not owned by the service. A wing commander had been marking officers down on their evaluation reports if their wives were not members of the base Officers' Wives' Club or didn't volunteer on base or didn't attend the wing social functions. The Air Force's investigation of complaints determined that the commander had indeed done as accused, but that it wasn't particularly a problem since he had the authority to consider this information in his assessment of the "whole person." An official shrug: "Yeah, he did it. So what?"

Military officers were once considered a two-for-one deal. They were expected to come with a wife who was devoted to her husband's career and would spend her days as an unpaid volunteer and her evenings as charming hostess or guest. But the days of the white-gloved, behatted Officers' Wives' Club luncheons of the fifties and sixties had long passed. More and more officers were single or had wives with their own careers—or were women themselves and not legally authorized to have a wife. The notion that in the eighties, a wing commander's old-fashioned beliefs could impact the careers of otherwise decent officers was noxious.

But the Air Force was going along with it. That official response on top of the commander's actions aroused a storm of fury throughout the Air Force. The five women in our office—two officers, two civilians, one NCO—discussed the subject hotly. We spent one afternoon, each composing a letter to the *Air Force Times*, then reading them aloud to the whole office. I don't remember much about mine, except for one phrase that makes me wince now, "wifely appendage," but the letter apparently dripped with just the right amount of righteous sarcasm and common sense. Everyone urged me to submit it to the paper's Letters to the Editor.

"But don't sign your name." This came from a surprising source, Velma, a civilian who worked for me. She'd always seemed so calm and sensible. I was surprised at this sudden surge of paranoia from her. But everyone else agreed. After all, the *Air Force Times* frequently printed anonymous letters, due to the fear some officers and NCOs felt for their careers (whether justified or not) if they dared to publically criticize Air Force or national policies.

"It doesn't seem right," I said. But everyone urged me to use common sense. I was a junior officer, female, my career just getting started. I didn't know how many influential people my letter might piss off. And, although no one said it aloud, I already had a serious strike against me from being on the Weight Management Program. Still, I couldn't shake the sense that submitting something in anonymity was a slick, slimy practice.

Velma looked at me shrewdly and said, "Don't throw your career away. Lynn knows what's what. Take it home to him and ask him before you mail it. He'll tell you the same thing."

I agreed to do so, though secretly I determined to send it under my own name or not at all. That evening, I showed the letter to Lynn. He admired it and agreed I should send it in.

"Everyone in the office thinks it could affect my career, that I shouldn't sign it."

He recoiled. "Why would you send something you were afraid to put your name on?"

I laughed and hugged him. "I knew you'd say that!" I grabbed a pen and signed the letter with a flourish John Hancock could have taken pride in.

Having gotten my ire out of my system, I didn't think much more about it. The issue raged through the paper—editorials, commentary, official responses—for the next couple of weeks. Then I received a small dime-store frame from a friend with a sticky note on it: "Cheryl – Your fifteen minutes of fame have now begun."

The frame held my letter as published in the *Air Force Times*. Besides the framed version, he had also included a copy of the new issue. They'd published a page and a half of letters on the same subject—fifteen or twenty in all. The headline across the section read "Readers Object to 'Wifely Appendage' Requirement." My letter was the first, directly under the headline. It was the only one that was signed.

For some time afterward, strangers meeting me would exclaim, "Oh, you're the one who wrote that letter!" and pump my hand and babble about how much they agreed. Even the colonels complimented me, and their wives loved me. If signing the letter affected my career at all, it was positively. I could hold my head up again, the WMP temporarily forgotten.

Soon afterward, the *Air Force Times* changed its policies to limit the circumstances under which they would print anonymous letters. More important, the Air Force changed evaluation regulations to forbid consideration or mention of an officer's marital status or any other "nonmilitary" factors as part of the evaluation report. I liked to think I played a small part.

## B. MRS. DIETRICH

A married lady, a Mrs.—that was me now. I'd always planned to keep my own last name if I married, but a few weeks before our wedding I realized that I was marrying not just Lynn but a family. I decided to take the family name. Besides, I liked the sound of Dietrich, Dee-Trick. It clicked crisply off the tongue, instead of grumbling in the throat, like Duncan.

I had also become the lady of the house—Lynn's house. We pretended it was ours, but really it was the house he'd bought with his ex-wife, raised Cathy in, a house full of his furniture and his history. It was not as crowded as I'd expected. His mother, Mabel, had decided to move back to Ohio as soon as we married; Cathy had gotten her own apartment. We made arrangements to rent my house to my lawyer friend Linda and her family, who were being reassigned to Randolph.

The day after we returned from our honeymoon, Lynn was scheduled to go on one of the many TDYs his job required. He'd not had a chance to clean out any drawers or closet space for me. I sat on the bed and sulked while he packed for his trip. "How can I feel at home here when I don't even have a place to put my clothes?"

Grumbling, Lynn flung things out of half his drawers, squeezed his clothes into half the closet. "There! Can you wait till I get back till you start moving furniture?"

"I'm sorry. I just feel kind of bereft. Like I don't have a home anymore."

"This will start to feel like your home soon."

The next night, with Lynn gone, I managed to lock myself out of the house that I was now the lady of. A fine beginning indeed. But it never occurred to me to remain in my old house till he returned. That no longer felt like home either. For better or worse I was wedded to all of Lynn, his name, his house . . . and his daughter.

Another new role—parent, Cathy's stepmother and now mother of the bride. Cathy and her boyfriend Pete had announced their engagement right after we did, with a wedding date only four months after ours. I spent my first few months at ESC rushing after work to countless meetings with coordinator, florist, caterer, baker, candlestick maker.

Pete threw himself into the wedding plans, making me long for the days of passive, acquiescent bridegrooms. Up to now, he had seemed sweet and good-natured, a tall lanky guy hovering protectively over tiny Cathy. But the closer we got to the wedding, the more demanding he became. He insisted on making every decision, often bringing Cathy to the point of tears trying to please him. He chose the church, the flowers, Cathy's headpiece. When she gave a brief thought to wearing a festive hat with her wedding dress, he exploded. If she showed up at the altar with anything but a traditional veil, he would walk right out, he told her. It was strange to see strong-willed Cathy back off so quickly. Only superstition kept him from also choosing her wedding dress, but he insisted it be white, no bone, no ivory—white, pure white.

We watched uneasily as the engagement progressed, afraid to talk to Cathy about it. Lynn's reluctance came from twenty years of fighting with her. "She's so stubborn. Ever since she was a little girl, she's always insisted on doing things her own way," he complained to me.

I pointed out that she came by her obstinacy naturally (a truly Teutonic quality).

He nodded innocently. "Yes, you're right. Her mother was also very stubborn."

He would say nothing for fear of making Cathy more determined to marry Pete. I stayed silent because I was just the stepmother, my position in the family still tenuous. Plus I felt guilty, as if our marriage had pushed her not just out of the house but into the engagement. So neither of us spoke up as Pete grew less reasonable and more truculent.

Pete's mother, like Cathy's, had died when he was a baby. We met his father only a few weeks before the wedding. At a rough-and-tumble western bar, Cathy's future father-in-law drank Lone Star after Lone Star and boasted about being hauled into court three times for child abuse. "But they never pinned nothing on me," he said and laughed.

Neither of us even attempted to smile, but Pete's father didn't seem to notice. I had the worst part that evening. I had to dance with the jerk, all hands and rank breath.

The week before the wedding Cathy was in tears every day. "Is this natural?" she asked. "Do all brides cry so much before they get married?"

Here was our opportunity to talk with her, to say, No—maybe a little weepy. There's a sense of loss when you move from one family to create another. But not this torrent of tears. We hesitated too long, and soon she was exclaiming over another delivery of wedding presents.

The evening before the wedding, I skipped the rehearsal, supposedly to entertain out-of-town relatives at home. Instead I paced the kitchen floor waiting for Lynn to return. Soon Lynn's three brothers and their wives joined me, mimicking me, all of us with heads down staring at the tile, hands clasped behind our backs, back and forth over the linoleum. We were like a sober conga line, not touching but all in step. The kitchen was small, just ten paces or so across. I could see Lynn's brother grinning at the tail of the line as I made the turn to go back. He was always easily entertained. Mabel fussed at us to sit down, but I was too tense to stay still.

When Lynn finally came home, he looked weary, his mouth twisted in disgust. Pete had caused a scene at the rehearsal. He blew up over some minor detail; the pastor threatened not to perform the ceremony, while Cathy cried and tried to appease Pete.

Hope poked its little feathered head up. "So is the wedding canceled?"

"No, they got it worked out. It's still on." His tone was glum.

Pete's grandparents were hosting a rehearsal dinner at the clubhouse of the complex where Cathy lived. When Lynn and I arrived at her apartment, we found the imprint of a fist in the thin metal of her front door. Cathy said she didn't know where it came from; she just found it there one day. We walked across to the clubhouse, all three of us silent.

At the dinner, the bride and groom barely spoke to one another. Cathy's eyes were red, Pete's face flushed. His father got drunk, yelled off-color toasts, and grabbed at the bridesmaids. He was the only one having a good time. Even the bridesmaids and groomsmen seemed subdued, making only the most cursory attempts at flirting. We brought an early end to the world's least festive party by pleading exhaustion and a busy day coming up.

Some of the bridesmaids had decided to hide Cathy's car, a desperate attempt at a light-hearted prank. They mistook Pete's keys for hers and hid his car instead. We were back at Cathy's apartment saying goodnight when he burst through the open door, trembling with rage, stuttering in his anger, screaming at Cathy. She was bewildered. She began simultaneously protesting her innocence and apologizing for whatever she'd done. Lynn, who'd known about the joke, got the keys back from Cathy's cousin and explained the mix up. Pete jerked the keys out of his hand and stomped out.

A heavy silence set in, even the giggling bridesmaids shocked and quiet. Cathy sank down onto the floor and sat cross-legged, her pretty face fragile and pale, her skin taut and almost transparent over the high cheekbones she'd inherited from her mother.

"Is it supposed to be this way?" she whispered.

Lynn knelt next to her. "No, honey, it's not. This is not what marriage is about." He gave me an inquiring look. I nodded. "You need to know one thing. Listen carefully." He spoke slowly, emphasizing every word. "You do not have to get married tomorrow. It is not too late. You do not have to go through with this."

She sobbed suddenly. "But I love him."

"You do not have to marry him."

She called us after midnight, said she needed to talk. We hadn't been asleep yet, hadn't gone to bed, hadn't even spoken much. We'd done nothing but wait. We found her still sitting on the floor of her apartment, bridesmaids hovering like uncertain ladies-in-waiting. Her face was red, streaked with drying tears. Her voice quavered, but she spoke decisively. We brought her home with us and tucked her into bed next to her grandmother. Mabel sat up. "The wedding?"

"It's off," I said.

"Good!" It was a crisp, satisfied judgment. She put her arm around Cathy, who eventually fell asleep, safe within the refuge of childhood.

Early next morning she called Pete. They sat on the front stoop and talked (with Lynn and three protective uncles secretly monitoring them from the windows). Both were crying when Pete left, not stomping away but dragging, his shoulders drooping. Cathy shut herself in her room for twenty-four hours. The following morning, she arose with new determination. She called Pete and arranged to meet him back at her apartment.

Lynn protested. "You know what his temper's like. He could be violent." He had a horror of Pete harming Cathy, even taking her out on a wild drive, a murder-suicide.

"He's never hurt me, Dad. Not physically. You don't have to worry. I need to try to work things out with him. Canceling the wedding was the right thing to do—for now at least." Her voice rose, strained and tense. "I can't throw everything we had away—no matter what you say."

I saw an argument brewing, perhaps even a rift—emotions were very high at the time, all of us on edge. So I stepped in. "Why don't I go along, Cathy? I'll take a book and read by the pool, while you and Pete talk. If you have any problems, just yell—I'll hear you."

Cathy agreed eagerly; Lynn, reluctantly and only after extracting a promise from Cathy that she wouldn't get into a car with Pete and that we'd be back within an hour.

Actually, after all the drama, I was delighted to have some time to myself. It was early, blissfully quiet, no one else out at the pool. I stretched out on a lounge chair and opened my book. But I couldn't read. I found myself listening for noises, not just a scream but perhaps a muffled cry through the French doors opening onto Cathy's narrow balcony. I stared up at those doors, afraid that I'd trusted too much to Cathy's assurances and not enough to Lynn's fears. I felt overwhelmed by the responsibility of keeping Cathy safe for just one hour. Sitting there, I realized what it would be like to raise a child, having that feeling all my life, always there in my heart: the fear that I couldn't keep her safe and happy and good. I was glad then that Lynn and I had decided not to have children of our own. This grownup girl was the only child I would ever have.

I began glancing back and forth up to the window, down to my watch. One hour passed, then another ten minutes. Just as I was starting to wonder if I should go up and pound on the door, Pete and Cathy appeared in front of me. I started. I'd been concentrating so hard on the balcony door, I hadn't noticed them coming down the stairs and walking across the courtyard. They were hand in hand, their faces glowing with happiness and hope.

"We're going to start again. Figure out what's wrong and work at it," Cathy said.

I kept my thoughts to myself, just said, "I hope you can do it." And I did. I understood Cathy. Love wasn't something to be tossed away without fighting for it, giving it every chance you could. Only then, if it didn't work out, could you hold your head up and move on without regrets. I'd learned that myself. Who was I to discourage Cathy from trying?

Pete said, "We think we need to sort things out the next few months, then after that we'll be ready to get married. We just rushed into it too soon, both of us under a lot of stress." He hugged her and looked at her with eyes that seemed to reflect only her. I believe he truly loved her. But love to some people means possession and power, and they don't change easily.

"Cathy, we need to go," I said. "Your dad'll be having a cow. Most of the family's leaving today, and he's fixing a big brunch."

She was so happy she could afford to be generous, to share the next few hours with her aunts and uncles and cousins. She turned to kiss Pete goodbye. It wasn't an instinct on my part but a well-calculated decision when I asked him if he'd like to come over, inviting him back into the fold. His face lit up. "Sure! I'll go home, get a shower and be there in half an hour."

When we got back, Cathy ran into her bedroom, announcing as she passed through the curious living room crowd, "I've got to clean up. Pete's coming over."

Lynn's face darkened. He was still sitting there, no move at making breakfast (which would have told me how upset he was even if I hadn't already known). "Why is Pete coming over?" He spat the words into the air.

Lynn didn't lose his temper much, but when he did, there was no hot explosion like in my family but an icy wall that shut me out into the cold. It terrified me. I usually tiptoed around anything I thought might trigger it. This time though I had such a sense of rightness about my decision that I barely quailed when I said, "I invited him." The look that prefaced his withdrawal started to frost his face. I went on quickly. "Cathy wants to try to make their relationship work. Do you want her to meet with Pete away from here? Wouldn't you rather have them here where you can keep an eye on them and stay part of Cathy's life?"

He stared at me, then I saw his face slowly clear. His body, which he'd held stiffly, tensed up for days, relaxed. He nodded, and with that acknowledgement, I truly became his wife. No longer merely a beloved visitor but someone who belonged in this house, a member of the family, his partner in life. We went into the kitchen and began to cook breakfast together.

Cathy and Pete's relationship lasted only another month. She left him the first time he shoved her against the wall. None of his pleading convinced her to give him another chance. She grieved but with her head up. She'd done everything she could. She had nothing on her part to regret, no second guessing.

I could write an article—and probably will someday—on the how-to's of dismantling a wedding on the day of, a subject on which I perforce became an expert. But that's not why I include this story here.

A twenty-year-old girl called her wedding off less than twelve hours before she was due at the altar. The beautiful ring, all those presents, the gown flowing with lace and her deceased mother's wedding veil, the cake and the flowers and the big party with dancing and two hundred guests, getting to be the princess that girls think they're entitled to be on their wedding day—she renounced it all and not from frightened impulse but resolute judgment. Remember the scene in *Private Benjamin* when Judy decks her arrogant bridegroom at the altar, then strides down the tree-lined avenue, martial drums in the background, flinging her veil into the air where it floats above her like an uncaged bird. Cathy's story didn't get to end triumphantly at that point, the music soaring while the credits rolled. She had to deal with her decision the next day and the day after. She had to face her fears and an unknown future.

Soon after the wedding that wasn't (as it's known in family lore), I attended a presentation by a colonel who taught ethics at the Air Force Academy. At one point, he asked the audience to name some virtues. People called out. "Love." "Independence." "Generosity." Even, "Punctuality."

"Good. Good. But what is the most important virtue, the quintessential military virtue?"

"Loyalty." "Patriotism." "Obedience." They were all wrong. I knew the correct answer. I'd always known. It was the strength I felt most lacking in. I shrank in my seat, afraid to call attention to myself. But when the colonel continued to press, I finally spoke, quietly, shyly.

He spun in my direction. "What did you say?"

I spoke louder. "Courage."

"Courage! And why is that the most important virtue?"

"Because the others are meaningless without it."

"Yes!" He began to expound on this, but I didn't hear what else he said, where he went with it. I was seeing Cathy again, flinging her dreams into the air and marching on without them.

# C. SOS

SOS, Squadron Officer School, was a refresher course for junior officers. Air University on Maxwell Air Force Base was like any other college campus, complete with three-story buildings flush with windows through which the sunlight poured cheerfully in, a campus quad where off-duty students could mingle in mufti, and a huge library—though its collection included more Sun Tzu and Clausewitz than Thackeray or Moliere.

I missed Lynn and Tippy, but it was a relief to be away from Security Hill, where I felt everyone knew about me and my weight failure. Here I could disappear into the mass of eight hundred-plus lieutenants and captains, my responsibilities limited to turning in papers and passing tests. And playing flickerball.

Flickerball was a hybrid game, designed to balance the skills of the athlete and the nerd. Played on a long field, with a football you weren't allowed to run with, only throw, it had goals mounted at each end like basketball backboards but with small square holes rather than baskets. One point for hitting the backboard with the football; three points for getting the ball through the opening.

We memorized pages of arbitrary rules, things like, "On overcast Tuesdays, players have to run backward." Maybe not that absurd, but close. Anyone who broke one of the rules had to spend time in the penalty box. My main achievement was staying out of it. My participation consisted of running aimlessly around the field, avoiding the football.

Our flight's strongest players should have been Henry and Malcolm. They were our only Air Force Academy graduates, the service's aristocracy. Both had played football there, and Malcolm had even been offered a chance to go pro. They despised flickerball, which they considered a "pussy game," and disdained its rules. Both spent too much time in the penalty box.

Still, our flight always managed to win, despite little help from the two of them and none at all from me. Our commander/coach/ instructor, a senior captain, finally took me to task. "You're not really taking part in the game. You're not even trying."

"I'm hopeless at sports."

"Maybe. But you owe it to the team to try."

Owe it to the team? I knew the words, heard them often enough, but like many women of my generation, I'd never internalized the concept of team. My brothers' childhoods had been taken up with Little League and Punt, Pass, and Kick teams, junior high and high school basketball. My opportunities to be on a team had been limited to drill and swim, but neither my inclinations nor skills had drawn me to those.

I began keeping a closer eye on the football, running more determinedly toward it, attempting to block throws—with little discernible success except for Captain Wallin's smiling encouragement. That was enough, since basically I was just trying to look like I was trying.

One day, however, my awareness was heightened by the subtle scent of leaves dying gracefully, fall carried on the breeze, the smell of football season I remembered from college. The opposing player nearest to me happened to receive the ball. His eyes and mouth flew open. He looked as startled as I was. Encouraged by his moment of hesitation, I sprang to block him, jumping like a maniac all around him (carefully maintaining the prescribed three-foot distance), my arms waving in the air. When he threw the ball, I managed to knock it off course. It hit the ground and I grabbed it—the only time I actually touched the football in the process of the game's play. A flush of triumph, then panic. *What now? What do I do with the damned thing?*

And there like a miracle stood one of my teammates, a solid, sturdy guy we called Buddha. He was a few feet away, holding out his hands to receive the ball. I threw a quick underhanded pass to him. He swiveled on one foot (allowed) and from yards away hurled the ball toward our goalpost. Right through the center of the square.

We ran to one another and high-fived. The rest of the flight surrounded us, hugging us both, all of us jumping up and down (except Henry, who was looking on from the penalty box). There you have it: the glory day of my athletic prowess.

SOS had its own version of OTS's "big blue bedroom," an auditorium where the whole class met for special lectures, programs, and news updates. Nothing but shades of blue wherever I looked, the air stifling with all those bodies so close together, eight hundred sets of lungs depleting the oxygen. One week, after the usual Cold War update, after every Soviet cough had been analyzed, the instructor cleared his throat. "Now, some special Air Force news."

Air Force policy had been changed to open up noncombat aircraft to women pilots, he announced. Forty-five years after the WASPs had proven women had a role in wartime aviation, the Air Force was finally catching up. The women in the crowd clapped enthusiastically, the men politely, an excited buzz running around the auditorium.

When the floor opened up for questions, an officer I didn't know stood up in the back of the room. "With women on Air Force planes now, does that mean we get a choice of 'coffee, tea, or me'?" His voice was sweetly mock innocent.

The auditorium exploded in laughter—all in the range of tenor and below. Even the officer at the podium smiled and let the laughter continue for a few minutes before saying, "Okay, okay. Are there any serious questions?"

Sheila, my only female flightmate, and I were livid, our anger shared by every woman I knew at SOS—and not understood at all by any of the men. "The guy's an idiot, everyone knows it, that's why we laughed," Buddha said later. "That's all."

In the eyes of most of the school the angry women became the problem—*can't take a joke, jeez, can't even rib 'em a little, no sense of humor, causing a ruckus over something so minor.* Sympathy shifted toward the guy, who'd been called on the carpet and persuaded to issue a public apology along the lines of "Sorry if anyone was offended." *Sorry you're so sensitive.*

Even that morsel incensed Malcolm, however. "Guy had nothing to apologize for—it was just a joke. You all made such a fuss over nothing. Now he's got a black mark on his record." Several of us were sitting out in the barracks hallway, a wide, carpeted corridor, the informal meeting area of our flight. He jumped up. "Aw, shit. You know what? Even though it was a joke, let's face it, it's true. Women don't belong in the cockpit." He stomped away.

Henry smirked. "Hell, it'd be easier to teach a monkey to fly than a woman."

"Shame on you, Henry," Sheila said—she was gutsier than I. "Not so long ago, that's what people said about blacks. How would you have liked it?"

Henry's dark face grew darker. He stood up. "It's not the same thing at all."

Sheila said softly, sadly, as he walked away, "Yeah, it is."

It was still dark when I was awakened by a thumping on the door. Captain Wallin's voice yelled down the hallway, "Fifteen minutes.

Downstairs and on the bus." Shit! This had to be Project X. It was a Saturday morning—on the weekend, *really*?

I'd been dreading Project X from the beginning. Not that I knew anything about it—no one did. But the mysterious X in the name would give any sensible person pause; nothing good ever came from the letter X. All we knew was it was a new exercise, developed as secretly as a war-fighting mission. Our class would be the first to undergo its challenges. We were less than two weeks from graduating, and I'd started to hope that the authorities had decided it needed more work. The next class could get the honor of being its guinea pigs.

Not so. Our flight was dropped off in a remote, deserted area, with just the drone of jet engines in the background to reassure us we were still on base. We looked around warily. A scrubby field lay before us with a small hut at the far end, a stand of trees in the distance. Captain Wallin seemed to be enjoying himself, as he summarized the task. "Your team was shot down in enemy territory. You have to make your way through various obstacles to where an evacuation helicopter will pick you up. If you don't get there in time, you won't make it out."

That was all the explanation we got, then information about our first challenge—to make it through the "mine field" across the way and to the shelter on the other side in five minutes. "Any questions?" But he didn't stop for any. He held up a stopwatch. "Go!"

We rushed away en masse, while he jumped into a golf cart and shuttled down the road. The mines were indicated by little red flags at foot level. There was no attempt to hide them, but there were so many to avoid that caution slowed the pace, fortunately for me. We all got through to the other side with no problems. Captain Wallin was waiting for us.

"Good, good," he said. Then he stood quietly, thoughtfully reviewing a sheet in front of him. After a minute or so with no further instructions, I started to feel uneasy with his silence and restless. *If we gotta do it, let's get this baby over with.* But I bit my lip.

Finally, Buddha spoke up. "Uh, sir, what's our next challenge?"

He looked up, beaming. "Nothing too bad, just a bit of uneven terrain. Unfortunately one of your teammates got injured in the minefield and can't walk. So you'll have to carry him." He pulled a litter out of the hut. "Buddha, you can't walk. Lie down and enjoy the ride." He showed us paper he'd been staring at. One sentence only: *The first one who speaks is the injured one.*

Buddha said, "Ah, shit," and settled his large frame onto the litter. Without comment, the four biggest guys each picked up a corner. They began running up the small knoll Captain Wallin pointed out. The rest of us followed, with me lagging at the rear and vowing silently that I would start speaking up more. A vow to start running more didn't occur to me.

Four hours later, after splashing through creeks, climbing over stiles (Buddha healed and on his own two feet already), crawling through itchy brush, and running, running, running, my energy, strength, and adrenaline had all drained out. I kept moving on sheer determination, and that was rapidly ebbing also. The cool, misty morning had given way to the noontime sun overhead, strong even in December. A ditch stretched in front of me, neither deep nor wide, but enough to require an extra effort in making the—at most—two-foot leap to the other side. For a moment, I was afraid my legs would refuse that extra demand and I'd fall face down in the grass, my feet in the narrow trickle of water. I stumbled but thrust my arms out and pushed myself back up before I hit the ground. My palms stung from some noxious plant in the scrub covering the sandy field.

I was far behind the rest of the flight. They were strung out in front of me, all headed toward a strip of concrete in the distance. A yellow school bus waited for us there, our "helicopter," the end of our ordeal. Up to now I'd kept up with the others, though getting slower and slower over the hours. Now I could barely breathe and even my sluggish jog had degenerated into a stumbling walk. The bus was a football-field length away. It might as well have been in the next state. I could just make out two stocky figures well ahead of everyone, almost at the bus. *Henry and Malcolm. Damn arrogant Academy jocks, they would be out in front.*

Not that I was in a mood to despise anyone but myself right then. While Henry and Malcolm rushed confidently ahead of the pack, I was faltering with the goal in sight. I grabbed for one of my favorite quotes: "Courage means holding on just one minute longer." But it didn't seem to help. I stumbled, pulled myself upright, and staggered forward. Stagger was all I could manage now. I didn't know if I could hold on for even one more minute. My legs no longer seemed connected to my will. Fear started to crowd out my little bit of remaining courage.

*I could twist an ankle, worse, break it. I'll fail. The flight will fail. Project X isn't important anyway. It's an exercise, for God's sake. I'm a Personnel officer. What does this have to do with me? I'll still collect the same paycheck. I can give up, lie down and rest. I can't make it anyway. I'm going to fail. Why not stop now? It's not real.*

I took another step and another. My heart pounded at me to stop. My breath came out harsh, quick, shallow. Now I had hyperventilating to add to my fears. I tried slowing my breathing, but my legs slowed also. Step, breathe, step, breathe, step, breathe. That was as much as I could manage.

The bus up ahead seemed further than it had been. Was that possible? I could just make out figures milling around it, haloed with the hard, hurting sunlight. I gasped for air and slid my reluctant foot a few more inches through the dirt. I didn't know if the moisture in my eyes was all sweat or also tears, but it was starting to blind me.

"Don't give up. You can do this."

For a moment I thought it was the fading voice of courage in my head making one last dying call. Then a hand grabbed my left elbow. "Come on. Let's go."

Another hand grasped my right arm. I couldn't see them, but I knew the voices. With Henry and Malcolm on either side of me, holding me up, I stumbled forward. They urged me on the whole way, words of encouragement. "Almost there. You can do this. Don't stop. A few more steps. Just a few more. Keep moving. You can do it."

We got to the bus with seconds to spare. The three of us were the last ones on, Henry and Malcolm helping me up the three mountainous steps. The rest of the flight began to cheer. They'd saved the first two bench seats for us. I collapsed into one and concentrated on getting my breathing under control. I wiped the warm stickiness off my face and out of my eyes. Captain Wallin handed me a plastic glass filled with cold water, lovely water I drained immediately.

"Good work, all of you," he said. "Let's go. We'll hold the after-action discussion till Monday." The bus started its rattling, bumpy way back to the barracks.

As soon as I could speak, I looked across the aisle to Henry and Malcolm. "Thank you."

Henry shrugged. Malcolm said, "Sure," and waved his hand in dismissal.

I sat back and rested my head against the bouncing window pane, a new thought rolling around in my exhausted mind. Henry and Malcolm hadn't rescued me for my own sake, I knew. The team couldn't pass without me. Every member counted—like Buddha in the litter, like my one minor assist on the flickerball field. Henry and Malcolm understood teams in ways I never had. If our positions had been reversed, I wasn't sure I would have gone back for them.

After my ten weeks at SOS, then a two-week Christmas leave, I returned to ESC in January, hoping my Top Secret clearance had finally come through. It hadn't, but there was an advantage to that. I got the good TDYs. For a change I actually did start to see the world in small bites at least: Italy, Greece, Germany, and Washington, DC.

It took a year for my upgrade to finally come through. I gratefully pulled off the "Visitor" badge, exchanging it for a photo ID that clipped onto my uniform collar. I found reasons to talk to people face to face, rather than by phone, just so I could walk down the hallways unescorted, free and equal at last. I could now go to the restroom by myself and take cigarette breaks on my own.

I flipped up the red covers from message after message and perused the read files that had been off limits up to now. "There's nothing here I haven't read in the *Express-News*! All that time and money just to have access to information that all the newspapers are printing."

"Yes, but the Air Force hasn't confirmed what you're reading in the newspapers." The boss's tone was dry. I was never sure if he was being serious or ironic—I leaned toward ironic.

Perhaps because it had taken a year for my security upgrade to come through, my memories of the two years at ESC are crowded with things that had nothing to do with my main responsibilities—TDYs, home, family, the Weight Management Program. Work seemed secondary. My last major project there was to identify positions in the headquarters for deletion. I deleted my own.

My year on Phase III of the WMP eventually passed. I checked the code on my computer record to make sure it dropped off. My stint on the program was over before I had to worry about my next assignment. If I had to be a fat cow, at least my timing was impeccable.

Soon afterward information about my next assignment came down. I approached Lynn nervously that evening. We could no longer avoid the issue: would he leave San Antonio or would I leave the Air Force? I waved the message at him. I could tell by the look dawning in his eyes that he knew what it contained; he just didn't know where.

I said one word. "Germany."

He expelled a long breath, then began to grin. "How soon can I start packing?"

## CHAPTER SIX

# "OVER ALL"

### 1988–1992: Ramstein AB, Germany

## A. DEUTSCHLAND, DEUTSCHLAND, ÜBER ALLES

It started with a familiar drum roll. I glanced at my watch. Five o'clock, time for retreat. I positioned myself at parade rest, preparatory to snapping to attention. The music started, but it wasn't the familiar, slow notes of "Ohhhh, saaay" with its upward swing to "seeee." Startled and unsure, I remained at parade rest. Then the music focused into mental words, into one of the few national anthems other than my own that I could identify.

I didn't know the protocol. I glanced around. German civilians were walking to their cars or smoking in doorways, while American military stood at attention and saluted the German flag. Quickly I snapped to attention. "Germany, Germany, over all,"—a little creepy when you think about it, which I did through the whole long rendition. As soon as it was over, another drum roll much to my relief introduced the notes of the familiar "Star Spangled Banner."

Next morning I asked Stacie about it. "Get used to it," she said. "On any base in a foreign country, saluting the host nation's flag is protocol." Though only a second lieutenant, she knew a lot, having served in the enlisted force up to the grade of tech sergeant before her commission. A friendly, outgoing redhead, she collected cats and dogs, a real menagerie in her off-base apartment. She gave them all names that ended in "o." I'd never before realized all the possibilities: Oreo, Rambo, Bozo, and Cheerio. Stacie and I both worked in the Ramstein Consolidated Base Personnel Office (CBPO) and yes, Stacie had a cat named Cee-Bo.

Ramstein Air Base was home to one of the largest and, during those days of the Cold War, most influential commands: United States Air Forces in Europe, known by its acronym USAFE (pronounced you-say-fee, or sometimes, just you-safe, pronunciation reflecting attitude, I suppose).

Even more than in the States, overseas bases functioned as self-sufficient entities. The Air Force took pride in the quality of life it provided—an American life no matter where you were assigned. On TV, you could watch *Golden Girls* or the World Series, thanks to the Armed Forces Network. You could read the daily news or comics out of *Stars and Stripes* newspaper; shop for food at the commissary, booze at the Class VI store, clothes and toys and dishes at the Base Exchange. You could get your hair cut or permed at the base barber and beauty shops; your clothes cleaned at the base dry cleaners. If you wanted an evening out, the movie theater got first-run films. The officer and NCO clubs were available for dining, drinking, and dancing to live bands. Most bases had gymnasiums and swimming pools; the larger ones like Ramstein, had golf courses, where sliding-scale green fees ensured airmen too could afford to play. Your kids could attend Department of Defense Dependent Schools while you earned a degree from the University of Maryland, which had a presence on each major base. You could go to church at the base chapel and make your will at the legal office. The doctors at the base hospital could deliver your babies, who would be considered born on U.S. soil in case, like John McCain, they wanted to run for president one day.

Like most Air Force bases, there was not enough housing to take care of every newcomer, so we had to find a place in the local economy (amply helped by the base housing office, which served as a kind of rental agency). This was fine with me, who got enough of the military lifestyle in my workday. Lynn and I rented an apartment in Bruchmühlbach, one of the few villages near the base with no pretensions to quaintness, not even a respectable castle ruin. But like all German towns in spring, the plain houses were enlivened with flower boxes extending from every window, trailing profusions of red geraniums and blue lobelia. To us, it was beautiful, and if we wanted ruins, they were a mere fifteen-minute drive away.

There was a civilian hiring freeze on overseas bases, so Lynn had taken an early retirement option before we left San Antonio. Now I had a house husband, and a damn fine one. More domestic and energetic than I was, Lynn even washed windows, loved to shop at the commissary and even more, the German outdoor markets. He had dinner in the works when I got home. I didn't do a single load of laundry all the years we were assigned to Ramstein.

Lynn's motivation was to get all the household chores finished during the week so on my days off we could explore. It turned out his wanderlust was as ferocious as mine, maybe more so. On weekends we threw Tippy in the car and hit the road. We explored Germany first: the Black Forest, Heidelberg, Rothenburg, Ludwig's castles in Bavaria, Trier with its Roman gate and coliseum. When we went further afield, to Paris, Venice, and Lucerne, Stacie took care of Tippy-o.

We had come at the best time, spring and summer so fresh and seductive here. We spent many of our evenings having lazy grill-outs with our landlords, Menachem and Brigitte, sharing food and culture. They practiced their English; we practiced our German. Their English improved faster than our German.

Menachem had learned most of his English playing keyboard in a pop band in his younger days. He was delighted to have us there to explain lyrics to songs he'd memorized by sound. "Jambalaya" was a very popular song in Germany, but the words were challenging. We finally confessed that few Americans knew what filé and "cherry-mio" (cher amio) meant, and that even gumbo and bayou were rather arcane (at the time). Another time, he asked about the word "trill." I explained it was a series of musical notes. His brow creased. "Does that fit?" I asked.

"Maybe," he said. "We used to sing 'I found my trill on Blueberry Hill.'"

"Thrill! Oh, that's different." He was delighted with the new explanation I gave him, and it became a favorite word with him, even though he couldn't say the soft "th."

"I found a trill at work today," he would say and talk about something that had happened. He owned a pest control business, which I doubted was all that trilling.

They had two daughters. Lisa was eight when we met her, a pretty blonde who liked to play circus in the backyard. She and her cousin pretended to be elephants and horses and clowns, while we were a silent audience on our balcony above them.

The older daughter Dafne was severely disabled, unable to speak or understand. During the week she lived in an institution but came home on weekends. She was confined to a wheelchair, patiently and lovingly attended to by both parents. One day, watching Menachem coax spoonfuls of pureed pork into her mouth, I said, "I admire you and Brigitte. You are so brave."

He stopped, his dripping spoon hovering in the air, and looked at me in surprise. "No, not brave. Dafne, she . . . she is my trill. She is the sunshine of my life." He turned back to her, and his face lit up as if she were indeed shining upon it.

Menachem's father came to visit, a genial, good-natured man who spoke a dialect of German as hard to understand as his bit of heavily accented English. In the heat of summer, wearing a short-sleeve shirt, he seemed unconscious of the faded numbers tattooed on his arm. I tried not to stare, sometimes successfully.

Menachem's father, a Polish Jew, had been young and strong enough to be brought to Germany to work on the Autobahn. After the war, he married a German woman. This lovely man was the only one of his family to have survived the war. I burned with anger for him, though he seemed to have none. He had settled peacefully and comfortably among neighbors who years prior would have turned him over to the Nazis. I wondered how his neighbors felt when they saw the numbers eternally identifying him as "Outsider." I wondered how his daughter-in-law felt.

We were too tactful, maybe too cowardly, to bring up the subject of Nazis and the Holocaust in German company. We mentioned it vaguely only once, but Brigitte immediately bristled. "Others did things as bad, maybe worse. Look at how the Turks treated the Armenians."

She could have thrown slavery and the genocide of Native Americans in our faces—and probably would have, if we hadn't changed the subject. But it seemed shabby to hide behind the offenses of others while not owning up to one's own. Of course, we never knew how she really felt. It's one thing to criticize your own country; quite another to listen to some damn foreigner do so.

There were two Germanys at that time. We visited East Germany only once, early in our Ramstein tour, flying into Templehof in West Berlin. We stayed in a small hotel right on the Kufürstendamm Strasse, the famous Ku'damm, the bustling heart of the city. The sun warmed the sidewalk cafes where we drank bright green Berliner Weisse, a light wheat beer flavored with woodruff, as fresh as the green leaves of springtime. I wanted to go to the zoo there, but the friends we were with resisted. "We've been to zoos," they said.

We got the same reaction when we suggested a cathedral. "We went to one in Cologne." "How about the art museum," I said.

"Oh, we've seen so many art museums."

"Well, what would you like to do?"

The wife responded immediately, "Go shopping."

It was tempting, but I resisted saying, "But haven't you been shopping before?"

On our last full day there we took a bus tour into East Berlin. As a military member, I was required to go in uniform, but I hadn't brought one with me. I hid my military ID in the hotel room before we left and went with just my civilian passport. Crossing the border in mufti made me a spy in East German eyes, and I could be detained and imprisoned if caught. We had to stop for a long time at Checkpoint Charlie, waiting to be cleared. My heart was thumping away loudly when a guard came on board the bus and asked any U.S. military members to step outside. A major calmly strode down the aisle to be processed separately, before meeting us at the bus on the other side.

I slouched in my seat, trying to look un-sharp and un-military, which fortunately wasn't difficult for me. Then one of our friends, despite having been informed of my ruse, began pointing at me and saying cheerfully, "Oh, she is, she's military." I knew she just meant for me to have my due and had gotten confused over what that would mean in these circumstances. Fortunately, her husband managed to shush her, and the strangers near us stared out their windows as if preoccupied.

East Berlin on a Saturday afternoon was empty, the streets devoid of traffic, no shoppers, the shops all closed in fact. One group of uniformed school kids passed alongside our bus as we were stopped at a pointless red light. They looked up at us through the windows, expressionless, no curiosity, no smiles, no jostling or laughter.

We went to a memorial garden replete with Soviet-style sculpture, Mother Russia mourning her lost sons, that kind of thing. Lynn was our cameraman, but as much as I urged him to take pictures, he refused. It had gotten cloudy, and he used that as an excuse. "Not enough light," he said but later confessed, "It's too depressing." We don't have a single picture of East Berlin, so it remains gray and dismal in my mind.

The only amusement we had was at the antiquities museum. A card sat on an empty plinth in the Egyptian section. It said something along the order of "This once held the beautifully sculpted head of Queen Nefertiti, which has since vanished. Its whereabouts are currently unknown."

Lynn whispered to me, "They should ask us. We could tell them."

We'd seen it on display the day before at the Ägyptisches Museum in the Charlottenburg suburb of West Berlin. We both started to snicker but stopped when a stern guard glared at us. Apparently in the East, even the most inconsequential information about the West had to be restricted. Something about the pointless little lie made the whole experience feel surreal.

I bought a small picture book while we were there, and in it are lovely old buildings, parks, monuments. We saw little of these. Our guide instead pointed out sparsely stocked shops, concrete block buildings riddled with World War II shell damage, the flimsy Trabant sedans parked on the empty streets. She used these to boast about the economic strength of East Germany. She took us to a tawdry cafe meant for foreigners and exclaimed over what she insisted was luxuriousness. To her, repression was freedom; scarcity meant plenty. Her enthusiasm seemed straight out of Orwell.

In 1988, we still saw West Germany as both the tip of the spear pointed toward an eternal enemy, the USSR, and its likely first victim if Mutual Assured Destruction didn't work. The Berlin Wall, however, was already vibrating with the determination of Berliners on both sides to tear it down. Checkpoint Charlie had only another year to operate. We didn't know it yet, but the Cold War was in its final throes.

## B. LOCAL SALTY NATIONS

Local Salty Nations or LSNs (who named these things?) exercised our ability to fight and function in wartime, whether conventional, chemical, biological or nuclear. In most LSNs we got the whole range. As the CBPO's chief of Personnel Utilization, I was more directly involved in wartime business than I had ever been before. At Carswell we had tested our readiness to mobilize forces and send them overseas. Here we were the forces already in place, the front line.

I brought my exercise chemical gear home to model for Lynn (the real stuff was sealed and stored on base) and giggled while he took pictures of me. I looked like an olive green Pillsbury woman, bulked up and sexless inside charcoal-lined chem pants and jacket. Heavy black galoshes, oversized as clown shoes, covered my boots. From a web belt a canteen hung on one side, a gas mask carrier on the other. I wore the mask, a huge rubber insect face with two oversized scratched lenses through which I peered. I had to have special eyeglasses made up to fit inside. Attached to the mask, a long plastic hood covered my head, hair, neck. Over that, I wore a metal helmet, chin strap securing it. With long black rubber gloves, no part of my skin was exposed.

At first, I thought it was funny, this strange garb turning wimpy me into a warrior. Then I took part in my first LSN. Fortunately, it lasted only three days, but in that time I learned to hate the mask and the rest of the gear designed to save my life. The second LSN was also short but came too soon and taught me too little.

By my third LSN, surviving the exercise was all I cared about. It was a big one, a full week to prepare us for an upcoming NATO inspection. By the fourth day, we were burned out. It seemed like life had narrowed down to the stark, windowless bunker in which we had set up the Personnel Readiness Center (PRC). We had a precious hour of peace and quiet that afternoon. I was luxuriating in the air coming through the bunker door we'd propped open, when I heard the base siren go off. Almost simultaneously, the phone rang. "Code Red" a voice from the command post said. One of the airmen swung the door closed and bolted it. All five of us inside the cramped, under-ground room fumbled with the clasps of our gas mask covers.

We were supposed to get the mask on and tightly sealed in seven seconds. I set mine straight against my face, held it there firmly while I pulled the straps over my head and tightened them. Some of my hair got entangled in them but I wasn't about to take the mask off to fix it. I'd just have to tolerate the uncomfortable feeling that someone was pulling my hair for the next . . . what? Ten minutes? One hour? Three hours? I had no idea how long I'd be wearing the mask. Its inside smelled like dirty sock feet. I checked the seal by inhaling deeply enough that the sides of the mask collapsed into my cheeks. I pulled the hood down, grabbed my helmet and disappeared into the keyhole leg space under my battered metal desk. I could hear the grunts of the others as they got themselves into similar positions, protected from debris in case we got a direct hit.

Under the desk, I put the heavy helmet on and lastly the rubber gloves. I hated the gloves almost as much as the gas mask. My hands began to sweat right away. Soon they would start to feel like something dead I was carrying, not a part of me at all.

I was a stickler for doing things right even when no one was watching. Lee, my NCO-in-charge, a tech sergeant, argued that if no inspectors were there, we should just lock the door and forget the rest of it. He was a short, powerfully built man with heavy muscular arms that disappeared in the bulk of the chem jacket. When he wasn't in a gas mask, his face glowed a rich brown burnished with the red gold of copper, smooth and polished, a vibrant contrast to my sallow skin. We had nothing in common, separated by race, sex, background, experience, but mainly temperament. He was a cynic and sneered at these exercises, while belief came as naturally to me as breathing. Besides, I had to insist we exercise properly, because—well, that was the point of exercising.

The phone rang after a few minutes. I grabbed it off the corner of the desk and down onto the floor with me. The attack was over. We pulled ourselves wearily, creakily off the floor.

The good thing about imaginary air and missile strikes was that they didn't last long. The aftermath was the problem. I sent two of the airmen outside to do the required sweep of the area around us. They would check for UODs, unexploded ordnance. While we were crouching under our desks, the inspectors, like perverted Easter bunnies, had been out sprinkling the base with dummy ordnance, such as small cluster bombs, no bigger than eggs lying treacherously in the grass. Worse, they put up signs and handed out cards, simulating destruction of planes, runways, hangars, and other buildings. They were grim reapers, handing participants notes that killed, injured, and maimed.

Fortunately, no little surprises awaited us outside the bunker, so we wouldn't be cordoned off to give the civil engineers or the medics practice in their wartime duties. We were small fish in this pond, and the inspectors seldom bothered us. The airmen came back inside and sat down, breathing harshly. We had to stay in full chem gear until we got the "all clear." This was the hard part, working while we could barely maneuver, barely move, barely breathe.

Our primary responsibility was to provide personnel strength and casualty reports. In case of an attack the wing commander had to know how many viable troops he had, where, and with what skills. We collected the information from squadron runners (more like waddlers in the bulky chem gear), collated it, and provided it to the command post in reports twice a day. We monitored the skill levels and prepared messages to simulate sending to USAFE asking for assistance. The headquarters was just on the other side of Ramstein, but they didn't take part in the exercises—neither did the CBPO itself nor any of the other agencies that had to stay open to support the HQ weenies.

As squadron input arrived, we got busy adjusting numbers and transcribing information into the report formats. We worked primarily in silence, our energy sapped by the gear that weighed us down and the mask that made the simple activity of breathing a struggle. The air inside my mask was so thick and stale I felt nauseated. I was thirsty too, but the technique for drinking out of a canteen in a gas mask was so intricate no one bothered to learn it—a failure could choke you, or at least make things even less pleasant inside the mask. So I waited and tried to keep busy, tried not to succumb to the lethargy that threatened the longer we sat inside the closed bunker. Every UOD on base had to be disposed of and samples of air and water tested until there were no lingering traces of chemical gas. Only then would we get an all clear. We had no idea what this scenario called for.

Lethargy, chaos, ignorance, discomfort—all bad, but what I hated most about the exercises were the constant reminders of how ineffective I was. Lee knew the personnel readiness business backwards and forwards, which I did not. I needed more of his expertise, but he provided only as much help as I specifically asked for, performing it slowly and passively, as if mocking my attempts to respond seriously to the imaginary attacks and their simulated consequences. Sometimes I read judgment in his eyes. *Who are you to think you're in charge? How have you earned it?*

I looked at the clock on the wall; the dial was hard to read through the smeared plastic of my lenses. It looked like we'd been in the masks over an hour. The attacks today had been coming more frequently, taking longer to clear up. In two hours it would be dark and time for the night shift to take over. Then we could remove the gear and go home—a luxury we probably wouldn't have in a real war, but there was a limit to the verisimilitude you could impose on an exercise.

As difficult as it was to work quickly and efficiently in chem gear, it was nowhere nearly as hard as Lee made it seem. The airmen followed his lead, however. I felt I was watching a slow motion tape, as they fumbled around with plastic transparencies, spilling them onto the cold concrete floor, the bulky gear almost upending them as they bent to pick them up with awkward gloves. Lee stood up to look over their shoulders, pointed out an inaccuracy or two, then threw himself back into his chair.

He did a Redd Foxx imitation. "This is the big one. . . . I'm coming, Elizabeth, . . . I'm coming." The airmen laughed, ghastly sounds coming out of their mouthpieces. I had to laugh too—he did it so well.

In my first LSN, I'd made futile stabs at organizing our work-space. By now I'd pretty well stopped trying, but my tidy spirit remained offended by it. Papers and slides were strewn every-where, on desks and on the floor, where transparency pens rolled and made walking a hazard. The supplies we brought down with us four days ago were scattered throughout, along with debris from potato chip bags, partially eaten sandwiches, and empty soda cans. Everyone shuffled through loose rosters to find the one he or she was looking for, then put it down somewhere else. "Where . . . calculator?" one of the airmen gasped and started a search which further dislocated everything. This would have been chaos, except chaos should involve fast, frenetic activity. We were as frenetic as sludge.

After another twenty minutes the phone rang. Everyone stopped, poised like Botero statuary. "All clear," the voice on the line said. "All clear," I repeated, and pulled off the awkward rubber gloves. I flexed my fingers, cramped and soaked with sweat. Then I pulled the mask straps over my head. I didn't wait to loosen them, so I tore out hair as I went. My hot, damp face luxuriated in the cool air of the bunker. I took deep long breaths that felt like miracles. I motioned the airman nearest the door to open it. The cool evening air felt like paradise, God's breath inspiring Eden.

"Okay, folks, no time to waste. Our report's due soon. Have we got all the squadron input?" I put them to work finalizing the slides while I felt around my desk for my glasses.

Lee handed them to me, then started an old argument. "Captain, we'd be sitting ducks if this was a real war. We can't see who's on the other side of that door. We open it up and blam! We could get blown to bits. We need to be armed. Bet the other centers are."

I bet the other centers weren't. The Air Force's commitment to reality in these exercises was uneven at best. I was tired of arguing the pros and cons of this issue with him. "Give it a rest, Lee."

"Well, why not, ma'am?" He dragged the last word out with an inflexion of sarcasm small enough for me to ignore.

"Because I don't want to be more afraid of who's inside the PRC than I am of who's outside." I laughed to show I was joking (I think I was). "Just one more hour to go, guys. Let's start neatening this place up for the next shift."

The airmen made a lackadaisical attempt to pick up papers, plans, and regulations. They piled them in stacks in no particular order. These were our weapons, what we in Personnel fought with, numbers and names and data, and we couldn't even keep them in order—thank God we weren't responsible for lethal weapons. Lee inspected the transparencies due to the command post and the typed messages we would simulate sending out. He grunted and handed them to me.

"Great," I said. "Good work, guys." I slid the documents, all stamped *"EXERCISE SECRET EXERCISE"* into an envelope and sealed it.

Just then, the siren began to scream. Everyone froze. The phone rang. Lee picked it up, listened, set it down. For a moment he did nothing but stare out into space. Then he pulled the door closed and fumbled with his mask carrier. We got our masks on and dived under the desks. I heard one of the airmen muttering low and steady, "fuck fuck fuck fuck," and I agreed with her.

The attack seemed to last a long time. As minutes ticked by— how many I had no way of telling—I started to wonder if we'd been forgotten, or if the command post had been destroyed and couldn't call to tell us it was over. I wondered if I should call them to check. I decided to give it another five minutes and began to count to myself, *one-Mississippi.* . . .

The phone rang, shrill, startling, and lovely as the crescendo of a symphony. The attack was over. I pulled myself stiffly off the floor, hoping there were no UODs outside to keep us cordoned off a little longer, to keep the second shift out and us in.

It was worse. For the first time since I'd taken part in these exercises, a tape stretched across the outside opening of the door with a sign on it. We'd received a direct hit. The PRC was destroyed, and we were all dead. This was definitely going to delay our departure.

Two inspectors appeared on the stairs above us. They walked down, removed the tape, and entered the bunker. They weren't hindered by chem gear or masks but wore the comfortable forest-camouflage battle dress uniform.

A major with a medical badge said, "Okay, folks, you're dead. Stop doing whatever you're doing, and just lie down on the floor. An ambulance is coming by to take you to the clinic for processing. We'll be carrying you out on stretchers."

I said, "But what about stuff . . . here? Can next shift come . . . take over?"

"What don't you understand about being dead, Captain? You don't get to talk. You don't get to stand up. And your bunker's destroyed. No one will be allowed to enter. They'll just have to set up at your alternate site. Now lie down and shut up."

I got down on the floor but immediately popped my head back up. "We need to . . . do something about . . . classified."

"What?"

"We have real . . . classified here, not . . . just exercise. Have to . . . lock it up."

"Okay, get up and put it in your safe."

"No safe here. . . . It's in CBPO. If you let me . . . take it, lock it up, I'll . . . come back . . . be dead again. Promise."

"Not an option," the major said. "The CBPO's not in the exercise zone."

I didn't know much, but after two years at ESC, I did know about protecting classified materials, so I persisted. I refused to leave without passing the material on to an authorized person or locking it in a safe. I tried to sound firm but didn't know how successful I was with my words coming out muffled and mechanical through the gas mask. I couldn't help but feel powerless and a bit ridiculous, lying on the floor beneath these open-faced, free-breathing creatures. Still, I stuck to my metaphorical guns.

"Captain, you can be in big trouble for refusing to follow an inspector's orders."

"I know. But . . . protecting classified takes . . . precedence over exercise."

They threatened. They cajoled. I refused to budge. The other PRC folks lay quietly on the floor listening or sleeping. The two inspectors finally moved to the doorway and whispered to one another. When the major spoke again, he sounded disgusted but weary. "Okay, you're all alive again." We struggled up off the floor, groaning. "But your center is still destroyed. You've got exactly one minute to gather up everything you want and get out of here. And you," he said, pointing to one of the airmen. "You've got a broken arm. Come with me."

We moved faster in our bulky gear than I'd ever known. We shoved all the classified, our papers, regulations, plans, supplies willy-nilly into cardboard boxes, then made our way up the narrow stairs into the darkness. The inspectors closed the door after us, placing a padlock and a sign on it.

*Exercise Off Limits This facility is destroyed No Entrance Exercise*

We trudged with our boxes down the street, moving slowly in the heavy gear. It took us fifteen minutes just to reach the one-story building two blocks away where an office was designated for use as our alternate PRC. This was the first time we'd had to use it since I'd been here. We unlocked the door and stepped in.

"Okay, find command post report. . . . Start covering . . . windows."

I called the command post and the squadrons to report what had happened and to let them know where we were. I didn't mention we'd been dead but miraculously resurrected.

My friend Stacie was the OIC of the night shift. They showed up before too long. She said there'd been a lot of damage on base.

"Looks like you guys . . . been having fun." We talked about the attack as seriously as if there had been real bombs, real chemicals. It felt real when we were struggling to make coherent sentences in between gasps of breath.

The "all clear" still hadn't sounded when I stumbled out to my car, but once inside what was technically a non-exercise environment, I hastily stripped off the helmet, the gloves, the mask. Now I could drive home where Lynn would bring me a martini to sip in a hot bath, while he finished getting a fresh meal on the table. I was lucky but found it hard to feel anything but exhaustion and frustration. I had to be back in ten hours to go through it all again. Three more days to go, an eternity.

Next morning, still weary to my bones, so tired even my short, permed hair seemed too heavy for my head, I returned to the base. It was still dark outside, though a faint glow of dawn held the promise of a lovely summer day I wouldn't be able to enjoy. The guard at the gate told me we were in an all clear condition. Not for long though. I barely pulled into a parking place in front of the alternate PRC when the siren went off. I stayed in the car breathing deeply till the next siren, then geared up. Lee showed up as I was walking into the building.

"Welcome back, Captain. . . . How you like this . . . change of shift?"

As soon as we entered the PRC, Stacie started in on us. "So there the hell . . . you are." Even in the physical restrictions of the mask, her temper came through. She was upset about every piece of data she couldn't find, couldn't understand. The place was even more disorganized than usual, stuff scattered all over from where it had been pulled out of the boxes. What should have been a simple passing on of responsibilities turned into a tirade of complaints and accusations.

I was still trying to force myself to wake up, having a hard time focusing. I finally realized that the night shift not only hadn't done the morning report but also hadn't sent last night's in. We were two reports behind, in the aftermath of an attack, and the place was still chaos. I remained calm; I didn't have enough oxygen to be otherwise. "You haven't turned . . . either report in?"

"How could we!" Stacie said. "We couldn't check . . . it, couldn't find . . . supporting data. . . and we had attack . . . after attack . . . all night."

It's hard to express rage in a gas mask without hyperventilating, but Stacie managed it. I felt a vein throbbing in my forehead. I didn't do the yelling thing well, but I couldn't have a lieutenant reaming me a new one in front of my troops. They were all here now, watching us intently, even the airman with the simulated broken arm.

"Release night shift . . . Lieutenant." I told Stacie. "Go . . . home, get rest."

She gathered her car keys and headed out the door, her shoulders slumped, her head down, her breath ragged.

"Hang on. I'll . . . walk out with you." I turned toward Lee. "Finish . . . morning report . . . please." He did a mock salute with two fingers.

Down the hallway, I found an unoccupied break room and guided Stacie into it. We sat together on a torn vinyl couch, the dim light of dawn coming through the closed blinds. "Listen, I know . . . you're frustrated."

"No, you don't . . . don't begin . . . to know."

I heard tears starting to thicken her voice. "Ah hell, let's . . . get these things . . . off." We pulled our gas masks off, then for good measure the gloves. I could see Stacie clearly then, tears in her eyes, her damp, bedraggled red hair slippery with sweat.

"You cannot understand what it's like for someone like me," Stacie said. I listened in silence, just let her spew it all out: the frustrations, the exhaustion, the heat, the difficulty breathing, the constant challenges, recalcitrant airmen, confusing instructions, angry commanders, incomplete data, arrogant inspectors. She described everything I experienced, everything I felt. Then she said, "You cannot understand. You know what you're doing. I feel so out of my depth with this stuff."

"Listen to me. I don't know what I'm doing. I try to figure it out as I go along. But mainly, I'm in over my head. I make lots of mistakes, and most of the time I don't know which decisions are mistakes and which ones are on target."

"Yeah, maybe, but here's the difference between us: it doesn't bother you."

"You think that?" I felt a howl rush through me, pressing inside me like it was trying to escape. I started speaking quickly, trying to outrace the howl. "Look, Stacie, you want to know what I did when I left last night? I cried. I drove home barely able to see, I was crying so hard. When I got home, I was still crying. I cried through a hot bath and through a dinner I could barely choke down. I went to bed crying. I could hardly sleep, I was so stopped up. And you know what? That's what I do most nights during an exercise. Just go home and cry." Stacie began sobbing. "Get it out of your system," I said through my own tears. "You know you can't cry in a gas mask."

That won a little gurgle of laughter from her. She wiped her eyes, then her nose on the sleeve of her chem suit. "I feel like I can't go on. It gets harder and harder to show up every night. How do you manage it?"

"I hate it! I really do. The only thing that keeps me coming back is the same reason you do. We have no choice. We have to."

The break room was dim, blinds down, we hadn't turned any lights on, but suddenly I saw a slight movement at the door in the corner. I glimpsed a figure retreating and heard the soft click of the door closing. It was Lee, I was certain of it, and I was just as certain that he'd been there for awhile, listening to our guts spilling out. Two officers, female officers at that, two pampered white women pretending to be warriors, our weakness on display for his entertainment.

I didn't say anything to Stacie. I was too exhausted to make myself care right then. I anticipated a hard time from Lee, but no point in worrying about it. We talked and cried, cried and talked for awhile longer, maybe fifteen minutes. But eventually we donned our masks and gloves again. She headed home for a short rest, before returning tonight to do it all over again—and the next night, and the following night.

I sat for a minute trying to collect some energy, trying to gather up the guts I'd been spewing all over the room. I readied myself to face Lee again, to face the PRC and its pretend wars. I struggled to turn myself back into an officer and a leader, even if a poor one.

When I opened the door to the PRC, I sensed a change before I could identify it. All the troops were up and active. One airman painstakingly printed the numbers another read off to him from the calculator. Another sorted through papers, putting them into file folders, which she stacked neatly inside the boxes. The desks were clear of their paper mess. Lee was just getting off the phone with one of the squadrons. He looked up at me.

"That's the last of . . . casualty reports . . . Captain. Negative from . . . Supply." He nodded toward the two airmen working together. "Morning report's . . . almost finished. Now let me . . . show you files . . . we're setting up."

In that short time, he'd gotten it all organized, neatly, efficiently. Our supplies were carefully stockpiled in one place; our rosters all on one desk ordered by squadron and date. The airmen were working diligently, with none of their usual lethargy.

Even through the plastic lenses, I could see mischief gleaming in Lee's eyes, but there was no malice in them. If it was a joke, I was being welcomed into it. I didn't know if he'd decided to pull this team together out of pity for my tears and weakness, or out of respect for my strength in standing up (metaphorically, at least) to the inspector last night. I suspected both. That in both cases I surprised him, turned out to be someone he didn't expect. Just like he was surprising me.

The siren outside shrieked relief through the windows. Simultaneously the phone rang. "All clear." We removed our gloves, our masks and turned them inside out to dry before the next alarm sounded. Then we got back to work.

## C. FLUGTAG

Ramstein's annual open house was blessed with a perfect day for an air show, the sky a brilliant blue seldom seen in Germany. The hot August Sunday felt Mediterranean, as if the Italian team had pulled it in on hooks behind their jets when they arrived last night. Over three hundred thousand Germans took advantage of the sunny weather to come out to the base open house. Every last one of them wanted a cheeseburger.

The duties of an Air Force officer include responsibility for unit morale, so I was doing my part in a crowded stand manned by my coworkers from the CBPO. For the last three hours, I'd been selling cheeseburgers and sodas to sunburned Germans, whose appetite for American junk food seemed insatiable. The six years I'd spent in German classes dedicated to reading Goethe and Schiller had come down to this: "*Zwei* burgers *mit käse und ein* Pepsi. *Acht mark, bitte. Möchten Sie*—" I couldn't think of the German word, so I just said "mustard," loudly, waving the yellow plastic bottle around. The square-faced man in front of me nodded and enunciated carefully, "Yess, pleasssss."

The soft German sibilants rose up with the sudden breeze that cooled the back of my neck, then disappeared leaving me as hot and sticky as I was before. I handed the man the bottle. He gave me eight marks. He began to squeeze huge plops of mustard directly on top of the buns. A voice crackled from the base loudspeaker, but after "Ladies and Gentlemen, *meine Damen und Herren,*" everything else was static and soon overcome by the engine roar that filled the air. The man stopped mid-mustard and stepped out from under the canopy to gape up at the sky.

I leaned across the rickety table that served as a counter, trying unsuccessfully to catch a glimpse of an airplane. The table was set far enough back inside the canopy to provide plenty of shade but it also limited our view, so I'd not seen a single performance all day. I'd counted on having a chance to pop out periodically to catch some of the aerial acrobatics, but it had taken all six of us in the stand to keep up with the German demand for cheeseburgers.

Flight Day. I'd heard about it ever since I arrived at Ramstein months earlier. My friends talked about it with gushing enthusiasm. "Just wait till Flugtag. It's—" "The planes, you've never seen—" "So many people, all—" "A big party—"

We'd spent the last few weeks in tedious preparation, cleaning and polishing all the buildings and equipment. "It's worth it," everyone assured me. But at this point, I didn't think anything that required me to be on base on a Sunday afternoon was all that great, especially since I couldn't even see the main event, the air show.

For the Germans it was a lively, good-natured festival, a glimpse behind the guarded gates at their huge American military neighbor. Static displays of aircraft allowed the curious to explore, to have friends take their pictures while they pretended to be pilots. Flight simulators were opened up for a lucky few, area mayors and the like. The security police put on working dog demonstrations. Squadrons like ours added to their morale funds by operating food booths. But the main event was the air show, the largest, most popular air show in Germany, with aerial teams from all over Europe.

The square-faced man stepped back in to give me the plastic mustard bottle. He said something, *"Danke"* or "Ssank you," I supposed, but it was lost in the screech of planes and the delighted cries of the crowd. He moved away, eyes staring upward, one hand automatically raising one of the cheeseburgers to his mouth. For the first time all afternoon, no one stood in front of me waiting to be served. I glanced at my watch. It was after three thirty. The day was almost over; the crowd would start to thin soon. I wiped the sweat from my forehead with the back of my hand. It smelled of grease. I rubbed my hands on my jeans.

Jerry, a soon-to-retire senior master sergeant, came up to me. I was the ranking person inside the tent, but he was the one really in charge and we both knew it. "Hey, Cap'n D. It's the last act. Why don't you go watch? It's the Italian team—they do all the showy, daring stuff."

I looked at the junior NCOs and airmen still serving the last few customers, and I hesitated. But RHIP—Rank Has Its Privileges. "Thanks, Jerry. I think I will."

I walked out the back to where Lynn was helping my boss grill the burgers. After the covered booth, the sun was so bright everything swam in its shimmer. A stray draft of smoke made my eyes burn. It smelled overwhelmingly of charcoal.

Major Cantore looked up from flipping meat patties and grinned at me. "Hey, Cheryl, you're fired. I want to hire your husband. He's a much harder worker."

"That works for me, sir. I'll stay home tomorrow and send him to the office."

Lynn closed the top of his grill and reached out to me. We stood together, his arm, damp with sweat, resting lightly on my shoulders. We watched the Italian team, *Frecce Tricolori*, the Tri-colored Arrows, go through their intricate maneuvers. Ten jets spiraled, slashed, slid, soared through the air, all in exquisite symmetry. I felt the muscles in my face relax into a contented smile.

Here is a truth so obvious Air Force members seldom bother to mention it. We were all in it for the airplanes. Forget service to country, forget the spread of democracy, forget career opportunities and free health care. Every one of us stayed in so we could be around airplanes. We thought God's skies were imperfect without the roar of flashing silver bodies streaking through them.

So as I stood there nestled in Lynn's arm, I wasn't the only one lusting after those flaunting, shining jets. All around I heard cries and gasps of amazement, the long sighs of satisfaction, so many in unison, they were even audible over the thunder of the planes.

The voice of the announcer came back over the loudspeaker. "Ladies and *krackle krackle screeee* a hand for their final *krackle krackle bitte die Italiener, Tricolori, Drei Farben!*"

The ten planes flew two by two to an invisible center point, at which they split off and continued to climb in opposite directions before swinging down and heading toward one another again to meet near the horizon. Their contrails painted a white shape against the azure sky.

"Look, Lynn, it's a heart," I said. He squeezed my shoulder.

As two planes met to close the heart's bottom point, a third ascended to the image's top left quadrant and cut across it diagonally—the arrow piercing the heart. Piercing the sky.

The wild blue yonder burst apart. The sky in front of me shattered into a prism of colors. Beautiful. Terrifying. Then a sound, as if the air itself were shrieking.

Fire rolled across the runway. In the distance in front of us, a blue and yellow pillar blazed up. A massive train of flame to my left raced behind the far side of a small knoll where the bleachers and viewing stands were arranged. And from this area came the first screams.

This took two, three, maybe five seconds. Shivering suddenly, despite the heat, I leaned bewildered into Lynn, who drew me closer. I whispered, desperately clutching an impossible hope, "Is that part of the show?"

His voice was as tender as if I were a child. "No, honey, that's not the show."

My mind couldn't take it in. While I stood there in shock, Major Cantore rushed away, toward the flames. Jerry was right behind him, along with a couple of the airmen. Smoke rose up from the area beyond the knoll. The cries had gotten louder and been joined by the sounds of keening and German voices calling out for help. An acrid, burning odor began to overcome the carnival smells of grilled burgers and popcorn and funnel cakes.

Above us, the Italian team was circling, continually circling. They had no place to go, no place to land. They reminded me of a flock of geese, bereft when a hunter kills one of its members. There were only seven of them. Three planes down.

I stood shaking and stunned in Lynn's arms. But while I stood, adrift in my own horror, the NCOs and airmen who had been selling carnival food less than a minute before were running through the crowd to reach the fires. Some emptied coolers of sodas and meat patties and lugged ice toward the victims. Others pulled off tablecloths and grabbed dishrags, towels, anything that could make a bandage. While I stood shaking and stunned.

Jerry spurred me into action. He'd come back to collect a heavy ice chest. "Cap'n, you'd better report to the office. The major's rounding up folks. He'll have work for you."

"Yes, yes, of course." I pulled away from Lynn's arms and tried to square my shoulders, tried to ignore the pleading cries, the smell of burning flesh, the seven planes circling overhead.

I walked slowly, selfishly savoring these few precious minutes between the terror of the flight line and the rush of involvement I knew awaited me at the office. Unbidden, the word *Senf* came to me, the German word for mustard. I wanted to call back time. I wanted to cry. But I didn't. Holding the tears back was as much courage as I could call up right now, and I clung to it.

We found out what happened almost right away. The plane forming the arrow had hit one of the two planes coming up from the point of the heart. The debris flung out from their collision brought down a third plane, which rushed blazing across the runway and into an Army medical helicopter on standby. The helicopter exploded, killing all seven of its crewmembers.

The worst damage was caused by the plane that formed the arrow. It struck an ice cream truck surrounded by hot, hungry spectators, many of them parents with small children. Then its fuselage, spewing fiery aviation fuel behind it, ploughed through the crowd.

Videotaped images of the colliding planes and even worse, the train of fire burning its way through a field of panicking humanity were on news channels all over the world within hours. Newscasters put on somber faces as they introduced the film clips and urged parents to keep their children out of the room. I never saw the clips. I was too busy the next few days to get near a TV.

My work began immediately. Besides compiling loss information for official manning reports, it was the CBPO's responsibility to put together teams to notify families of a serious accident or death. So the major ordered me to nearby Landstuhl Army Regional Medical Center (LARMC) to report casualty information back to him as injured Air Force members were brought in.

Though little time had passed, triage tents were already set up on the Ramstein flight line. The base theater had become the meeting place for individuals missing family members or friends, clinging to hopes that they were just mired in the chaos of the crowd. Teams cleared smoldering metal from the runway to make a place for aerovac planes and medical transport helicopters. The base was closed tight, no one allowed to drive on or off. The only exceptions were ambulances and buses to shuttle medical personnel from the base up to LARMC, perched on a hill ten miles away. I tried to get a ride on one of these, but my function was not considered a high enough priority to make room for me. So I walked.

A mile from the base was tiny Ramstein village, where many Americans rented houses. There I found a master sergeant I knew and asked to borrow his car. Mike was obviously reluctant, but when I suggested that instead he could personally drive me to the hospital, he thrust his car keys at me. "Here. You take it. But I need it back in time to go to work in the morning."

*Work in the morning.* I wondered at those words as I drove away. The morning was a concept I couldn't wrap my mind around right now. I felt locked into this day, as if the future would never be anything more than an extension of it. *Please, God, let this not be real. Let this be a dream that I will wake from.* But one cannot mistake reality for a dream.

It took an hour to drive the few miles to LARMC. Roads were blocked to allow the ambulances free access. I drove a wide loop away from the base and approached the hospital from the back. I rolled down the car window and lit a cigarette, automatically holding it out the window as I drove. The day's beautiful blue was fading into gold by the time I got there. It was such a gentle evening, I wanted to stay outside in the parking lot, lifting my face into its cooling air. The massive hospital looked hostile. I heard sirens screaming and forced myself to go inside.

I made my way through wide corridors, crammed with staff rushing toward the emergency room, some pushing empty gurneys. I found the ad hoc administrative command center and squeezed myself into a mass of people milling around too few desks, too few telephones, too few computers. Hardly anyone was in uniform or medical whites or even scrubs. Most people, like me, were still in off-duty clothes, jeans or shorts, a contingent of summer weekend pickups, people pulled away from the open house or from their own outdoor barbecues, people in muddy walking shoes and shorts, just in from a ten-kilometer Volksmarch. Our real life had been interrupted by a demanding nightmare, so screw the uniforms, the rank, the nametags, the service designators. I found it disconcerting not knowing anyone's rank. I didn't know where I belonged in this world.

I bugged everyone I could with questions about identity and nationality of the victims who were brought in. But there was little information about casualties at this point. Many of the victims couldn't be identified. Their identification lay lost in the ash of purses and shoes and souvenirs abandoned in the panicked push away from the flight line. Or melted from the heat, right in their pockets. Of those who were conscious and could speak, few were Americans, and none Air Force.

In the administrative center, I didn't see any of the patients or witness their treatment. But frenzied orders roared constantly into telephones and out of loudspeakers.

"Clear out the semi-private rooms, roll them into ward three and sterilize the rooms. Stat!"

"Call Dr. K to the ER for surgical assistance."

"Team B to the helipad."

"All available lab techs report to the third-floor conference room."

Urgency drove the medical staff. I envied them because they had something productive to do. My useless questions couldn't fill the huge void of helplessness inside me. I looked for other things to do. I made coffee and took it around to the busy staff sitting two and three to a desk. I directed newcomers to the people in charge. I trotted back and forth with messages. Even the smallest task kept me a part of this great, horrible happening. Not to be part of it was unthinkable, because nothing else was real.

Finally, someone grabbed me and gave me a chair, a telephone, and a job. I answered the flood of calls from tearful strangers, inquiring about loved ones: *Do you know if my husband, my wife, my teenage son, my parents have been brought in? They haven't come home.* Sometimes the desperate voice on the line was speaking half in German, half in English. The only answer I could give most of them was we didn't know yet, but everyone was getting good medical attention. "Don't worry. Be patient."

Every thirty minutes or so I called my boss. "Nothing so far, sir." Each time, he grunted and said, "Okay, keep in touch." Around two a.m., he released me.

I drove home through empty, starlit streets under a sky that glittered with innocence. No danger here, it seemed to say. And I might have believed it if I had never seen how quickly a lovely sky could turn deadly.

Lynn was waiting up for me. He told me about sitting in his car on the base, waiting for the gates to open. Wanting to be home, in the quiet sanity of our own apartment, our own life. But also wanting to stay and be part of the rescue. Wanting to do something but not knowing what he could do. Feeling leaden with uselessness.

He told me about arriving home and how Frau Keller, Brigitte's mother who lived downstairs, came barreling out her door when she saw him. She threw her arms around him and sobbed. After a few minutes he realized she was afraid something had happened to me and managed to explain that I was okay. I was working. At that she patted his arm, took his hand, and led him inside to feed him. They watched the news together, the news clip playing over and over on German TV.

Around three o'clock we went to bed. I tried to sleep, but whenever I closed my eyes, I saw the flare of a yellow-blue explosion. The phone rang and continued to ring on and off all night as worried family members and friends called in from the States.

"Are you all right? We've been trying to reach you for hours." Yes, we were all right, we told them. And this was true, but not entirely.

The morning I couldn't conceive of finally arrived, the dawn of another perfect summer day. Mike was pacing back and forth on the sidewalk in front of his house as I pulled up.

When he stepped in, he sniffed the air. "Captain, have you been smoking in my car?"

For a moment, I just stared at him. "Oh, for God's sake, Mike, one, just one."

I felt like saying: *What does one cigarette matter now that the world has come to an end?* But of course, the world kept going. We still had to go to work, and we still had assignments to process and evaluations to write and records to maintain and meetings to attend and phone calls to return. And everything began the slow fade into normality.

Almost. Later that day I found an airman crouched in a shadowy alcove off the hallway where we kept stacks of supplies. I knew him, a big, pasty-faced bruiser of a boy not that far from his glory days on the high school football team. He was crying big, round tears like a hurt child, his fist stuck in his mouth to block his sobs. Next to him, on a crate of typing paper, perched a buck sergeant. He held a box of paper clips which he was hooking together into a long chain.

"A little German girl died in his arms," the sergeant told me. "He grabbed her and got the fire out, but she up and died on him while he was carrying her." He hooked another paper clip onto the chain, held it up and inspected it. "I saw her. She was small, maybe five or six—about the same age as my little girl."

I had nothing to say to them. I left them sitting there in a silence broken only by the airman's muffled sobs and the click of the sergeant's paper-clip chain swinging against an old typewriter.

August 28, 1988 was Ramstein's last Flugtag. Within seventy-two hours, the West German Bundestag passed emergency regulations banning air shows altogether. They removed the ban three years later. Ramstein renamed its open houses and restricted them to static displays.

Investigators looked for a cause, for someone to fire, for something to make sense out of tragedy. They finally settled on the catchall, "pilot error"—a split second of inattention. A pilot coming in too fast, too soon, unable to correct course in time. A rumor flew around base that he had been drinking, though it seemed to spring from nothing more than the fact that he was Italian. "Everyone knows Italians have to have a little *vino* with their lunch," the rumor-mongers said.

It was never announced who approved the questionable maneuver that allowed the "arrow" to fly toward the crowd.

Over one thousand people at the air show required emergency medical care from burns and trauma. Almost four hundred and fifty were critically injured. Seventy people died: forty-four German adults, sixteen German children, seven American medics, three Italian pilots.

# D. DESERT STORM

The Berlin Wall defined our mission, our purpose. When Mary visited us the summer of 1989, she told us about the final thesis she'd written in a joint air command and staff course for new majors. "It was on the political and military implications if the Berlin Wall came down."

She'd done well of course (I never had any doubt of that where Mary was concerned), but she was piqued about a comment she'd received. One of the reviewers—some Army colonel—had written this snide remark: *Your time would be better served researching something real rather than fantasy.* Mary took another sip of beer and added her own, typical critique, "Fucking asshole."

I laughed and lifted my stein. "So here's to when the wall comes down." But it seemed fantasy to me too. The Berlin Wall had formed my view of the world I grew up in. I thought of our visit there: the massive wall covered with graffiti, the bleak no-man's-land between West and East.

In early November that year, we were returning from a trip back to the States, where we had been visiting Cathy. At Schipol Airport in Holland, we trundled our carry-ons past a bookstore on the way to our gate. A headline and photo leaped out at me as we passed. It took a second to process before I grabbed Lynn's arm. "Did you see that?"

The lead story of the *International Herald Tribune* had a huge picture of a mass of people with sledge hammers tearing the Berlin Wall down. My first thought was, "Well, right on, Mary!" My second, not so well formed, more uneasiness than cognition, was that the world was about to change. I wished I'd read Mary's paper.

The assignments officer at MPC had assured me that after a year in the CBPO, USAFE would pull me up to the headquarters staff. But after two years, it still hadn't happened. My promotion board for major would meet in a year, and I needed a position of greater responsibility to make the promotion. In the Air Force's up-or-out system, no promotion meant pack your bags and find a civilian job. By now I was hooked. I wanted to stay, not be sent back to the States, my tail between my legs, with no future but to find an administrative position in an office somewhere.

I began calling the assignments office at Headquarters USAFE. I was their resource to assign. I kept getting the same response, like a recording: "You're doing fine where you are. You were assigned to the Ramstein CBPO. Why should we move you?"

"MPC told me that would only be for one year, then I'd be moved up to the headquarters. Sir, it's been over two years now."

"You have a four-year commitment to the Ramstein CBPO."

"No, sir, I have a four-year commitment to Ramstein. Besides, you can move me anywhere in USAFE." But USAFE had no need to move me and so let me sit.

I wondered if image problems were behind the difficulty I was having moving into a better job. The weight I'd barely kept down at ESC had come creeping back the moment Lynn first came home from the Ramstein commissary, flushed with excitement. "Look! Danish butter—even cheaper than margarine. And good German *Brötchen!*"

A captain I worked with, a skinny woman, offered unsolicited advice. "Every morning I eat an unbuttered slice of whole-wheat toast and a piece of fruit. Every noon, a plate of sliced bell peppers. Every evening, I pop in a Lean Cuisine." She looked me up and down as she talked, eating a rainbow of peppers from a plastic container. Her eyes said, *Now you know the formula. If you don't follow it, it's your own fault. Fat cow.*

This woman appalled me. I wanted to cry out to her, "We're stationed in Germany, for God's sake! *Wurst! Schnitzel! Spätzl! Strudel!*" All those good German food words that filled the mouth with their esses thickened like sauce. "What about German beer? *Pils! Weizen! Doppelbock!*" (Don't even get me started on the culinary pleasures of traveling in France.)

So once again, for a week before weigh-ins, I would eat grilled chicken and asparagus, and I would just scrape past, sometimes by terrifying ounces. Still, I managed to avoid the Weight

Management Program, thanks in large part to the German woods and Volksmarches we enjoyed even in cool, drizzly weather. But image wasn't controlled as easily as pounds and ounces on a scale.

At my request my boss called the USAFE Assignments Section. Major Cantore told me afterward, hesitantly, but plunging in with a grimace, "Cheryl, I'm sorry, but he said there was no way you'd get a headquarters position because, uh, well, he said you're too ugly."

The nasty word smacked me like a club in the face. I could handle "plain," even "obese"—but "ugly"? I was too stunned to speak and stood there like stone, silent, staring.

He hurried on. "Hey, look, I'm an ugly guy. I know how it is to be ugly."

*Do you think you're making it better?* I slowly came back to life enough to say calmly, "Thank you for making the call, sir. I appreciate it." I could almost hear him congratulating himself (Well, that went better than I thought it would), as I walked out of his office. I had to find a way into a better job on my own. No one was going to help me.

Later that day, I called a colonel I'd known at ESC. She was the highest ranking female officer I knew at the time. She exuded warmth along with a calm inbred sense of authority. A single woman in her forties, she had a square face with short blonde hair and a firm body that leaned toward stocky without being stout. She now had an office at Ramstein, in charge of overseeing all the ESC units throughout Europe. She patiently listened to me talk about what I'd done in the two years in the Ramstein CBPO and how unhelpful USAFE was being at moving me up to a position that would make me competitive for major. She agreed to keep me in mind for any upcoming jobs in ESC, then rose, skilled at bringing meetings to an end.

"Actually, ma'am, there's one more thing," I blurted out. She sat back down, shrewdness in her eyes. I told her the rest, stumbling a bit over the word, "ugly."

She sat back and studied me, looked me up and down. I had the sense she may have had to fight her way over this barrier too, since the Air Force image of the perfect female officer was a youthful Mary Martin playing Peter Pan—sexy in a boyish way. She gave me practical advice, not least of which was the number of her hairdresser. What she mainly gave me was someone to talk to about the hurt.

I had told the major about my appointment with someone outside the command structure. Like any good subordinate, I reported back and told him she would keep an eye open for an appropriate ESC job for me. (I may have exaggerated the probability of that happening a bit.)

Within two weeks, Colonel Collins, the new support group commander at Ramstein offered me a job working for him. Major Cantore took credit: "I marched right up to the squadron commander and told him we had to do something for you or the wing would lose you altogether," The squadron commander took credit: "I recommended you strongly for this position." And I took credit for not passively accepting the situation. All three of us were right.

Desert Storm began for me around oh-four-hundred on 18 January 1991. The phone rang and pulled me out of one of my frequent dreams in which the sky exploded into a horrifyingly beautiful blue and yellow blossom. I hoped it was Cathy and not a recall. I punched Lynn.

"You get it," I mumbled, pulling the tacit she's-your-daughter card.

Even with the pillow over my head, I heard his sleepy, "Hi, Cass," and then a change in tone as if he suddenly woke up. "What? . . . Really? . . . When?" A few vague statements, and finally, "Okay, sweetie. Thanks for letting us know."

"What?" I asked when he came back to bed.

"We're at war with Iraq. We sent planes." The line in the sand had been crossed.

I realized my leisure was over for awhile. I got dressed and drove to the base. There was no other traffic at the gate, in or out. The guard checked my ID—there would be no more being waved through because of the decal on the windshield. He also walked around the car with a flashlight, looked underneath, inspected the contents of the trunk. I was lucky I got in when I did. Later that morning it would take two to three hours for cars to get through the gate.

The parking lot was dark and empty, except for the colonel's official car. I dragged my hand along the wall down the dark hallway. The light was on in the colonel's office. I could hear the thin tones of an announcer's voice. Colonel Collins and his deputy stared at CNN on TV. They started when I said, "Good morning, gentlemen."

"What are you doing here?"

I explained I was on the Cathy Alert System. "I figured I should come on in."

We watched the TV in silence for a few more minutes, all of us wincing as a reporter stood outside Incirlik Air Base in Turkey with a microphone in hand saying something like "Twelve F-16s have just taken off, heading south." The two colonels exchanged sober looks. So much for the surprise factor in warfare.

"Well, I suppose we need to hold a meeting to figure out what we should be doing," Col Collins said. "Let's plan it for eight."

"I'll take care of it, sir," I said. But first things first—I put the coffee pot on, the first of about twenty we went through that day.

I didn't leave the base again till well after midnight. We had a planeload of journalists stopping at Ramstein that night on their way down to the war zone. We arranged for the Italian restaurant in the O'Club to provide a late buffet for them. I was assigned to herd them around, keep them out of mischief and Ramstein out of trouble.

"And Cheryl, wear civilian clothes, why don't you?" Colonel Collins said. "Of course, if they ask if you're military, don't deny it."

But they wouldn't ask and we both knew it. That's why I'd gotten this assignment. I was a woman and had none of the giveaways a male captain would have—the too-short haircut, the ramrod posture. In uniform, I would be fair game for their questions and could be quoted in their articles or TV shots. "An Air Force official told us today . . ." If I didn't answer, it would read just as damningly, "Air Force officials refused to comment."

Fortunately, no one paid me any attention at all. I greeted them in the pantsuit Lynn had brought for me earlier that evening and pointed the way toward restrooms and the restaurant. They were exhausted and hungry. Most traipsed eagerly to the buffet. I found only one of the big-name personalities missing, finally rousting him out of the empty O'Club ballroom, where he was whispering a description of its ornate chandeliers into a small recorder.

We didn't know how long Desert Storm would last of course, so we busily prepared for the worst. Despite the thorough checks at the gates, every public building on base also had a security checkpoint. Lynn volunteered at the NCO Club, where every day the same few women acted amazed when he asked to check their handbags.

We expected major casualties to be medevaced into Germany and prepared for these. Colonel Collins tasked me to work with LARMC to identify housing for dependents who came to be with their wounded spouses. I was too slow. I spent two days working on all the details I needed to hammer out with them. By that time, the colonel had already passed the job on to a go-get-'em lieutenant, who reported her first interface with the hospital as I was still typing up my list of contacts. I felt like I was at Flugtag again, shocked and stultified while others were acting. Still, the colonel never said a word of blame to me, just gave me tasks that better suited my slow but thorough style.

Among other things, he sent me to represent him at a meeting of Army commanders working out the details of opening up an emergency hospital in the Black Forest. My job was just to take notes and report back. This emergency hospital was maintained by a skeleton crew that could be augmented quickly in wartime with medical reservists. The main purpose of the meeting was what to do with them, when/if they were called up: how to feed and where to house them. I sat quietly at the end of a long table, listening to the Army colonels discuss possibilities. It seemed like a no-brainer. A French casern was located nearby, and the French military had offered to house our reservists in apartments there and feed them in their dining hall. Problem solved.

Until one colonel said, "You know, the French eat their big meal at midday."

"With wine," another added.

"I don't know if our folks could adjust to that."

"And they'd be surrounded by people speaking French."

I couldn't decide whether to laugh or cry as they talked themselves out of the French Army's generous offer and into providing our troops MREs (Meals Ready to Eat). And instead of being comfortably housed in apartments, the medics would all sleep on cots in the hospital's gymnasium. I bit my lips, but I wanted to say, "War is hell, gentlemen. Tell your troops to suck it up and have a glass of wine with lunch."

As it turned out, Desert Storm was over in forty-three days, with few American casualties and no need to open emergency hospitals or dependent housing.

In a seminar a few months later, I talked to a pilot who'd flown combat missions in Iraq.

He told me, "After two weeks, there were no new targets left to bomb. We were basically rearranging rubble. Then one day we got sent to destroy some jets that the Iraqis had tried to hide by parking them around a traffic circle on the outskirts of Baghdad. Well, we flew in and took care of them okay, but on the way back I started thinking about one time when I was a kid. A pilot had performed an emergency landing on one of the highways coming into town. My dad came and got me. He said, 'Come on, let's go see the plane up close.' And we did. We wandered all around it. I was just a little guy, already in love with airplanes."

He stopped to take a sip of coffee. "Anyway, I couldn't help wondering as I flew back to the base, if there was some Iraqi dad out there, showing his kid the planes." He stared into his cup as if he saw them, then changed the subject.

I remembered the captain at OTS who had so firmly drummed into our heads the reality behind that bland phrase, "collateral damage." And I thought, *This guy's a good pilot and a good officer, because he never forgets what he does—and that's killing. He knows the price he's agreed to pay isn't necessarily his own life.*

I didn't have his nightmares to face. I managed meetings and information, supervised people, worked with words and numbers. The closest I'd ever gotten to real warfare was in the LSNs, surviving the attacks of a chimerical enemy. My biggest challenge during Desert Storm had been herding journalists. No one ever shot at me or set off explosives near me. My life was never in danger. I never had to look someone in the eye and pull a trigger. I never had to drop bombs and not know who they might destroy.

# CHAPTER SEVEN

# "IN COMMAND"

## 1992–1996: Spangdahlem AB, Germany

*"This is the land of peace, love, justice . . . and no mercy."*
—BRUCE SPRINGSTEEN,
INTRODUCING "THUNDER ROAD" IN CONCERT

## A. PEACE AND LOVE

Tippy lay snoozing on the front seat of the car. Another forty miles and we'd be there. A chilly mist floated like ghosts across the night. I slowed down to seventy miles an hour as a nod to the poorer visibility, but there were still cars whizzing past me—left lane only since this was the fast but orderly Autobahn.

After four and a half years at Ramstein we were moving on. Only two hours away, our new town, Manderscheid, was ancient and picturesque in ways Bruchmühlbach had never been.

"Castles," I said to Tippy, reaching over to stroke her rough fur. She thumped her stub of a tail. I could feel the rough lumps under her skin. They'd multiplied beneath her coarse black hair. The vet said they weren't cancer, nothing to worry about, so I tried not to. It was her smell that bothered me sometimes. It seemed to ooze out of her as if part of her were rotting. Still, at sixteen, she seemed happy and content. Deaf as a post, sure. A little confused at times.

"We have two castles we can see from the house," I told her. "We have a babbling brook. We have woods and pathways all around us. The house is old, way way old." I talked to while away the time, to make the drive shorter. Lynn would be following in our other car in a couple of hours, after he finished the few things remaining to do in our now empty apartment.

The fog ghosts thickened into a white wall, and I slowed to creep uneasily along the right lane. A signpost appeared briefly, then disappeared back into the white. Another thirty kilometers. I did the rough math in my head. About eighteen miles. "By now you'd think I'd be used to using kilometers, wouldn't you?" I said. Tippy's arthritic paws twitched in a dream chase.

When I found my way along a narrow, windy road to the cobblestone courtyard of the old inn we'd found to rent, I breathed out all my tension, sat back for a moment and relaxed. "Ready to go, girl? Welcome to your new home." I lifted Tippy out, stroked her ears, kissed the soft dimple between her two coffee-bean eyes. I set her down on a verge of grass to pee before we went inside.

I could hear the sound of the brook splashing in the gulley below us. Perhaps she could smell the water. Something energized her, sent her darting into the shadows and down the steep, dark hillside, through the thick underbrush. I called and whistled, hoping the shrill note would reach through her deafness. I turned the car lights on to guide her back up the hill. I could hear her crashing through dried leaves and bare branches and began to get worried. At the nearest house, where I ran for help, a middle-aged Frau opened the door with a cautious *"Was?"* I stumbled through an explanation in bad German. She loaned me a flashlight.

With the help of its light, I found a way down the hill, sliding on my butt as far as I could. I saw Tippy below me, pacing along the top of a bank that dropped down several feet into the stream. I looked for a way down to her but couldn't find one my clumsy human form could negotiate in the dark. I turned the light on her. She looked up, her face expressionless. I tried moving the light from her up the slope to me. I showed her my face and hoped she'd follow the light back to me. Instead, she turned toward the water and stepped out into air, falling into the stream.

Frantically I looked around for a way down to her. I held on to branches to balance myself as I struggled. In my mind, I prayed— a habit I had never been able to break. *Dear Lord, dear Lord, please please please.* Formless prayers. I didn't even know what I wanted for my old sick dog, just not for anything to happen now. I wanted a gentle ending, with Lynn's arm around me. I kept the light on Tippy and called out soothing things she couldn't hear. Before I could reach her, she was gone. One moment I saw her in the water, literally dog-paddling below me, looking around with great interest; the next, she was below the surface. By the time I made it to the top of the bank, she'd disappeared. I sat down on the frozen ground, staring into the water below.

Eventually I made my way wearily back up the hill, trudged over to my neighbor's house and returned the flashlight. She inquired about my dog. *"Tot,"* I said. *Dead.* A look of appalled sympathy rushed into her face, but I turned away before she could say anything else.

I sat on the stoop of the house for another hour or more waiting for Lynn. I couldn't bear to go into the house on my own so I stayed outside, huddled in my coat, freezing in the winter cold. I cried and rocked back and forth to warm myself. Perhaps trying to comfort myself.

When Lynn arrived, he assumed I'd been worried about him. "It's okay, I'm here now," he said, then suddenly, sharply "Where's Tippy?" I started to cry again.

Later, in the daylight, we found Tippy in water so shallow we could see her form lying just underneath the surface. Lynn convinced me that she did not drown ("You didn't see her struggle, did you?") but had a heart attack in the cold water. I eventually came to believe that she'd had a gentle death for an old, ill dog and that I was blessed to be there to witness it, the last gift of many she gave me. Lynn took to referring to her as "our little Ophelia."

We wrapped her in her raggedy, pink blanket and buried her next to the hillside. A rosebush in our new garden produced an unseasonable bloom. Lynn plucked it to set on the grave. "Rest in peace, little girl," he said. With a grave here, Manderscheid already felt like home.

After Desert Storm, I had moved up to serve as the Ramstein wing commander's executive officer. The general liked to say, "I'll work you to death for a year, but then, I'll help you into a good job." He was a man of his word. A year after that, I was sitting at a desk in HQ USAFE, down the hall from the officer who'd thought I was too ugly (not that it rankled or anything). I worked there only five months when three bases in the command lost their CBPO chiefs and needed replacements ASAP. I was the first to volunteer. With my experience and wearing my new grade of major, I was immensely eligible and got my pick of the three. I chose the most challenging.

"It's not that I don't like it here," I explained to my boss at USAFE. "It's just I'm convinced CBPO chief is the most important job a personnel officer can do."

He nodded, then reminded me that we didn't have CBPOs anymore. They'd been redesignated Military Personnel Flights, MPFs. (The Air Force's answer to everything is to rename it.)

My new base, Spangdahlem, was in the Eifel, the German extension of the Ardennes Forest. It hosted no higher headquarters and no competing missions, just a single fighter wing supporting four operational squadrons of A-10s, F-15s, and F-16s. Its CBPO, I mean MPF, had recently failed a USAFE inspection.

"They had seventy write-ups, worst I've ever seen," the inspector told me. "But we gave them a Marginal instead of Unsat because we didn't want to demoralize the troops completely."

I had never known a base like Spangdahlem. Set in an idyllic wooded, pastoral area of Germany, "Spang" should have been a great assignment. But discontent poisoned the base, distorted reactions and relationships. Suspicion and hostility imbued most interactions.

As the head of a major support agency, I had to attend the weekly wing staff meeting. It began with a prayer from the chaplain (don't get me started on that practice), only to degenerate into a free-for-all of accusations and arguments. The flying commanders ganged up on the support folks. I was often the target.

"My guy got there at 5:10 to review his records and the MPF was already closed."

The wing commander would turn toward me. "Cheryl?"

"Our hours are 7:30 to 5:00." Not that there weren't a lot of people still in the MPF after that time, trying to catch up on the work they couldn't do while they were busy with customers.

"How nice for you. I wish we could keep business hours." So while they were out saving the world, we were lazy bureaucrats. I wanted to say: *What if we extend the hours to six and your guy comes at ten after? Or seven and he arrives at five after?* But I kept my mouth shut. It was one of my skills, not saying anything. (I did initiate a test of late hours every Wednesday but after six months with no customers we went back to the old schedule.)

"Somebody lost my guy's paperwork!"

"Cheryl?"

"Sir, if you'll give me the details after the meeting, I'll look into it."

"Why should I do your work for you?"

It wasn't all against Personnel, of course. Transportation, Finance, Supply, Civil Engineering, all the support agencies took it at wing staff meeting. When the operational squadron commanders got bored with attacking us, they turned on one another. A few of the senior officers seemed to egg on the pit-bull behavior with grins and snide remarks, almost licking their chops in delight. Of course, even at Spang most pilots were gentlemen, but the macho minority swaggered around base with a disdain that was tacitly approved by some commanders.

This attitude might have sprung naturally from "winning" the Cold War. Strategic bombing was no longer the answer, as localized conflicts sprang up like Desert Storm. The bomber, with its multi-man aircrews—pilots, navigators, even enlisted gunners—was no longer king. Thus began the reign of the fighter pilots, lone shoot-'em-up cowboys of the air or the occasional dynamic duo, the Lone Ranger and his sidekick Tonto. Teams? Who needed them?

SAC shrank into the background with its hulking bombers and clumsy missiles, deposed by the flashy, sleek jets of Tactical Air Command. (Of course, SAC and TAC were also reorganized and renamed in the shuffle of the nineties.) The time had arrived, it was announced at the highest levels, for the warriors, the gun-fighters to take back the Air Force from the deskbound wee-nies—the planners, the analysts, the comm guys, the women. Not quite in those words, of course, but we could all read between the lines.

When most people hear "Black Hawk Down," they think Somalia. I think of the no-fly zone that our planes controlled over northern Iraq. Spang's squadrons rotated in and out of Incirlik Air Base, Turkey flying Operation Provide Comfort missions to protect the Kurdish population.

One day, two of Spang's F-15 pilots mistakenly identified two U.S. Army Black Hawks as Iraqi war helicopters and shot them down in the no-fly zone. The investigations that came afterward revealed a mess of discrepancies by all players involved: the pilots, their trainers, the Airborne Warning and Control System (AWACS) Army and Air Force officers who monitored the whole zone, even the Army helicopter pilots. All of those discrepancies, some of which had seemed trivial to the officers involved, added up to the death of twenty-six innocent people from friendly fire—a few Army military members, but also UN observers from France, Turkey, and Great Britain, as well as the United States.

It was also suggested that some of the fault lay in the natural competitiveness that had arisen between F-16 and F-15 pilots. With the bombers deposed, the fighter pilots had only one another to compete with. So far, only the F-16s had accomplished "kills" in Provide Comfort II. Perhaps an unconscious thrill lurked in the back of the two F-15 pilots' minds that they could be the first of their kind to intercept and destroy enemy aircraft in this mission. Besides, if you're carrying a loaded gun in your holster, your fingers itch for the trigger.

The pilots were sent home from Incirlik while everything was being investigated. One of them was a lieutenant colonel and a squadron commander. He seemed not to notice anyone who wasn't a rated officer. In staff meetings, he sat coldly, silently. *Arrogant*, I thought. His eyes normally passed over me with nothing but indifference. I avoided sitting next to him.

I had never spoken to him except for the verbal greetings that came with the mandatory salutes when we passed on the sidewalk, but entering wing headquarters one day as he was leaving, I looked into his eyes. Instead of saluting and moving on, I stopped. "How are you doing, sir?"

"I'm, I'm . . . getting by. Thank you, Cheryl. For asking."

That was all to the exchange. But I had seen ghosts in his eyes, a haunting he would live with the rest of his life. I began to notice that even the other flying squadron commanders seldom spoke to him as if afraid of being infected with his nightmares. Eventually, he was allowed to retire.

In three years the Spang MPF went from the worst in the Air Force (according to the USAFE inspectors at least) to receiving the Gerrit D. Foster award as one of the best. I can't take credit for the award, except for being the one who grunted and swore and shoved it up the first few steps. The officer who replaced me hoisted it higher, and the officer who replaced him did the same. All three of us were present at the awards ceremony. I would have been content to remain the MPF chief longer, but one doesn't get to pick the timing of one's opportunities. After a year, I was offered what most officers call "the best damned job in the Air Force": squadron commander. Of course I said yes. Who turns down command?

A cold January day at Spang, the 52nd Fighter Wing change of command ceremony was taking place in one of the drafty hangars. We'd marched in almost an hour ago, fifteen squadrons in full blue uniform. We paraded in front of the reviewing stand, heavy with American and German VIPs, then around the inside corners, saluting, wheeling, eyes right, about face. Now we stood in orderly squares, squadron commanders in front to pass commands back to their troops.

Standing at parade rest is harder than it appears. After all the ceremonies and speeches, my back and shoulders ached. My hands, loosely clasped behind my back, began to cramp. Surreptitiously, I rubbed my fingers together, careful to let no change of expression cross my face. I remembered an OTS warning: never lock your knees; it's the surest way to keel over. I allowed myself a slight bob, like a modest curtsey, to make sure my knees were soft. Ever since I left OTS, I had managed to avoid marching in a military formation—I couldn't walk and chew gum at the same time, much less pivot, swing arms, and stay in step. But now it came with the position.

I stood in front of the 52nd Mission Support Squadron—the newest, most junior, and only female squadron commander on base. I shifted my weight slightly and tried not to think about falling over, about the military ambulance waiting discreetly outside. If I fell, I would shame my whole squadron. My male counterparts would smirk next time they saw me. My weakness could be used to justify not appointing another woman to command. The pride of my squadron and the future of Air Force women everywhere depended on my staying upright and still. The responsibility was overwhelming. The back of my neck tightened with tension.

When I heard a muffled thud to my left, instinct urged me to turn and look, but training kept my eyes facing forward. I heard people scurrying, soft murmurs, heavy footsteps moving along the concrete floor and out the open doors behind us. An engine turned over and a vehicle pulled away. A ripple of whispers made its way through the squadrons. Someone had fainted.

The Germans have a word, *schadenfreude*, which is the joyful relief you feel when misfortune falls to someone else. One of the maintenance squadron commanders, a lieutenant colonel, had keeled over and been hauled out on a stretcher. I was surprised. Despite my anxiety, unless it was under a hot sun, hardly anyone ever really collapsed on parade—especially not commanders. He was a strong, hefty man too, a reliable rock of an officer. But I had heard him mention to someone that morning that he'd driven all night to be here, hadn't even had time to get something to eat. So no wonder. I tried to feel sympathy, but I wanted to dance. The odds of two commanders collapsing today were just too high. The pressure was off.

The new general wound up with the expected words about how honored he was to be entrusted with this wing and its outstanding men and women. The guests on the platform and bleachers applauded. Those of us in formation on the hangar floor remained silent, motionless.

The adjutant shouted a preparatory command, "Wing!" In unison with the other commanders, I called over my shoulder, "Squa-*DRON!*"

The adjutant called, "Ten *HUT!*" I snapped my arms to my sides and my heels together. From behind me came the sharp click of perfectly synchronized movement.

"For-*WARD.*" We squadron commanders repeated, "For-*WARD.*"

"*HARCH!*"

I stepped out with confidence, right foot first. It felt great to move.

Mission Support Squadrons were fairly new in the Air Force, a mishmash of only loosely related activities: Personnel (both military and civilian), Education and Training, Professional Military Education, Base Administration, and the Post Office. At least I knew something about the largest, Military Personnel, so I could concentrate on learning the other agencies.

Besides the two hundred or so military and civilian personnel who worked in my squadron, I also provided administrative and command support to the one hundred military members who worked in the wing headquarters, directly for the wing commander or his deputy. So I was both a squadron commander and a headquarters squadron commander, which is a confusing enough distinction when you're in the military. As a squadron commander I was responsible not only for people, but also for squadron operations: making sure the mail got delivered, the base records accurately maintained, people properly processed for assignments, airmen provided the training required to become NCOs, hiring rules for civilian personnel enforced, and on and on and on.

As a headquarters squadron commander, I was only responsible to maintain squadron records and to perform the personnel actions necessary to support the wing staff—command post, finance, social actions, safety, even the legal office—all sorts of cats and dogs. Occasionally that meant I got to do happy stuff, like announce promotions and attend graduations. But mostly, those personnel actions meant discipline and counseling. All told, it was wearying work.

The old house in Manderscheid was my sanctuary. The landlord's mother had run it as a pension, a European bed and breakfast. Three stories with only a bath and a half, but seven bedrooms, each of which had a number on the door and a sink in the room. Cold as ice in the winter, but the first signs of spring pulled us outdoors. We had a lush yard from which we could see two castles, a tenth-century one near us with little left but a wall and a tower, as well as a massive eleventh-century ruin below us along the Lieser River. Spring and summer evenings, we sat drinking beer on the small paved patio enclosed by the old lady's ornamental bushes and trees, now overgrown, until the sun went in and the evening chill drew us back inside.

Mary, now a lieutenant colonel, had been assigned to a NATO support office in Belgium. She and her husband Steve came to visit us one weekend. They brought their current Irish setter, Mollie, a mellow lady who lay at our feet, exuding a soothing canine presence. We sat with her on the patio one morning. She leaned her long body against my leg. I looked up to see Lynn gazing at her, chewing his lower lip. I caught his eye.

He said, "It's time, isn't it?"

I said, "I'll put the word out at work."

It took less than a week for an eager staff sergeant to appear at my office door first thing in the morning. "Major, in our village—puppies! A new litter playing in our neighbor's yard."

Her German neighbor's prized purebred beagle had slipped out one night while in heat. Not anxious for a litter of mongrels, the owner planned to have the subsequent pups aborted until a friend of hers talked her out of it. This friend worked as a telephone operator on the base. "I can find homes for them," she promised. "The Americans—they don't mind mixed breeds." (I took her comment as a compliment when I heard about it.) She offered to pay for the puppies' vet bills and food.

Thanks to this generous woman's intervention, we found The Amazing Dog, a.k.a. Maisie, a good-natured, beautiful, long-legged beaglette who entranced everyone who met her. She took us on long walks every day. We made good use of the winding woodland paths that radiated out from the edge of town, right next to our house. She was such a pretty dog, strangers would stop to admire her and ask what kind of dog she was. Lynn got tired of the response whenever he replied honestly, *"Eine Mischung"* (a mixture). Often their noses would go up and with a dismissive, *"Ach,"* they would lose interest and stride away. So he began telling people she was an *Eisenschmitter Hund,* an unknown breed, therefore obviously exotic. They would admire her all the more. Eisenschmitt was the village she came from.

Lynn went back to work a few months after Maisie joined us. His years managing DEERS and ID card policy/implementation for the Air Force had impressed the folks in the Department of Defense main office. When they decided they needed a government employee to oversee the program contractors in Europe, a friend let him know about the position. He applied and to no one's surprise, got the job. He arranged for an office at Spang but traveled frequently to Landstuhl where the contractors worked, about eighty minutes away at the speed he drove.

So more than five years after retiring, he appeared one morning dressed in a suit and tie, carrying a new briefcase, ready to face the contractors as the official voice of the U.S. Department of Defense. "What was I thinking?" he asked. "They were already paying me for not working."

I wondered too. My days with no household responsibilities were officially over. I eyed the German-style washer and dryer. "Lynn, you're going to have to introduce me to this thing."

# B. JUSTICE

My first official action as an Air Force squadron commander was to initiate court-martial proceedings against a Staff Sergeant Reston. I had little say in this. The investigation had been completed, the initial steps taken with the former commander, the sergeant familiarized with the charges, an Air Force Area Defense Counsel (ADC) assigned to him. Everything was prepared to move the drama on to the next stage, but a judge advocate (JA) could not press charges; only a commander had the legal authority to do so. I'd had that authority less than twenty-four hours.

So there I was, my first full day on the job, reading aloud the charges JA had prepared. In front of me stood an attractive young man at attention—motionless, emotionless. I sat at the commander's desk in an office so new I hesitated to call it mine. I felt like an imposter and wondered what I was doing there, reading legal documents in a flat, clear monotone.

The charges started with words like "lewd and lascivious behavior" and continued with specifics that required me to read the phrase "your penis" several times surrounded by legalese, "whereupon" and "to wit" and "your penis" and "wherein" and "insofar as" and again and again, "your penis." Throughout the reading neither of us so much as blinked an eye or twitched a lip, nor did any of the witnesses from the ADC and JA staffs, for whom such scenarios must have been commonplace. We all maintained good military bearing.

I had met SSgt Reston only once before, about six months earlier. He'd applied to be a recruiter. As MPF chief at the time, I had to review his record, his application form and its attachments, then interview him, and make a recommendation regarding his suitability to represent the Air Force. Recruiting duty was strictly for the best and brightest.

Reston's record had impressed me, a sterling account of fast promotions and challenging assignments, documented in raving reports from enthusiastic supervisors. Even his official photographs—full-length, one frontal, the other in profile (to eliminate anyone with unmilitary pudge)—fit the recruiter image. They showed a professional noncommissioned officer, slim and compact, with well-formed and even facial features, but with no hint of delicacy or prettiness. He projected intelligence, health, and energy.

In person, SSgt Reston had been equally impressive. His uniform pants and shirtsleeves had knife-sharp creases pressed into them. His eyes were a bright blue I hadn't expected to go with the dark hair of the black-and-white photos. He had a clear, pleasant voice and expressed himself well, neither overly familiar nor mawkishly subordinate. I had given him the strongest possible recommendation for recruiting duty.

He was equally military sharp at this second meeting, standing at attention while I read charges involving his penis.

He was one of a dozen men our deputy group commander had dubbed "the hole-in-the-stall gang." At Ramstein, the base librarians had received complaints that the plaster wall between two of the stalls in the men's room had a round hole the size of a fist knocked out of it. The worthy civilian women who worked there had Base Engineering repair it, then forgot about it. Until it reappeared and again had to be repaired. Then reappeared again.

By the time someone reported the situation to the base branch of the Air Force Office of Special Investigations (OSI), it must have been pretty obvious what it suggested. The OSI sent agents undercover to find the men who used the hole as a conduit for communication and sexual pleasure. The newspaper, *Stars and Stripes*, in each of its reports of the arrests that came out of the OSI's investigation described the men's restroom as being located in the children's books section of the library. It was accurate, but the paper's emphasis on that detail created an image of a parade of predators amidst the innocents. The American military community in Germany was particularly riled up about this ("In the children's section, for God's sake!"), though there were no allegations that I knew of that any of the men caught had targeted children or minors. I'd read about the case as it unfolded in the daily *Stars and Stripes*, months before I realized I would be professionally involved. No names were reported in the paper at that time. There were twelve "busts" before the investigation closed down, including airmen, NCOs, officers, and civilians. All but one of them was stationed at Ramstein. The exception was from Spandahlem and attached to my squadron.

When I read the transcript of the OSI agent's arrest of SSgt Reston, I wanted to laugh. I did laugh—then felt ashamed. But I forgave myself long ago for that laughter. After all, sex is seldom solemn, seldom dignified, not even when it's the expression of the most tender, enduring love. And never in the quick, desperate encounter of two strangers. My imagination embellished the transcript with the images it didn't bother to provide. I pictured the professional investigating agent sitting on the john, his pants around his ankles. He must have done so to be convincing in case his prey looked under the door—lust made suspicious through military necessity.

According to the agent's report, they didn't speak. Their contact was limited to notes passed through the hole in the wall, penciled on strips of toilet paper. SSgt Reston initiated contact; this was essential if the encounter was to legally avoid the label "entrapment." There were rules to this game, after all. Their short-lived, deceptive relationship began with a greeting and moved quickly to personal matters. There would be little time to waste in a library restroom.

SSgt R: HELLO
OSI: BACK ATCHA
SSgt R: HOW OLD ARE YOU
OSI: TWENTY-TWO

Reading this initial part of the toilet paper dialogue, I felt a rush of relief that SSgt Reston had taken pains first off to identify the person in the other booth as being of age, not a minor, not a child. So this was a meeting of two consenting adults, distasteful perhaps, but legal—anywhere else perhaps except between two military members in a public restroom on a military base.

The remainder of the transcript was short and as vague as possible on the agent's side. He couldn't be the one to suggest this was anything more than a weird pen-pal arrangement. So, SSgt Reston's notes became more graphic, suggesting other uses for the hole in the separating wall. The agent waited till the moment SSgt Reston's penis thrust through the hole, then sprang out of his own stall (pulling up his pants with one hand, I imagine) and forced open the other stall door. SSgt Reston in the few seconds this took had pulled his penis out of the hole and crammed the toilet paper correspondence into his mouth. He couldn't get the paper swallowed, so he pulled it out, threw it into the toilet, and pushed the lever. As he read SSgt Reston his rights, the OSI agent was bending over the toilet bowl, rescuing the clump of toilet paper from the swirling contents of the bowl. You may laugh now or say "eww."

The agent arrested SSgt Reston and walked him out of the restroom with as little fuss as possible. Neither of them would have wanted to upset the children, so they walked out casually, inconspicuously, the clump of wet toilet paper in an evidence bag in the agent's pocket. The toilet paper was sent off to a forensics lab, where the writing was eventually deciphered. It, as well as the agent's testimony, made up most of the case against SSgt Reston. That was enough to lead to that day in my new office, when SSgt Reston listened emotionlessly as I read the charges against him.

After we finished the formal part, the signing, the rituals, the "will that be all, ma'am?"—as if this had been nothing more than a duty roster assignment—he did a sharp left turn preparatory to leaving the room. The lawyers gathered up the paperwork, ready to file out after him. The squadron first sergeant opened the door.

As SSgt Reston marched proudly to the door, I heard a voice, my own, call weakly through the commander's mask. "Wait, Sergeant Reston," I said. The staff JA, Lieutenant Colonel Alster, looked up sharply. "Have a seat. I'd like to speak to you for a few minutes."

Alster's hard eyes bored into me. "Do you need us to stay?"

"No, sir. Thank you, but that won't be necessary."

Actually I wasn't as sure as I sounded that I wanted to speak to SSgt Reston alone, with no legal backup, and in my own voice. But I felt like I'd been handed a role to play, a starring position, true, but still one where I was reading someone else's lines—which I literally had been. Now I was stepping outside the script, ad-libbing. What I was going to say might not be "commanderly," might prove me unfit for the position. My heart raced, my palms were damp, but I met Lt Col Alster's eyes steadily.

The ADC said firmly, "I'm staying with my client."

"Of course." I motioned SSgt Reston to the chair beside my desk. The ADC sat watchfully a few feet away. We waited for the other lawyers to file out, with one last meaningful, warning look from Alster at the door. My first sergeant closed the door behind them and remained standing next to it, like a sentinel. SSgt Reston sat stiffly at attention, arms tight to his side, elbows bent, palms of his hands placed symmetrically on his thighs. He stared straight ahead, his face blank. Silence filled the room. It was up to me to break it. I cleared my throat. I reached for papers on my desk to fiddle with, caught myself, pulled my hands back, felt one brush against a pen, picked it up, set it back down. I turned to look at SSgt Reston. He was so young, twenty-four, twenty-five maybe.

"I want to say something to you, Sergeant." I spoke slowly, picking my way through a minefield of words. "I do not know if you are guilty of these charges or not. That is for the court-martial to determine. But I feel I should say something to you in case these charges are true."

No change in him. He continued to stare straight ahead, respectful but distant. The ADC shifted in his chair. I cleared my throat again before going on.

"Whether your future is in the Air Force or in the civilian world, I want you to know that you are . . . valuable. Yes, valuable. You have a lot to bring to whatever you endeavor. And . . . the, the, well, the kind of encounter described in these charges is dangerous. Dangerous to you in oh so many ways." I saw his hands tremble now, the hardened blue eyes covered with a softening mist. "And I just wanted to tell you that you need to take better care of yourself." I swallowed. "Because your life is valuable. Do you understand what I'm saying to you?"

"Yes, ma'am." His voice was soft, barely a whisper. He swallowed. "Thank you."

I leaned back then and sighed. "Very well. That will be all." When the door closed behind him, I sank back in my seat. My hands were shaking, and I felt exhausted, wrung out.

The court-martial lasted less than half a day. SSgt Reston's only defense lay in his sterling record and the enthusiastic endorsement of supervisors and coworkers. He was convicted and sentenced to three months at the military prison in Mannheim and a bad conduct discharge.

When I became a commander, I had not expected to spend such a large portion of my time conferring with lawyers. I'd pictured myself . . . well, commanding: leading, inspiring, ordering, supervising, managing, heroically in front of my troops in the day-to-day battle to slay the paperwork Goliath. Despite my best intentions, however, I found myself constantly tied up in legal and personal concerns affecting the military and civilian employees who worked for me. As a commander at an overseas base, I also had the family members to deal with. I saw a lot of the legal office.

Lt Col Alster had hair as dark as SSgt Reston's and eyes as bright blue—but cold. They reminded me of the pictures I'd seen of glaciers in Alaska. He was a bachelor and as far as I could tell had none of the warmth of human relationships to soften the stern, unyielding principles he lived by. No, they weren't principles— they were laws, regulations, rules. None of them seemed to come from his own sense of what was right. But he had an icy passion for defending the law to the letter.

"This is the reality, Cheryl," he told me. "Most commanders spend 95 percent of their time addressing the problems caused by 5 percent of their people. The slugs. And it's a shame you have to waste so much time dealing with them." There was no place for slugs in Alster's Air Force. He was a lawyer. He saw guilt and innocence, black and white. "Too bad you had to start with a big case like Reston's. Fortunately it was an open-and-shut case."

He slapped one palm against the other, as if doing the shutting. Book closed, from his perspective. Another slug squashed between the heavy covers of a legal tome.

In reality, it was easier to be handed a case where all decisions had already been made, even one as questionable to me as Reston's, than to have to deal with my own conscience and uncertainties.

The first disciplinary action to begin and end on my watch concerned a staff sergeant named Fletcher, who served in the APO. The base SPs arrested him as an accessory after the fact, trying to help a friend. All the facts, which no one questioned, indicated he'd been well intentioned and ignorant that he was assisting with a larceny. Nevertheless, he'd broken significant rules involving protection of post office funds. This was the second time he'd done so. He'd received a Letter of Reprimand the first time. This time, I reluctantly agreed with the JA that an Article 15 was in order.

Article 15 was the most significant of administrative actions (that is, nonjudicial—no courts or judges involved) that a commander could take to discipline troops. It was used for serious infractions, and could affect other personnel actions as well (assignments, promotions, etc.). Unlike Letters of Counseling and Reprimand, an Article 15 could impose punishment. Commanders could choose from a menu of options, singly or in combination, including a Letter of Reprimand, withholding a promotion, demotion, a monetary fine.

The day the captain from JA gave me the Article 15 package on Fletcher to review and complete, with places for my signature and initials carefully indicated with sticky orange arrows, I stared at it as if he'd handed me a pornographic photo—both disgusted and titillated. It included the Letter of Reprimand I'd asked him to prepare, then a memo signed off by Lt Col Alster recommending other punishments: demotion and removal of SSgt Fletcher's NCO status, which would bring him down to senior airman with substantial cuts in status, pay, and benefits; also immediate forfeiture of five hundred dollars. All of which I could make happen with no more effort than a few scrawls on that prim form. *Power*, I thought. *Command. Authority.* Words that scared and excited me.

I picked up my pen. I held it over the first signature block for a few seconds, then set it down. I put the Article 15 package in my office safe and went out for a cigarette. And to think.

Every day for a week I pulled the Article 15 out of my safe and read it through and thought and thought and thought. Every day, the JA captain called me. "Have you signed it yet?"

"No, I'm still thinking."

Alster called me. "Have you signed it yet?"

"No, sir, I'm still thinking."

"For God's sake, Major, what's there to think about?"

I didn't answer him. After all, if he didn't know, what could I say to him? I spent a week thinking about power and responsibility, realizing that whatever I did could affect this young man forever. Finally I signed the Article 15. Huge relief on the part of the legal staff, who set up an appointment for me to present the Article 15 to SSgt Fletcher that very afternoon—obviously afraid of my changing my mind.

The usual cast of characters gathered in my office, my first sergeant, lawyers for both sides, Fletcher's supervisor. Before we went into the formal part of the punishment, the ritual as it were, I had SSgt Fletcher sit down. "I want to make sure you understand why you're receiving an Article 15, Sergeant Fletcher." He looked at me sullenly, anger in his eyes. "A year ago," (surprise flickered in his face) "an airman you supervised at the post office came to you and asked you to cash a check for her out of postal funds, something you knew was absolutely forbidden. But you were a nice guy so you helped her out. And you were found out and you received a Letter of Reprimand. Do you see a connection between that incident and the one you're here for today?"

He had the good sense to look abashed. "Yes, ma'am."

"Good. You have been entrusted with a huge responsibility, and you are expected to follow the rules that govern it. If you don't, do you think the airmen who work for you will? The impulse to help out a friend is a good one, a natural one, but you have to learn to stop and think. You need to exercise better judgment."

This was the only part I actually liked in these proceedings, the erstwhile preacher in me rising up before the captive congregation—no one got to slip out of the back pew when the commander was talking. At least I kept the sermon short and to the point. "You're not an airman anymore. You're a noncommissioned officer. You set the example. So this disregard for the rules has to stop *now* or you'll find yourself in bigger trouble one day." I paused to allow the congregation to call out "amen," but no one did. "All right. Let's get this over with."

SSgt Fletcher rose to attention while I read the Article 15 to him and the Letter of Reprimand attached to it. Then I read the punishments I had initialed. He winced when he heard demotion to E-4 and removal of NCO status. He winced again when I read forfeiture of five hundred dollars. "Signed, this date." I stopped reading, picked up my pen, and signed. Then I initialed two more blocks at the bottom of the form, signed again, and continued to read. "Demotion and removal of NCO status to be suspended for one year. Forfeiture of funds to be suspended for one year."

"Wha—" I heard the JA captain start, then catch himself.

"Suspended?" SSgt Fletcher asked, a catch in his voice.

"Suspended," I said. "So keep your nose clean for a year. Show me you've learned how to be an NCO, and it all goes away."

When Alster heard about it, he told me I was nuts. "He'll be in trouble again. Just wait. He won't be able to resist some buddy coming up to him, suggesting something else—but it'll be worse next time, just wait. Now he thinks nothing bad's going to happen to him."

He didn't say, *you're soft, you're not really a commander, you're not fit for this job.* But I heard it behind his words. I heard it in my own mind, whispering to me. And I was afraid he might be right. That maybe I had been too soft with SSgt Fletcher and that in the long run he and the Air Force would suffer because of my incompetence. For the next few months, I was on tenterhooks, waiting for the phone call from the SPs, from the OSI, from a supervisor or coworker that would lead to SSgt Fletcher standing at attention in front of my desk again. But nothing happened. After six months, I removed the Article 15 early so he could take an assignment to the Philippines.

The following Thanksgiving, I received mail from a base in the Pacific. The return address read *Technical* Sergeant Robert Fletcher. Inside was a card decorated with childlike pilgrims and a complacently smiling turkey, the words "Happy Thanksgiving," and scrawled across the bottom:

> *Thank you,*
> *From*
> *Bob Fletcher*

Bob Fletcher is the only one who ever thanked me and perhaps the only one I deserved thanks from. When he got in trouble, I'd been green and fearfully aware of the sudden power handed to me. I was thoughtful and cautious in using that power then. Later my decisions came faster and easier but not necessarily better. Nevertheless my early disciplinary cases left me with a feeling of relief. Yes, I could do this stuff. I could enforce the rules, yet also be true to the person within me who wanted to heal and to help, be both Major and Cheryl. But just as I was patting myself on the back for maneuvering the pitfalls between justice and mercy, comparing my empathy smugly against Lt Col Alster's unyielding cynicism, Jack Sorenson walked into my office. Jack Sorenson was—in Alster's parlance—a slug. And for the first time, I agreed.

He was also popular, bright, hardworking, a senior master sergeant poised for selection to chief master sergeant on the next promotion board, the fair-haired boy of the 52nd Fighter Wing. A few months previously, he and his soon-to-be ex-wife Nina, also an NCO, had been in the bedroom of the house they once shared. She'd come back to pack up some things. He said she was sitting on the ledge of the open window as they talked. He saw her sway suddenly and reached out to grab her as she began to fall. His story.

Her story: he pushed her out the window. Whichever is true, what's certain is that Nina fell out of that second-floor window while he was in the room. She landed on grass and got by with cuts and bruises, a broken arm and more fodder for their nasty divorce. They were not nice people. What I got to know of Nina convinced me she was perfectly capable of falling out a window, then filing a police report accusing her husband of trying to kill her. There had been no witnesses, just a he-said/she-said situation, so the charges against him were dropped. In a peculiar compromise, both parties were given Letters of Reprimand for disorderly conduct.

This all happened before I became commander, so I got to know of it first when Jack made an appointment to come see me to discuss early removal of the Letter of Reprimand. I asked Col Starr, the deputy support group commander about him. I'd known Starr since he was a lieutenant colonel at Ramstein, a tough but genial black man with a bushy mustache just within Air Force limits. He told me the story, sitting back in his chair, chewing on an unlit cigar. He finished in his slow drawl, "Doesn't matter that there's no evidence. Sorenson pushed his wife out that window, sure's I'm sitting here. Can't say as I blame him. But that son of a bitch is guilty, guilty, guilty."

It wasn't Col Starr's opinion that influenced me when Jack showed up in my office the next day. I'd known the colonel long enough to realize he was right on target 75 percent of the time and way off target the other 25 percent. But when Jack Sorenson approached me, he leaned toward me a little too closely, his voice smooth and quiet, his eyes catching and holding mine as he informed me, not asked me, what I had to do.

From another man that good-looking, his approach could have been seductive, but from him it felt threatening. I saw and smelled bully all over him. Every word and movement of his told me he was stronger and more powerful than me. He meant me to be afraid of him, and I was. I was glad I had the first sergeant, a large, burly man, at our meeting.

I said little at first. I listened to him, his voice slick and polite, but always that undercurrent. Then I told him I had reviewed his file and thought it too soon to consider removing it. His face turned red, and he began to shake.

He got right in my face and hissed at me. "You'll regret this, *Major*. Who are you? You're nothing. You fucking bitch. You know I can get you fired."

When I responded that he'd just bought himself a Letter of Counseling, I thought he was going to lose it then and there. If it hadn't been for the first sergeant's presence, he might have hit me (which might have worked out better in the long run).

After he left, the first sergeant turned to me, admiration in his voice. "Well done, ma'am. He used to treat Major K just as bad, but she never did nothing. She was scared of him." I was too. I was terrified of Sorenson in fact, but I knew I couldn't let him see it. When I gave him the Letter of Counseling a few days later, he refused to sign it. The next day my boss, the support group commander, chided me.

"Come on, Cheryl," Colonel Boston said, "an LOC just because he was upset?" He had been more than upset, but I couldn't make the colonel see it. Jack was so good on the job, so personable, so tied into the good-old-boy network. He was the sort of senior NCO who golfed with the general and exchanged bawdy jokes with the colonels in the locker room.

For over a year he was the monster under my bed. The battle between him and Nina began to revolve around their kids. I had to assign the first sergeant to go with him Saturday mornings and Sunday evenings when the two parents exchanged children in a mandated public parking lot. "Exchange of hostages," Col Starr called it. Since both parents continued to play nasty tricks on the other, hardly a week went by without Jack demanding I do something about the stunt Nina had just pulled or Nina's commander calling to insist I do something about Jack. Both of them were expert at playing the Transactional Analysis game, "Let's You and Him Fight."

Jack crossed the line when he removed his personal gun collection from the base armory without permission. The order to leave them there had come from the wing commander after the window incident, well before me. It had never been rescinded. After a week with his dad, the Sorensons' ten-year-old son told his mother that he'd seen Jack sitting in his bedroom, drinking, pointing a gun at a picture of her, clicking the empty chambers while saying things like, "You're dead, you bitch." The son claimed to be terrified to go back to his father's again. Nina marched him down to the Security Police to tell his story.

"It's all lies," Jack yelled when he heard. "He's lying. His mother made this story up and made him tell it. She's just trying to get sole custody of the kids." Whether she was lying or not, she succeeded. Nothing shook the boy's story, and no one disagreed with me this time when I presented Jack with an Article 15 for disobeying the order to leave his guns in the armory. He hated me more than ever then.

One night he walked into my office around seven thirty. My staff had gone. I was trying to finish up paperwork while it was quiet. The three-story office building was mainly dark, though I knew the colonels would be working long after I went home. SMSgt Sorenson swaggered in like a gunslinger into a saloon. He stood in front of me, leaned over with his palms planted solidly on my desk. I schooled my face into nothingness, hoped he couldn't see the pulse I could feel pounding away at my temples. I kept the pen in my hand to keep from shaking.

"What do you need, Sergeant Sorenson?"

"What do I need? What do I need? I need my little girl, that's what I need. I need you to make my ex-wife hand her over to me tonight." He spoke slowly, with barely restrained fury.

We'd been through this issue recently. I felt sure enough of my ground here that I let go of my pen lifeline, let my forearms rest on the desk, and wove the fingers of my hands together—the body language of the one who's in charge. "We've been over this before, Jack. She's got custody now. You need a court order if you're going to change that. Do you have a court order?"

He began to yell. "I shouldn't have to have a fucking court order! Don't you get that? This is my daughter. I don't need a court or a commander or anyone to tell me that I can't see my own daughter!" He began stomping around the room. I waited quietly and calmly for him to settle down—a technique that usually worked well for me. He finally stopped, came back to my desk, leaned over it. "Are you going to help me or not?"

When I asked if he had a court order again, he resumed stomping around the room. "Ah, man! This is my flesh and blood! I want my daughter. You don't care, do you? You don't care whether I ever see my kids or not. A commander's supposed to support their troops but you never have. You've always been against me."

He hit a sore spot here. I *didn't* care whether he got his daughter. As far as I could see both children would be better off with neither parent in the picture, poor little prisoners of their mutual hatred. I constantly had to struggle to be impartial, to support Jack when he seemed to have right on his side. But at that moment I truly wanted him to have that court order. I wanted him to be happy and to win this foray in the war of the Sorensons. I wanted him out of my office and out of my hair. When I spoke, I dripped sympathy—and actually felt some.

"Look, Jack, we went to Colonel Alster with all the documents. He told you what you needed to do to get a court order to allow you visitation. Have you got the court order?"

"Oh, fuck it all anyway. Why on earth did I think I'd get any help from you? You're a pitiful excuse for a commander." His voice rose as he went on, spewing hatred at me. I found myself straining to hear noises in the hallway, the sound of other life in the building. I thought of his guns. I thought of how it would feel to fall from my three-story window onto concrete.

"That's enough!" I yelled above his ranting. I stood up, but stayed behind the desk, near the telephone. "Get out of here! I don't have to put up with this. Get out! I'll deal with you tomorrow when you've had a chance to calm down." When I would have the first sergeant with me and an office full of staff outside the door. "Get out now!"

It was a gamble of my authority. What if he refused to leave? Fortunately, I thought, he stopped, looked at me through slit eyelids. "You haven't heard the end of this, *maa'aam*." Then he was gone.

I listened for his footsteps to sound down the hallway, then went to the door and watched him disappear down the stairs. Breathing hard, I rushed into my office, grabbed my hat and purse, and locked my office with papers still strewn all over my desk. I would come in early in the morning, finish up then. Of all the emotions caroming through me, foremost was terror. *Some warrior you are*, I thought as rushed down the stairs. There was still light coming from the support group office on the second floor, a muffled sound of voices from behind the glass doors, the comforting sense of bustle in an office after hours. I hesitated there, but it seemed too wimpy to involve Col Boston and Col Starr. I should be able to solve this without bringing in bigger guns.

My heart didn't stop pounding till I was in my car, doors locked, heading out the front gate, ashamed and relieved. The drive to Manderscheid took half an hour through curvy dark forest roads and gave me a chance to gradually let go of the fear and the stress. As I slowed to take the hairpin turns, my pounding heartbeat also slowed. I relaxed, the pressure eased its way out of my shoulders, the tautness in the back of my neck loosened. By the time I got home, I felt calm and confident again. Lynn was back in the States for a conference, but Maisie came rushing to greet me when I opened the door. The phone was ringing. It was my boss.

Half an hour later I was back on base. The colonel's office was full. He sat at the head of his conference table with Col Starr next to him. Lt Col Alster was there with one of his young captains, also my first sergeant, Nina's squadron commander, his first sergeant, the wing's senior enlisted adviser, and the head chaplain. And sitting righteously in the midst of them, SMSgt Jack Sorenson. He was the only one who didn't turn to stare at me as I entered the room.

"Ah, Major. Now that you're finally here, we can get started." Col Boston's greeting was chilly. That word "finally" spoken with just the slightest emphasis—so they'd been gathering, waiting for an hour, time for me to get home, answer the phone, turn around and come back. I slid into the chair waiting for me, right next to the colonel and gave a thought to the poor dog, without her walk, probably peeing in the house that very moment. "Senior Master Sergeant Sorenson," Col Boston said, using the full title, always a sign he was irked, "needs help to get his ex-wife to release their little girl for a visit. Apparently he came to you for assistance—the right thing to do considering the restraining order. When you wouldn't help him, he came to me. Now, Major, I'm sure you had your reasons, so I wasn't about to step in until you had a chance to explain them."

Jack's bland expression barely bothered to hide a smirk. The others stared at me with tired hostility. It was almost nine and I was the reason they weren't home yet or having a beer at the club. Only the genial chaplain smiled, and Col Starr chewed his unlit cigar with half-closed eyes and a twist of amusement on his lips. I felt small but also right and righteous and angry.

"Colonel Boston, Sergeant Sorenson and I have addressed this issue with Legal. He has to have a court order to require his ex-wife to give him visitation rights."

Lt Col Alster spoke up. "He has a court order. I reviewed it earlier today."

"What!" I turned to Jack. "I asked you three times tonight if you had a court order. Three times! You never answered me. You just kept going off about it."

"I was frustrated, ma'am. I was going to show you the court order but you kicked me out before I could do so." Jack looked hurt, innocent, just a father wanting his child, bewildered by the mixed-up world of red tape and bureaucracy complicating the simple matter of a parent's love. I could feel all those other men around the table aching with him, picturing having their own children somehow denied to them.

I didn't buy it. This had nothing to do with wanting his daughter, who, along with the son, was little more than a pawn in the power games he and Nina played. What he wanted was what he had right now, a roomful of base officials witnessing my incompetence and unworthiness to be a squadron commander. He'd set it all up to get at me, to undermine and humiliate me in front of my peers and superiors. Okay, that's definitely me projecting. It's what I thought and felt, surrounded by all that hostile testosterone. Jack Sorenson was probably less interested in me, than he was in being the center of the little drama playing out in this room. All those officers on his side tonight. *Big score, Nina. Top this if you can.*

I summoned as much dignity as I was capable of, trying not to sound like a whiny kid. "Colonel Boston, I'm sorry you had to be bothered with this. I asked Sergeant Sorenson for the court order three times. He never told me he had it. Instead he was threatening and belligerent."

Col Boston cleared his throat. "Well, that's neither here nor there. So what do we do now?" It took just five minutes to put together a team—one that didn't include me—to accompany Jack to pick up his game trophy, a six-year-old girl. Surrounded by this entourage, Jack left with just one smirk at me. Col Boston waved me away when I tried to say something.

I walked outside with Col Starr, who shook his head back and forth. "Lord, I hope those kids have enough money when they grow up to pay for all the therapy they're going to need." He lit his cigar and walked away laughing to himself.

For the second time that night, I drove home, this time despising myself, feeling the humiliation, the public glare highlighting my incompetence. Even the quiet of the woods couldn't spoil this bad mood. It would almost have been preferable to be thrown out the window. To end the episode with a bang instead of a pitiful, whiny whimper.

In memory, it feels like the very next day that Alster appeared in my office, angry and agitated, though it may have been several days or even weeks, given how slowly paperwork moves in the government. He threw a file down on my desk. "Damn! The Article 15 on Sorenson—Seventeenth sent it back." (Seventeenth Air Force was the Numbered Air Force our wing reported to.)

I grabbed the file and started to flip through it. "Back? What's wrong with it?" We'd been so careful, knowing what a slippery slug Jack was—for once we'd been on the same wavelength.

He didn't even sit down, just paced in front of the desk. "My fault. I should have known. I did know." He spun around and stopped in front of me. "*You*," he said, pointing an accusing finger at me. "*You* are not authorized to give Article 15s to seniors or chiefs. *You* are only a major." Impatiently, he grabbed the file from me and flipped through to a chart copied out of a regulation. Highlighted in yellow was a footnote saying that to present an Article 15 to a member of the top two enlisted grades, the squadron commander had to be a lieutenant colonel or above.

"Oh, shit," I said. My head immediately started to pound. Just like that—instant headache.

Alster dropped into a chair. "It's not your fault," he said, though grudgingly. "It's my job to catch this stuff. I'm supposed to know. Hell, I did know. It just hadn't come up before. Most of the commanders are LCs, and let's face it, we don't give a lot of Article 15s to senior NCOs."

"So what do we do now?"

"Just move it up the chain. I'm redoing it for Col Boston's signature."

"Well, I guess we need to go tell him." I started to get up, but Lt Col Alster waved me back down. He looked abashed.

"I already have. He's not happy about it, but he's going to do it."

I bit my lip. So I was no longer in the loop on this, not even entrusted with the responsibility of being part of the screw-up, responsible to explain and to recover. The message was clear. As far as Jack Sorenson was concerned, I'd shown myself to be incapable. Col Boston presented the new Article 15 later that day under his own signature. I was not invited to be present. When it returned, all duly signed off by higher headquarters, my only function was to get it on file. A glorified administrator, that was me. It burned, but there was an upside. Jack stopped bothering me with his demands, instead going directly to Col Boston.

## C. MERCY

In my two and a half years as a commander, I remember only one woman who received disciplinary action from me. A senior airman, she kept going AWOL, wandering all over Germany. Military police would eventually track her down, bring her back, then a few days later she'd be gone again. The base psychiatrist diagnosed her with a behavioral disorder and prescribed a stay in an Army psych ward while we processed an administrative discharge for her. The hospital determined she didn't need to be there, let her loose, and she disappeared for two weeks.

And where was kind, concerned Cheryl at that point? Glad to have her gone, not concerned about her well-being at all, just relieved to have a few weeks reprieve from dealing with her. When the SPs hauled her back again, I was pissed. I ordered her into barracks confinement, though I had no way to enforce it. She must have been tired from her wanderings though, because she stayed put and left on schedule. Out of my hair. Finally.

I can't even remember what she looked like. Just one image of her remains in my mind and that's of her walking away, the first sergeant escorting her down the hall after she had signed her discharge papers. So all I can picture of her is her back, a short stocky figure topped with flyaway black hair, moving away from me, away from the Air Force. I might have felt a tinge of sympathy then, maybe guilt that in some way I'd failed her. But what I primarily felt was relief. Thank God! Another problem gone now.

The women were more likely to present themselves as the accusers, the victims, the injured wife, or righteous neighbor. I had no sympathy for them either. They demanded pounds of flesh. I was to be judge and executioner, while passing the tissue box to mop up hysterical tears.

Lt Col Alster requested that I take part when he had to interview two female tech sergeants who were making allegations of sexual harassment. They worked for one of the wing functions. Denise Valdi, a quiet, reserved woman, had only recently arrived. The other woman, Ellie Firmen, had worked in the office for two years. A vivacious blonde, Tech Sergeant Firmen did most of the talking. She described an office in which casual friendliness with the boss had led first to flirtation, then sexual innuendoes.

"Nothing serious, you know." She had big blue eyes, which she kept trained on Lt Col Alster. I wasn't sure she even saw me in the room. "It was just a way of letting off steam, of being friendly. I certainly never took it seriously. Did you, Denise?"

Denise looked startled to be appealed to but dutifully shook her head. "No. No. Not at all."

"But then Willis, I mean Master Sergeant Johnson, he started grabbing at me—and Denise." We turned to look at Denise, who nodded. "And then it got uncomfortable to be around him. He was always trying to get me or Denise somewhere alone."

Alster asked how long this had been going on. Weeks, maybe months, it seemed. Ellie leaned forward toward him earnestly, pure piety dripping from her voice. "I didn't want to say anything because I really hate getting someone in trouble, but he just wouldn't stop, and it got worse and worse. Right, Denise?" Denise nodded, still looking scared and unhappy.

The story that came out was a sordid one of an office atmosphere that reeked. I thought of the other people working in the small office. I looked past Ellie to quiet, pale Denise Valdi and her unhappy eyes. As soon as the door closed behind them, Alster exhaled as if he'd been holding his breath. "Shooo. Every time

I'm around that woman I feel like I need to go wash the slime off my hands."

So it wasn't just me who sensed the sordid come-on and the sick power game. I had little sympathy for MSgt Willis Johnson, who after all was a senior NCO and should have known better. But so should Ellie Firmen.

"The funny thing about this case," Alster said, "is it was just a matter of who got the accusation in first. He could have had an equally good case of sexual harassment against Firmen, I suspect. But," he shrugged, "she got here first, so she gets to play victim and he's the culprit."

"Any legal grounds to do something to her too?" I asked. He shook his head. "Seems a shame. She seems just as guilty."

He pursed his lips, placed his fingertips together and quoted. "When the scene is set in hell, you don't get angels for witnesses."

An investigation and interviews with the other office members confirmed MSgt Johnson's guilt. Great, another wing NCO to deal with. I called him in to see what he had to say about the charges. A tall, forty-something man with smooth skin the color of coffee with cream, he'd always been an outgoing friendly sort, the kind of person I couldn't help liking. Even knowing he was in trouble, he walked in smiling, greeting me with a hearty, "Hallo, ma'am, hallo!"

According to him, they'd just been joking around, and he couldn't understand why the two women had taken his friendliness the wrong way. If only they'd talked to him about it. But soon he changed the subject. "You know, Major, I hear things, being in my position. Stuff goes on all over this base. Not everything is handled fairly. People treated differently 'cause of their skin color or their gender. *Every* squadron, there's favoritism goes on."

I let him talk, uninterrupted, for fifteen minutes. His veiled comments became less and less veiled with my lack of response, but more and more personal, aimed at me and my squadron. My first sergeant, who was new, looked at me curiously as I let Johnson ramble, insinuating systemic racial and gender bias in the squadron ever more directly in the face of my silence. I heard frustration in his voice as he continued to talk. *Is this white woman too dense to know what I'm talking about?*

Finally, I interrupted him. "Okay, Sergeant Johnson, I've let you have your say, and it's been very interesting, though nothing to the point. My only response to your . . . *implications*, is to say that I have done nothing to be ashamed of. So if you wish to initiate the investigations you seem to be hinting at, go right ahead. I'm not concerned."

"Oh, no, ma'am. Why, I didn't mean to imply, no, nothing like that." He stumbled all over himself, backtracking, eager to placate. He went back to his ultimately meaningless version of what had been going on in the office. Meaningless because it was a game that could only be played as long as neither side complained. After that, victim and perpetrator were identified, winner and loser proclaimed.

But was I as innocent as I claimed to be? After the two men left, I felt—like Lt Col Alster—a need to wash the slime off my hands, the slime of playing a part in an archetypal drama, white woman accuses black man, with the ending preordained. I reminded myself that archetypal as it was, this was also its own unique case. There was no question that MSgt Johnson was guilty of sexual harassment as charged. He probably misread the compliance of women who were afraid to seem prudish, who wanted to be part of the macho culture that the military so exemplified. The line he inevitably crossed he saw as one of the women's making, a trap they snared him in with a big "gotcha."

When the day came to present MSgt Johnson with an Article 15, he came alone. There were no lawyers in the office, just the two of us and my first sergeant. Johnson stood proudly before my desk, an NCO with a spotless record after more than twenty years of service. I began to read the charges. His ramrod figure swayed suddenly. I looked up. "Are you all right, Sergeant Johnson?"

"Yes, ma'am. Go on."

I looked down at the paper again, began to read. Then his body toppled like building blocks to the floor. I ran around the desk to him. His face had turned gray; his breathing was fast and ragged.

The first sergeant called to my secretary from the door, telling her to send for the base ambulance. I sat on the floor holding MSgt Johnson's head and shoulders in my lap. "Willis, Will? Are you okay? Are you okay?" Of course he wasn't. Stupid question. He was receiving an Article 15; his career lay shattered, that bright, shiny career he'd taken so much pride in. And he'd found himself standing at attention in front of a squadron commander's desk, like any disorderly eighteen-year-old airman. No wonder he'd fainted. Probably locked his knees, my analytical mind noted, while my feelings were screaming, *You cold bitch, you killed him! You killed him!*

He groaned, his eyelids fluttered, his eyes opened—just like in a movie. It was interesting to note that Hollywood had gotten it right. "I'm sorry," he said and pulled his head up. The first sergeant and I helped him into a chair.

"The ambulance is on its way," the first sergeant said.

"I don't need an ambulance. I just fainted."

"Yes, you do," I told him. "The medics need to check you out." We sat in silence for a minute, waiting. Finally, hesitantly, I spoke as gently as the subject and situation allowed. "Willis, you know, I still need to finish giving you the Article 15. We can wait and do that another time or we can do it now. It's up to you. What do you want?"

He nodded, his breathing starting to slow, but his face still a sickly gray. "Get it over with."

He made a move as if to rise, but I stopped him. "Just stay there, just sit." And I finished reading the charges. I signed and dated the paper, then handed him the pen. He signed. We didn't talk, just listened to the siren of the ambulance getting closer.

The next time I was in Col Starr's office, he took the unlit cigar out of his mouth to say, "I hear you're so tough even strong men faint when they have to stand before you." He laughed.

I wanted to ask him, "Have I done right? Am I doing right? Did I let his color influence my judgment? Would you have done the same thing?" I had denied so firmly and disdainfully the accusations against me MSgt Johnson had hinted at, though I never knew if he had anything specific in mind or was just fishing in a pond stocked with white guilt. But I wasn't so sure of my innocence. Centuries of history had helped create me. Where race was concerned, could any of us truly claim innocence? I wanted to ask Col Starr to put the cigar and the laugh away and talk to me. Tell me I was right. Or wrong. Or both. But I didn't.

My last significant disciplinary action occurred not long before I was due for reassignment. Senior Master Sergeant Sean Pendleton, stalwart, reliable, smart, and good-humored, had been my right-hand man for many projects. I'd always been able to count on him—honestly, to *lean* on him. I was sorry when he announced his retirement. The base would lose a good NCO.

I knew he was a heavy drinker, but that was hardly unique in the Air Force. As long as he didn't drive under the influence or let it affect his work, it wasn't really a problem. He lived on base and did most of his partying at the NCO Club, walking home in the evenings. He walked everywhere, his lanky frame and easy lope not varying, whether he was coming to work sober in the morning or heading home with a buzz on after happy hour.

One of the other sergeants complained to me once that he'd come back from lunch with alcohol on his breath. She seemed shocked at the notion, but she was the easily shockable kind, her nose always sniffing around for a scandal. I reminded her that there was no rule against drinking during duty hours. None written at least. Still to be on the safe side I held him back after a meeting to caution him. "Are you having problems, Sean?" I asked, perhaps too delicately.

"No, ma'am. You know me. I just like a beer at lunch, a little whiskey at night."

"Everything okay at home?"

He laughed. "Yes, ma'am. Me and the little woman doin' fine," he drawled.

"Well, just be careful. And come talk to me any time you need to, okay?"

And that was that, for almost a year. Then a few months before Pendleton was due to retire, with his replacement already on board and more time on his hands, he started going to the club earlier and staying longer, not just drinking but also playing the slots. It was money that got him in trouble at first, not the drinking. The club manager complained that he hadn't paid his club bills for over two months. It turned out he had other debts too.

Air Force regulations established the steps to take in these situations. First, a Letter of Counseling and mandatory sessions at the Family Support Center, where a financial expert would work with him and his wife to set up payment plans and a budget. He undertook these steps humbly, with proper regret. Then slipped back into the same ways. More late bills, more complaints, including some from people who claimed he was getting belligerent at the club. He and his wife were having problems, I heard, and he spent more and more time there. "What's wrong, Sean? Talk to me. You're walking into trouble."

He kept assuring me everything was fine, that the reports of his drinking were exaggerated, that the bills were his wife's, that he'd take care of everything. But the situation kept getting worse and I kept upping the administrative actions, hoping to get his attention. Another Letter of Counseling, then a move up to Letters of Reprimand. I started counting the weeks till he would retire and depart the base.

Mere weeks before his retirement, his drinking led to a fray at the club. I wanted to ignore his behavior, but it had been too public to be swept under the rug, even if I could have brought myself to do so. "You know, you're going to have to take sterner action," Alster told me.

"Yes, sir, I know." I looked for some sympathy in his blue eyes, but they were as icy as ever. *Another slug,* I could hear him thinking. "Time for an Article 15, I guess."

"Right. We'll get the paperwork done by the end of the week."

I avoided looking at him as I said, "He's retiring so I need to sign and present it soon."

The silence was so heavy I glanced up at him. The cold eyes were staring at me, his expression unfathomable. Then he nodded. "Okay. We'll have it ready for your signature as soon as we can. You'll let the colonels know?"

I found both of them in Col Boston's office and told them about the new problem and what the JA and I had decided. Col Starr chomped down on his cigar and shot me a shrewd look.

Col Boston harrumphed and said, "JA's preparing it for you to present?"

"Yes, sir." I kept my gaze on him, looking as innocent as I knew how.

He shuffled some papers on his desk. "Well, okay then."

The letters I'd given him would disappear as soon as Sean retired, but an Article 15 would be a permanent part of his record. When I presented it to him, he signed it with an angry scrawl. He never spoke to me again. He refused a retirement ceremony and left Spang a bitter man. It took a couple of weeks for the Article 15 to work its way through Col Boston and our wing commander before being mailed off base to the Seventeenth Air Force commander. Sean Pendleton had been gone three weeks when Alster got the Article 15 back.

"Man, those guys at Seventeenth *really* think we're idiots now," he said.

He handed me the file and pointed to a caustic handwritten note attached to the formal letter of disapproval: *What does it take to convince you folks that this major is too junior to give Article 15s to seniors and chiefs?!! DON'T SEND US ANOTHER ONE OF THESE!* Something that might have been a slight smile loitered on Alster's lips.

"Oops," I said. "Sorry, sir. You'd think I'd learn. I guess we could redo it for the colonel to sign like we did Sorenson's. Of course, we'd have to recall Pendleton. That hardly seems worthwhile."

"Colonel B agrees. We all do. It's just not worth it. I guess we tear it up and forget it."

"Works for me." I wondered how long it would take Sean to realize that sterling Air Force record of his remained unblemished. Every now and then it felt good to be a commander.

Not often enough though. I'd been singing "Take this job and shove it," for two years now. My next assignment had finally come through: the Pentagon, not a place I was thrilled about, but at least I wouldn't be in charge there. But before I could leave Europe, I had another job to take on.

# CHAPTER EIGHT

# "ON DEPLOYMENT"

## 1995–1996: HQ Commander for Support, the Netherlands and Croatia

## A. IN THE ARMY NOW

NATO's Armed Forces Central Command (AFCENT) was a three-and-a-half-hour drive from Manderscheid. I lingered over a big breakfast the day I was to report, reluctant to leave home. I thought wistfully of walking through the crisp leaves covering the forest floors around us; of climbing down the narrow, winding path to the Burgweiher, the "tears of the castle," two ponds that nestled inside a bowl of hills; of lazy weekend afternoons reading and napping in my easy chair.

"It's only thirty days," Lynn said when he kissed me goodbye. I pretended to believe it. Col Boston's reaction had been, "Thirty days? Holland? This reeks of Yugoslavia. I won't expect to see you for six months, Cheryl. Not once NATO gets hold of you."

It was after two when I got to Headquarters AFCENT. Light poured into its empty, silent hallways from glass doors and windows. When I found the room number I needed, the door wouldn't respond to my push. A number pad next to it was the obvious means of entry for those who knew the code. I found a buzzer and pressed it. The door opened so suddenly I was startled. A man, whose uniform and accent I couldn't place, said, "Yes?"

I handed him my orders.

"Ah, yes. Welcome to the Vault. Come in, Major."

Noise assaulted me as soon as I stepped inside. The Vault was a huge room but packed full of desks and people, most of them on phones or in pocket-sized meetings. Almost everyone was talking. There were no windows, and overhead fluorescent lights cast an unearthly glare. Besides U.S. uniforms—mainly Army—there was a sprinkling of foreign officers I would later learn to be Dutch, British, French, Canadian, and German. Everyone wore a version of the Battle Dress Uniform (BDU) in forest camouflage. I didn't see another U.S. Air Force person there. Inside me, someone began screaming, *Get me out of here! I don't belong!*

My escort led me through a maze of desks to a small office in the corner where I met my new boss, a U.S. Army colonel. "Welcome to C-Support," he said.

Commander for Support (C-SPT) was an ad hoc command set up to provide logistical direction and assistance to NATO participants if the warring parties in the former Yugoslavia could come to a peace agreement. NATO would then take over for the beleaguered UN forces and send its own troops in. C-SPT had 250 authorized positions; I was only its 33rd member to show up. Now that peace loomed, we needed to grow. I was the C-1, in charge of Personnel, so getting NATO nations to cough up the augmentees they owed us would be my first priority.

Even though I was now in NATO, it felt more like the U.S. Army to me. They had the lead here, all the way from the two-star general who commanded our mission to a handful of NCOs. This was the closest I'd ever been to so many Army folks, the first time to be immersed in their culture. I thought guiltily of all the Army jokes I'd made or laughed at. They almost certainly had their Air Force jokes too. Instead of reassuring me, that thought dumped a load of anxiety on me. It had been bad enough bearing responsibility for all the women in the service, now I had to be responsible for the whole Air Force too. I vowed I would not provide fodder for another Air Force joke. I broke the vow every day.

It didn't start out too well. Battle dress seemed to be *de rigeur* even though we worked behind desks in an office. When I showed up the next morning in my BDUs, one of the Army colonels stared at me for a moment, then yelled, "Snakes!"

"Uh, what, sir?" I asked.

"Snakes," he repeated and pointed to my boots. "Your laces. They drag like snakes. Cynthia, take her away and teach her to tie her boot laces properly. Jeez!" He walked away shaking his head, murmuring something to himself. Cynthia, an Army major, stared down at my boots.

I'd tied my laces sensibly, the Air Force and incidentally the civilian way: threaded through the eyelets, tied in a bow at the top. Cynthia showed me how to wind the long laces around the top of the boots and knot them so no straggly ends showed or got caught in something or unraveled. For good measure, she showed me how to roll up my sleeves the Army way and advised me to have the cleaners use medium starch on the uniform so it would hold up crisply for two or three wearings. Starch on BDUs seemed absurd, but I was in the Army now.

We were billeted in a hotel in downtown Heerlen but spent little time there. Our hours began at eight o'clock, which seemed late to me, but most of us worked a solid twelve hours, five days a week—frequently longer. Our commander figured we were in this mess for the long haul, so he closed the organization down on Saturdays. On Sundays, we didn't start till one o'clock, a nod to the church-goers. Those weekends kept me sane. After work every Friday, I rushed to the hotel to find Lynn and Maisie waiting for me. I was the envy of the other Americans there, most of whom were based stateside.

During the week, the officers in charge of the other functions besieged me with their needs. "I have to have an explosives expert here ASAP." "We've been hurting for an admin troop for weeks."

"The Norwegians promised us a plans officer." I spent my days calling Personnel functions all over Europe, nagging them to send us augmentees. One by one, they started to arrive, a Turkish captain, a Scottish group commander, a Danish NCO, each greeted with joy and put right to work.

As Thanksgiving approached, the general announced that C-SPT would close three days for the holiday. At that point we were holding our breaths to see what would come out of Dayton. If the peace accords were signed, we'd move down to Zagreb, and I'd be in for the whole 179 days TDYs were limited to. If not, we'd pack up and go home.

The evening before Thanksgiving, I was flying back to Holland from Naples. I'd been there at NATO's AFSOUTH headquarters working on a panel standardizing Personnel policies. I'd planned to drive directly to Manderscheid for the holiday but as we approached the runway, a flight attendant walked down the aisle, calling, "Major Dietrich. Major Dietrich."

Hearing your name paged on an airplane is not a great sensation. My imagination flipped through images of gruesome accidents. When I unfolded the paper the attendant handed me, it said simply, "Call your office as soon as you arrive at the airport," not a message designed to relieve anxiety. It was almost eight when I found a pay phone at the airport and dialed the C-SPT number. An unfamiliar voice came on, the accent obviously English, but so heavy I could barely understand it. After a few, "What?" "Say that again," and "Huh?" interjections on my part, I finally worked out that the peace accords had been signed, leave had been canceled, and I was to drive back to Heerlen for instructions. The next morning we would fly down to Zagreb.

"We? I'm sorry, but who are you?" I asked.

Through his accented mumble, I made out, "I'm Chris, mum, your new assistant."

The colonels were already in Zagreb negotiating with the UN for their property and equipment. Chris and I were to snap up military personnel already in place to help fill out our headquarters. I was relieved to hear this was a three-day trip, not the big move—yet.

Chris was a chief petty officer in the Royal Navy, due to retire after this tour. We got along great, despite his accent which was virtually incomprehensible. A typical exchange went like this:

Chris: Mumblemumblemumble . . . mumblemumblemumble.

Me: Uh, yeah, okay, fine.

Chris: You didn't understand a word I said, did you? (Words he spoke perfectly.)

Ten days after Thanksgiving, C-SPT officially established headquarters in Zagreb, temporarily leaving a five-person crew in the Vault to close out accounts with AFCENT, turn equipment back in, and serve as a staging point for new arrivals. I was in charge of that small contingent, so I avoided the big move for a few weeks.

The work got even harder in the Vault, as augmentees started flowing in. I was exhausted, working eight a.m. to midnight many days. I kept the general's weekend schedule, though; weekends with Lynn provided my frantic life a dose of normality. I had a U.S. Army major working with me, a good-natured, bullshit artist, who liked to quote from "The Wind Beneath My Wings." There were also three enlisted members: a gruff, hardworking U.S. Army staff sergeant; a sharp young U.S. Air Force buck sergeant; and a lackadaisical Dutch corporal, who argued every direction he was given and demanded to be paid for overtime, expecting me to follow Dutch Army union rules.

My reply was always "So? Keep track of your hours and send your Army a bill."

In mid-December, seventeen red-eyed, drooping Canadians stood before me in the Vault. They'd flown in overnight on mil-air, not a trip particularly conducive to sleep. I was prepared with plenty of hot coffee. "We've got a plane scheduled to forward you folks down to Zagreb tomorrow, but first I've got a short briefing on C-Support to give you, then we'll take you to the hotel where you can rest till tomorrow morning. Everyone, that is, except, uh, who's . . ." I hunted down my listing again looking for the name, "Captain Levasseur?"

"I am, ma'am." A slender young woman stepped forward tentatively, her eyes wary, her stance saying: *Please don't send me home; let me take part in the adventure.*

I smiled at her. "You'll be working for me, Captain. I'm going to keep you here a few days to train you, then send you to Zagreb early next week." So I got my second Chris working for me, one Christopher, one Christine. A French Canadian, she was impressively adept in both French and English and a fast study. She gobbled up the information I gave her, digested it thoroughly, and was immediately ready to use it. In two days, she'd learned what had taken me weeks to figure my way through.

Late Friday night, snuggled in bed with Lynn, Maisie snoring on her mat on the floor, I got a call from Christine. "Ma'am, I'm sorry it's so late. It's just, well, this friend of mine called and said he can get a quick flight to Paris this weekend if I could meet him there. And oh, ma'am—Paris! I know it's a lot to ask. But I've never seen Paris. I've looked up the train schedule and everything, and it's so close. I can be back in the office first thing Monday morning. Could you—? I mean, can I—? I mean—Paris!"

This was insane. She was, in C-SPT's reckoning, not a person but a personnel resource, and I was the one responsible for that valuable resource. She might oversleep and miss her train, get hurt in Paris, just decide to stay a few extra days, elope with the boyfriend. How well did I know her after all? But—Paris! I gave her my approval, even as I thought, *I'm such a wuss!*

Lynn asked sleepily what was up. I told him about the call. "I said she could go."

"Well, of course," he mumbled into his pillow. "It would be a crime not to see Paris." His judgment, always so sound, reassured me, and I went back to sleep.

Of course I still worried incessantly until Monday morning, when Christine showed up nice and early, her face aglow, bubbling with the excitement of her weekend. "Thank you so much, Major D. It—Oh! Do you mind my calling you that? I don't mean it disrespectfully."

"I like it," I said. "It's what my folks always call me." *My folks— hey, I have folks now!*

New Year's Eve, Lynn and I sat on the window sill of my third-story hotel room, drinking champagne and watching fireworks go off all over the city. Maisie cowered under the bed, but we lured her out with a treat when things eventually settled down.

"This is cozy," Lynn said, as we crawled into bed. "Wish you never had to go back to work, that we could start the new year off slowly. Lazily."

"Well, you have to go to work too." I lay quietly for awhile, not sure how to tell him. Blurt it out, that was the only way. "We're closing shop here this week, leaving for Croatia on Friday."

Lynn turned away to stare at a few Johnny-come-lately sparks out the window. I wanted to cry but was afraid if I started, I couldn't stop.

The Vault was virtually bare. Two desks and three phones remained, a fax machine and five metal chairs. The Army sergeant eschewed hers, and sat cross-legged on the floor with one of the phones. They'd been ringing all morning with questions from contributing nations, from C-SPT officers down south, from bewildered augmentees. I'd come to work early, and by late morning I was beginning to fade. When the phones finally stopped their shrill ring for a moment, I jumped up, grabbed my cigarettes. "Going for a smoke," I announced. My voice echoed in the emptiness.

A spot was set up at the end of the hallway for smokers, which meant me, those festive weeks around the holidays, when NATO virtually shut down. If I hadn't already had the smoking habit, I might have developed it just to have those occasional, quiet breaks. It wasn't quiet for long though. The Army major came bustling out of the Vault to join me. He bummed a cigarette—as Chris liked to say about himself, Don had "never developed the nasty habit of *buying* cigarettes."

For awhile we smoked in silence. "So, Cheryl," Don said finally, "you okay?"

I was surprised at the question. As far as I could see everything, including me, was normal. "Yeah. Sure. I'm really tired, got here early, but that's all. Why?"

"You just seem, I don't know, a little absent, as if your thoughts were far away."

"No, no, I—" Then it hit me, a fact I'd not consciously thought of for hours. "Oh, my father died. My brother called me this morning to tell me."

Don almost fell through the glass doors and onto the icy sidewalk outside. "What! I mean, why are you here? Shouldn't you be on a plane, heading for home or something?"

The thought hadn't even occurred to me. "Nah. I barely knew the man, hadn't seen him in years." I put my cigarette out. "Come on. Time to hit it. Lots more work to do."

"Did you ever know that you're my hero?"

The phone had rung about four that morning. It was my brother David. We were close but not known for making overseas phone calls just to say, "hey."

"What's wrong?" I said immediately.

"Nick died."

"What! What happened?"

It had been about a week ago. He'd walked out to the mailbox, then keeled over with something, maybe a heart attack. It was pretty much instantaneous. David and I spent a few minutes arguing over how old we thought he was, finally settling on seventy-two-ish.

"Joe and I went to the funeral. The family there kept asking where you were, why you didn't come. I told them you were overseas with the Army—"

"Air Force."

"Right. Anyway, we saw all the old family again, Wilma and Pam and Junior and—oh, hey, we saw Kevin. Had a good long talk. He seems like a really neat guy."

"Kevin!" I'd forgotten I had another brother. He'd just been a red-headed baby the only time I saw him. Nick, our mutual parent, had been a serial monogamist, selecting his next wife before he divorced the current one. We never knew how often he'd been married but had counted up to at least six wives. David, Joe, and I had the distinction of springing from his first and longest marriage in the dewy days of youthful love, when life would have been full of promises—the least likely of which Nick had chosen to believe in.

I'd been nine when he and Mom separated. I woke up late one night hearing them quarreling in the living room, the words too distant to understand, but the tone unmistakable. This fight sounded like sorrow as well as fury, a finality in the voices I'd not heard in previous quarrels. I crouched in the dark hallway, listening. When one of them said, "So I guess this is it," I burst into the room, dramatically, like a kid in a movie I'd seen. "Daddy, don't go!" But he did.

The first couple of years he stayed unreliably in touch with his kids. He'd often make plans to pick us up, then never show. His excuse was a charmingly frank, "Kids, you know I keep promises as well as pigs can fly." Then he became more reliable at disappearing altogether. He gambled away a respectable law practice and spent the rest of his life as a traveling salesman, using his charm to pitch products, straying south in the winter to follow the horse races. I used to say he was like a seven-year locust because he could be counted on to show up only once every seven years. Even seven years became too frequent for Nick. I was in seminary the last time I'd seen him.

David described the funeral service. "We were amazed at how many people were there and how many got up to tell about Nick helping them out some way or another. Joe and I kept looking at one another like, *Huh? Is this the same Nick we knew?"*

"He was a nice man," I said. I could be objective. "He just didn't like responsibility." That was what we meant to him. He'd loved us but didn't want to be saddled with us.

"Here's the real kicker," David said. "You're going to love this. Of course he didn't have a pot to piss in, so everyone seemed to think *we* would pay for the funeral expenses. You, me, Joe, and Kevin. We told them no way, but hey, I can't speak for you." I laughed. We began to joke and moved onto other subjects, just chatting for half an hour. After we hung up, I sat in bed smoking and thinking about Nick, whose death didn't touch me, and about my other two parents, whose deaths still left me bereft.

There is a picture of my mother seared into my memory. While I was still the wing commander's exec at Ramstein, Lynn had gone to Florida for a few weeks to visit Cathy. They drove across the state to visit my parents on the Gulf Coast. Of the photos he took that trip, there was one of Bob, Cathy, and toddler Stanzi, with Mom in the foreground staring into the camera, not smiling. Her eyes, red-rimmed and large, ate up the image with longing. Her face was thin and gray, her lips slightly parted as if she was trying to tell me something.

"She thinks she has cancer," Lynn said.

"Does she?"

"Her doctor says no."

"Well, then. The doctor must know." But he had not. By the time he discovered the mass of malignity in her colon, the cancer had already metastasized to her liver.

I took leave while she was still healthy enough to go shopping, to lunch, to a movie. The film she wanted to see was *Fried Green Tomatoes*. We hadn't expected one of the characters to die young of cancer. We both cried; the tears we couldn't shed for one another, we released for a movie character. We shopped. I bought her a scented body cream she admired, all the while she complained about the cost. "Fifty dollars for a jar of moisturizing cream!"

Five months later, when Mom slipped into her final coma, Lynn and I flew back to Florida on emergency leave. The earliest flight we could get was military air, on a huge C-5 Galaxy whose engines roared through the cabin the whole ten-hour trip. It had no windows, only dim lights, beneath which I tried to distract myself by reading *The Mill on the Floss*. We were in the back row across from the only latrine, which stank after a couple of hours. Its door wouldn't latch from the outside, so it swung and banged constantly. A hellish flight with my mother's death accompanying us silently throughout.

Mom lay in a hospital bed set up in the living room, surrounded by our bustle, the presence we hoped she could sense. A hospice nurse instructed me to keep her lips moist with ice. "And every now and then," she said, "rub her hands with this stuff. She seems to like it. She smiles when you do it." She handed me the jar of scented cream.

Mom died the next day, as Bob, Lynn, my stepsister Joni, and I held her and one another's hands. "Talk to her, Cheryl," Bob said, his voice hoarse. So I murmured over and over, "It's okay, Mom. You can let go." What I wanted to say was, "Don't leave me."

My real father, in the truest sense, was my stepfather Bob. For his first date with Mom, he included me and my brothers in an invitation to the Cincinnati Zoo. He carried a slide rule in his shirt pocket and showed me how to use it. He took us by his house later that day to see the caiman that lived in a tub under the piano. We sang as he drove us back.

Where was Nick when I came home dejected the afternoon of my senior prom? Not in my life by then. I'd had a fun day out of school, one of a dozen girls decorating a hotel ballroom for the prom. The other girls had been so tactfully silent all day about their dresses and dates, it didn't really hit me until we finished: I was the only girl there who had no need to rush home to bathe and primp for the most exciting night in a normal girl's high school life. I maintained my stoic smile until I got home. I resolved to spend my dateless evening dissolved in tears, locked in my room, immersed in as much misery as a teenage girl could call up—which in my case was quite a lot.

Then Bob called from work and asked me out. The stepfather/stepchild relationship still being a delicate one, I didn't feel I could hang up on him like I wanted to.

"Oh, won't that be fun," Mom had chirped, as if she'd had nothing to do with it. Her, I scowled at, and I'm sure I came up with some sarcastic remark. But she ignored me and made me dress up. Bob took me downtown to an expensive, elegant restaurant. We talked, but not about the prom. He asked me about things I was interested in, the most solicitous of dates. It was a wonderful evening, just me and my dad.

He died of a stroke two years after Mom. Again, Lynn, Joni, and I were at his bedside, holding his hands. I was forty-three, married, independent. Yet with Bob's passing, I felt like an orphan.

When the black night outside my hotel window had lightened to a dark gray, I put out my cigarette and swung my legs out of bed. *Too late for any more sleep. Might as well get ready and head out to the Vault early.* I got in the shower. Standing under the clarifying stream of water, something else David said came back to me.

"Aunt Wilma asked me about a little horse Nick had in his belongings. You know he didn't have much because he moved around a lot, mainly living out of a suitcase. But she said he had this bronze horse figurine for ages that he always kept with him, wherever he moved. She wondered if I knew where it came from. I told her no. Do you?"

Still half asleep at the time, processing the news he'd brought, I'd said automatically, "No idea." The conversation moved on, and with it, the little horse. But as the shower spray rinsed off the last vestiges of sleep, I remembered. Like many little girls, I had loved horses. I collected them, all sizes and colors and materials. That night long ago, when I burst into the living room, flinging my arms around Nick, sobbing "Daddy, don't go," he had gently rubbed my back and soothed me by saying things like, "I have to go. But I'll see you a lot. I'll always be your daddy."

"Just a minute. Don't leave yet." I'd rushed back to my room to grab my favorite horse, a sturdy bronze piece about six inches high, hollowed out for use as a bank. I took it to him. "Keep this to remember me by." (Definitely channeling some kid in a movie.)

"Wouldn't you guess it," he said. "A racehorse!" He laughed as he turned it over in his hands, a harsh burst of sound that I realized only many years later meant he was hurting. At the time though, I felt foolish, and I pulled away from him.

But he'd kept my horse all those years, the only thing he kept. I found this very touching and stood quietly under the shower, giving myself permission to cry, waiting for sobs and tears. But what came was just a sense of pity for him. He'd carted around a little horse bank wherever he went, when he could have had his children instead.

Later that day, the colonel called me from Zagreb. "Cheryl, you okay? Don told me about your father. We're all sorry to hear about it. Do you need to take emergency leave to go home?"

I assured him I was fine. And truly I was—the only part of this story that makes me sad.

## B. THE STREETCARS OF ZAGREB

It was still dark. I stepped carefully down the icy sidewalk to the shuttle bus waiting at the corner. It already looked full to me, packed with sleepy people in variations of heavy BDU jackets. As I searched for a seat, I heard a voice from the back, an Army lieutenant colonel I'd known in Holland yelling, "It's the Cee-One! We finally have our Cee-One!" The bus burst into cheers and applause. I felt like an award winner making my way past the seats, hands reaching out to shake or slap mine. That first morning in frozen Zagreb started with a warm welcome. I was back among the fold.

A few days after I arrived, C-SPT finalized the deal they'd been working with the local transportation officials, and we were able to ride for free on the local streetcars. No more warm, friendly shuttle, just the clanking streetcars swaying down the avenues.

As with any old city, Zagreb's streets were incapable of moving the traffic of the 1990s, so cars and trucks idled constantly within the town center. The electric streetcars, the most efficient system of transportation here, became the chain that linked the two locations that made up my world now—the hotel where I slept and the office where I worked. Electrically powered and running on their own tracks, the trams buzzed right past the stalled city traffic. Their few seats faced forward in single file along the sides of the car. Most people stood crammed in the middle of the aisle, swaying with the curves while clinging to plastic straps hanging from the ceiling.

The Croats were used to seeing foreign military uniforms around the city and generally ignored us on the trams. We must have all looked alike in our combat boots and camouflage uniforms. They probably didn't distinguish minor differences in colors and rank designations. The important thing was we did not wear the blue berets of the UN, which was hated throughout the country. Our identifying feature was the NATO badge we wore; it said IFOR in both the Latin and Cyrillic alphabets.

IFOR stood for Implementation Force. NATO had benefitted from the lesson the UN painfully learned, that it's impossible to "keep" a peace that doesn't exist. We therefore were in the business of "implementing" it. Success was guaranteed by thousands of well-armed troops backed by the political determination of the Western powers. In C-SPT, we were not armed and had no need to be. We worked in an office building in a Croatian Army compound in the city. NATO was paying to renovate the building, which had been a boarded-up shell before we moved in. At first we worked at rickety, borrowed desks, sneezing from the sawdust generated by the ongoing renovation projects. We conducted business holding the receivers of antiquated telephones tight to one ear while blocking the other ear against the noise of pounding hammers and the high-pitched whine of electric saws. Add to that the ever-increasing international staff jammed into the finished offices and the place was as noisy as the Vault had been in its heyday.

Nevertheless, this dusty, noisy building was a haven compared to the oppressive, sullen silence that dominated the bleak city streets. In here, we were alive—laughing, arguing, shouting above the din of the constant construction. C-SPT echoed with the constant jabbering of accented English. While two-thirds of the military there were native English speakers, even among these, accents ranged from soft, lilting Welsh to crisp, professional Army British to the French tinge of Quebecois like Christine. We Yanks, the largest national group, added our mix of southern drawls, Brooklynese, and midwestern twangs into the lingual stew. "I didn't understand you. Say it again," peppered our staff meetings.

That early January of 1996, white Christmas lights still decorated the city center, but their brightness did little to lighten the dismal street corners. Tawdry booths dotted the pedestrian walkways leading to the Hotel Dubrovnik, which I was to call home for the next four months. They sold the favorite seasonal fare of European marketplaces—grilled sausages hinting of paprika, sugared almonds, hot mulled wine. But the smells, which should have been cheering, were slightly off, as if the food and drink they broadcast had been prepared days before and were being kept warm just in case a customer should appear. I seldom saw anyone stop at these isolated stalls, whose proprietors stood stiffly behind scarred wooden counters, unsmiling, like crudely carved nutcrackers. The stalls, a ghoulish travesty of the bustling Christmas markets in Germany, taunted me.

In its winter dress, Zagreb was plain and treacherous. Snowfall arrived like clockwork every day at midmorning, its cleansing, white cold providing a brief relief in the January gloom. Too soon though, traffic and pollution dirtied the new snow. It lay piled along the roadside, charcoal-gray and oily to the touch, the pavement always slick with ice.

That dreary winter, Zagreb looked like the shell-shocked remnant of the Austro-Hungarian Empire that it was, a poor man's Vienna. Its past glory had barely survived in Yugoslavia, the slumgullion cooked up by the victors of World War I. Years of Nazi occupation, communism, then civil war had destroyed whatever charm the city must have had. Its stately buildings, once painted a proud Hapsburg yellow, had degenerated into putrid khaki, like a molding dijon mustard. Their white trim was now gray and peeling. Chunks of plaster, gouged out by time and shrapnel, still littered the ground surrounding the once majestic palaces. Any beauty it had left was lost on me.

Bleak Zagreb became the daily reminder of all I didn't have: Lynn, Maisie, home, my comfortable routines, my sense of self. I began to lose Cheryl somewhere in the dirty snowdrifts, in the chill cold of an angry, wounded city.

The work continued to be exhausting, even though I now had a full staff, not just the two Chrises, but Frank, a U.S. Army master sergeant, and Nia, an airman from the RAF. We made a great team. British Chris established our office's enviable phone greeting: "Ceeeeeeeee-One! First Chairborne!" The latter part was added partially to tease Frank, who took his red beret and membership in the 81st Airborne unit very seriously. But Frank soon became proud of the "chairborne" designation also and spoke it with the gusto it demanded.

Besides the continual struggle to bring augmentees in, C-1 had daily manning reports to submit, accounting for all the NATO troops in the former Yugoslavian nations. We had evaluations and decorations and all the other Personnel processes to enforce and monitor for the members of fourteen different nations and four different services that made up our headquarters. We had civilian hiring and management. We had manpower functions, deleting, adding, changing slot requirements. Gradually, however, the hours started to lessen, the pace to slow down. We could almost count on an eleven-hour workday, which seemed glorious luxury after the Vault.

I was at my happiest in the office, but even there, I couldn't entirely escape the city. I was drawn too frequently to the large windows that looked down onto the street below. From there I could see the United Nations compound across the street and the Wall of Shame that bordered it. The wall stood almost three feet tall and extended three sides of the city block the UN inhabited, with just a couple of openings to allow access into the compound. It consisted of red bricks balanced on top of each other, with flowers and the occasional picture tucked into the spaces between them. Croatian families built it brick by brick in grief and anger. Each brick bore a single name scrawled in white paint, the name of a loved one who died in the civil war while UN peacekeepers were in the country. The wall was meant to humiliate the UN, to remind the world of its failure, though no one I saw coming or going across the way seemed to pay it any attention.

The bricks numbered in the thousands, and those were the Croatian fatalities only. Perhaps somewhere Serbs and Bosnians were building their own walls. But I realized early on that the Croats had it wrong. All those names on the wall—the UN hadn't killed them.

I seldom heard Croatian spoken except in the restaurants, where hearty beer and taut-skinned, juicy sausages loosened the silent tongues and gave me a glimpse of a Zagreb I was not welcomed into. I dutifully took the lunchtime language classes offered by one of our translators and learned to say *"hvala"* (thank you) and *"molim"* (please). When I had a day off, I wandered the streets looking for a key to unlock the secrets of this sullen city, maybe searching the self that kept slipping away from me. I used my limited Croatian in shops, restaurants, and cafes but never received so much as a smile in return.

One afternoon I heard a slight noise behind me. At the foot of one of the streetcars, an old woman sprawled, hands still grasping two shopping bags. Curious bystanders stared at her, saying nothing, offering no help. I started toward her but she was already struggling unassisted to her feet. She limped away and disappeared into the crowd. The incident reminded me of a man who had slipped and fallen into the side of a passing streetcar outside our office. He lay bleeding and alone in the road, with passersby surrounding him but doing nothing. It had taken our NATO guys rushing out through the gate to assist him, offer first aid, and move him out of danger.

Dependent on the help of a bunch of foreigners, that seemed the only hope for this region with its sorry history of hatred and genocide, torture, rape, mines, and booby traps. Centuries of conflict and violence in the Balkans had kept the area's three ethnic and religious groups in a perpetual struggle for power and vengeance, periodically exchanging victim, ally, and aggressor roles. Only Tito's leadership had held the warring groups together in one nation. That nation no longer existed, and the best we could do was hold the groups apart.

A friend told me of a Croat he'd gotten into conversation with over a beer. The young man had smilingly confided that he was just waiting for NATO to leave so he could kill some Serbs, any Serbs, because after all, Serbs had killed members of his family. To him, this was a personal feud, not a war fought for political differences that could be resolved by impartial outsiders.

With military members nowadays in never-ending desert deployments, living in tent cities, eating MREs, always under the threat of danger, I know it seems churlish of me to complain about my Zagreb deployment. I lived in a large, comfortable hotel room in the middle of a city. I ate at restaurants. There was a store right next door that had an excellent collection of English language books. If there was danger, actual physical danger, it came mainly from the unexploded ordnance, including mines and booby traps that could still be found in the city. But these had mostly been cleared by the time I arrived.

The danger there was of a different kind. The hatred I sensed infusing the bitter air made its way into my spirit. The icy wind carried its fierce passion, its bite all the worse for being frozen. It was not directed at me, but even so, I returned from my walks carrying it within me, transmuted into despair and depression.

One morning, I studied my face in the mirror, shocked at what I saw: sallow skin with patches of a rough rash; gray semicircles under the eyes; nose raw from the sinus flu I'd been battling for two months. My hair frizzed and drooped waywardly over my head, the result of a bad, last-minute perm I'd received before flying down to Zagreb. Worst of all were the dull, lifeless eyes, opaque as if no light reached beyond their flat surface. The person I saw in the mirror looked like a stranger, one I didn't particularly care to meet. Sighing, I plugged in my curling iron and reached for foundation and makeup sponge. Then I was struck by the absurdity of it. Here I was in my BDUs and boots, getting ready to face another day in this forbidding city—and applying makeup to prettify myself!

I made a decision. All I would be these next few months was a United States airman. That was the only identity I wanted to hold on to in Zagreb. I set down the makeup and unplugged the curling iron. I ignored the earrings I had put out to wear, dragged a comb through my frizz, and pulled on my uniform. That afternoon I took myself to a barber shop where the staff spoke a little German. I told the young woman hovering morosely over me to cut my hair—short! "Kurz?" she repeated to confirm. "Ja, kurz!" I emphasized, removing my glasses. So it was my own fault that when she finished and handed me a mirror, I found myself sporting a haircut just two grades longer than a marine's buzz cut. I couldn't see any trace of myself in that mirror, but that was what I'd wanted after all.

When I got back to the office, none of my staff commented on it, though I noticed them glancing at one another. The general, not so restrained, said, "Whatever got into you, Cheryl?" It was more a matter of what had gotten out of me. I was only a uniform now; there was no Cheryl here in Croatia. She might have gotten lost altogether except for two encounters on the streetcars.

The first was in early March. It was still blustery and cold, but crocuses gleamed in the filthy snow and promised an end to the bleak winter. It was dusk, and I was leaving work with Lewis, a U.S. Army captain also staying at the Hotel Dubrovnik. We clambered aboard a crowded streetcar and pushed our way into the middle.

After several stops, the tram started to clear out a little. That's when I heard from somewhere ahead of us, the distinct but heavily accented words, "New York. Washington. Kennedy. America. Ya-a-ay!" I looked around and spotted an old man sitting two seats up, staring eagerly at us and repeating, "Kennedy. New York. America." I smiled and carefully articulated one of the few phrases I'd learned in Croatian, "*Dobro vece*" (good evening). His face glowed, and he responded, "*Dobro vece*," then began a fast spiel in Croatian. I shook my head and interrupted, carefully sounding out the syllables I had learned for "I don't speak Croatian. Do you speak English?"

The old man grimaced with exaggerated sorrow, jerked his upturned palms into the air, shrugged, and repeated, "New York. Washington. Kennedy. *Ich spreche Deutsch. Sprecht ihr Deutsch?*" Lewis's blank look clearly said, "*Nein*," but I replied that I spoke a little German. The old man sprang from his seat and pushed his way back to us.

He was tiny, thin from the depredations of old age and illness, but he was still a dapper man, neatly dressed in a threadbare suit whose style was popular forty years ago. His face was smoothly shaven, his hair impeccably cut. He had an air of old-fashioned courtliness. He disdained the straps we were clinging to but swayed along to the streetcar's movement with the grace of long experience. His German, while only slightly less elementary than mine, was clearly spoken and well accented. He began eagerly questioning me. How long had we been in Croatia? Did we like it? (I politely lied.) Where were we from? Such a pleasant old gentleman, but when he invited us to have coffee with him, I refused without hesitation. Unfortunately we didn't have the time, I informed him; it just wasn't possible. I didn't tell him the truth—that nothing dwelled inside this uniform but depression. All I wanted was to sit alone in my darkened hotel room, smoking and looking out over the dim lights of the city. The old man repeated his invitation. I again refused.

"What's he saying?" Lewis asked.

"He wants to take us out to coffee."

"Oh!" Interest brightened Lewis's eyes, "That would be wonderful!"

"I told him no, we can't go." The excitement in his face faded. Disappointment struggled with obedience. The soldier won out. He nodded and schooled his face into indifference.

Another stop, and we paused while commuters struggled through the narrow tram doors. Once we were again underway, the old man began a new subject, raising his voice as the streetcar clattered over intersecting tracks, a sign we were nearing the city center.

He asked my rank. "Major," I responded, articulating "maiyor" as the Germans did.

"*Ach, du bist so jung.*" (You are so young.)

"*Nein,*" I said, "*Nein.*" I informed him I was a grandmother, a "*Grossmutter.*" I was surprised when he looked puzzled.

"*Ich verstehe nicht.*" (I don't understand.)

So I repeated a little louder, enunciating a little more clearly, "*Ich bin eine Grossmutter.*" When he still looked puzzled, I switched to the colloquial "Granny." "*Oma. Ich bin eine Oma.*"

Comprehension flooded his face, and with an amused chuckle, he kindly corrected me. "*Ein Grossvater.*" (A grandfather.) "*Du bist ein Grossvater.*"

*"Nein,"* I said firmly, *"Ich bin eine Grossmutter."*

He couldn't help himself. Astonishment overtook that well-schooled courtesy and he blurted out, *"Du bist eine Frau?"* (You are a woman?)

He was so dismayed, I had to take pity on him. I assured him in as kindly a tone as I could manage in German that it was all right, I was not offended. He recovered from his distress and with innate courtesy, apologized charmingly. He blamed his own old eyes for his error and assured me that he thought it was fascinating that I, a woman, had achieved what he insisted on pretending was a high officer rank. In fact, more than ever he wanted to talk with me. Would my companion and I please honor him by taking the time to join him for coffee? Again I refused, making my regrets more elaborate to match the style of his invitation. This time a flicker of relief crossed his face. Lewis and I got off at the next stop, bidding the gallant old man a friendly, *"Dovidjenja"* (See you later—except of course we wouldn't; I had destroyed any possibility of that). Lewis's eyes had skipped curiously back and forth between us during our last exchange, and now he asked one last time, "What did he say?"

"He invited us for coffee again." I wasn't about to tell him the old man thought I was male. I wasn't completely honest with myself, either. I had enjoyed my only real conversation with a Croatian. I thought I would like him if I got to know him. But I couldn't allow this kindly gentleman to give a face to the silent people around me. If I began to pay attention, I might see other old men who'd survived decades of brutal history with humor and geniality intact. I might see mothers shopping for that night's soup, grandmothers steadying toddlers just learning to walk, fathers worrying about their jobs, young couples holding hands. If I started seeing these people and hearing their stories, I might begin to care. Then I would have to bring Cheryl back, and she just seemed like too much trouble.

Spring brought some relief. Rains replaced the daily snow and rapidly washed the filthy snow piles away, flooding the streets and gutters. I began to feel the pull of the early spring air, the sun warming its chill during the daytime. I spent my days off walking in Zagreb's meager Botanical Garden, searching for new growth since my last visit, longing to be on the familiar woodland paths at home in the German Eifel. I had begun to count down to my departure date, forty days, thirty-seven, now thirty—just a month.

In C-SPT, we were not allowed to be out alone in Zagreb after dark. I had obeyed faithfully until the evening I escorted a visiting officer to her hotel. I had counted on being able to meet up with some other NATO officers in order to get back to the Hotel Dubrovnik, but I found no one around. I was weary, so I decided to hop on the streetcar alone for the four stops it would take. The streetcar was virtually empty, but I chose to remain standing next to the exit since I was going such a short distance.

There was no one else in uniform in the car, which made me uneasy. So when a young man sitting near me got up and with insistent gestures indicated I should take his seat, I became tense and watchful. It seemed bizarre for this stranger to demand I take his seat when there were plenty of empty seats all around. But demand he did. My polite refusal was met with an even more determined sweep of his arm toward the seat. Seeing no practical alternative, I muttered *"hvala"* and sat down, trying to seem composed and natural.

Instead of moving to another seat, the young man positioned himself in the aisle and stared down at me. He was dressed in what I thought of as "Euro youth chic"—all in black, tight jeans, T-shirt, leather jacket, a silver stud in his nose, and a silver cross dangling from one ear. His hair was short and dark, his eyes even darker, staring at me with a ravenous intensity. I found his silent scrutiny discomforting. I turned to the window and looked out, trying to ignore him. Every now and then I caught his reflection in the window. Each time he noticed me doing so and responded by moving his hand up to brush his eyebrow, then staring at me even more intensely.

He remained standing over me, unsmiling and stern, until we reached my stop. I was concerned that he might try to block me from getting off or that he might follow me, but he did neither, just stepped aside to let me pass. I nodded in noncommittal acknowledgement and stepped down from the streetcar. Puzzled by the encounter, I couldn't resist turning back to look at him once I was on the pavement. He'd slipped into the seat I'd vacated and was looking out at me. We stared at each other through the window for the few seconds the streetcar lingered at the stop. With obvious deliberation, he again brought his hand up to brush his eyebrow.

His actions clicked into place now. I came to attention and saluted. He didn't smile, but the sternness around his mouth relaxed, the dark eyes softened. He nodded as the streetcar pulled away. I knew what he wanted to say as clearly as if he'd been able to use words I could understand. For the first time in many years, he was living without bombs, mines, booby traps, snipers. He was living safely and doing normal things—like riding a streetcar on a gentle spring evening. For now, he, his parents, his sister and brother, his friends, his girlfriend, they were all living the kind of life I had always taken for granted. To him, my uniform meant security, a world in which he didn't have to be afraid. Just because the peace we provided might not last forever, didn't mean he wasn't grateful today. And the only way he knew how to say thank you was to give up his seat in an empty streetcar and offer an awkward civilian salute.

When I returned his salute, I felt someone stir within my uniform—Cheryl, beginning to make her way back.

On the 179th day of my deployment, I returned home to Manderscheid. When I stepped into the long hallway of our house and flipped on the light, I heard the clink of Maisie's tags coming down the stairs. She turned into the half-flight landing at the end of the hall, saw me and stopped. She didn't bark, didn't move, just stood there as if frozen.

"I'm home, Maisie," I said.

She moved then, fast, into the air and down to the hall floor without touching the steps. She ran to me and flung herself, all thirty-five pounds, into my arms. Like the young man in Croatia, she couldn't tell me what she was thinking, but I understood her just the same. The look in her eyes, her body all a-wiggle with joy told a story. To her, I'd been dead. Now I was alive again. Resurrection. A miracle.

# CHAPTER NINE

# "FROM THE TOP"

### 1996–2000: the Pentagon, Washington, DC

## A. THE PUZZLE PALACE

The Pentagon would be my final assignment. I was not a volunteer. Like any sensible officer, I'd resisted the "Puzzle Palace" as long as I could. My first day there, after I showed my ID card and orders to a guard at the entrance, I passed through its dreaded portals, feeling as if a large sign above them should read, *Abandon Hope.*

I found myself in a brightly lit concourse, a lively place full of shops—bookstore, beauty salon, pharmacy, bank, bakery, and more. People scurried through the broad hallway and up gently sloped ramps into the heart of the building. I saw the uniforms of every military branch, plus some from foreign militaries, and the conservative suits and jackets of government civilian employees. A blonde major rushed breathlessly down one of the ramps toward me.

"Cheryl!" she said. We'd met briefly once before. I smiled and greeted her, pretended not to be scared to death. She led me up a ramp, along the corridors, through hallways, up stairways. I was lost, but by the time she delivered me to my new office on the fifth floor, I was halfway to falling in love with the building.

The Pentagon was once the world's largest office building, built to meet the contingencies of World War II, able to double as a hospital if needed. Roosevelt wanted no looming skyscraper with banks of elevators blocking the view of the capital, so George Bergstrom designed it as a pentagon to create a large but low building that fit the rough shape of the property it was to be erected on. When the location changed, neither time nor money was available for a redesign.

Seventeen miles of corridors extend through five floors plus two underground levels, in a structure with five angles and five sides. Each floor contains five concentric pentagons nested inside one another. The largest, known as the E-Ring, runs along the outside perimeter and has great views of the Potomac, the Washington Monument, the Kennedy Center, the skyscrapers of Rosslyn. Here, the biggest of the bigwigs have large office suites (modest by private company standards)—the generals and chiefs of staff, the service secretaries, the secretary of defense.

From the angles of the five concentric pentagons, corridors wide as highways lead directly from the E-Ring office suites, through ever-decreasing rings D, C, B, to the smallest, A-Ring, dividing the building into wedges. Equidistant between the large corridors, five narrower halls cut across the rings also. Diagrammed it resembles a spider's web. They say you can walk between any two points in seven minutes or less. This is true. As soon as I figured out the obvious tricks (like using the smallest pentagon, A-Ring, to find your corridor) and learned which inner hallways didn't go all the way through, I could make my way anywhere easily within seven minutes. I know because I used to time myself.

I am still in awe of the brilliance of this design, its practical use of basic geometry. I'm amazed that no one else has picked up on its elegant practicality, that the American landscape isn't dotted with pentagons. What entrances me most is the symmetry of the building, the beautiful, logical order of its design, those multiples of five like mystic symbols of power. Built in little more than a year, the groundbreaking took place September 11, 1941, fifty-five years before I arrived and sixty years to the day before American Airlines Flight 77 crashed into it.

At the center of the nesting dolls of pentagons was an open-air, pentagonal (of course) courtyard, a pleasant park with giant magnolias that flanked the broad stone stairs leading down into it from A-Ring. There were park benches to relax on and large communal ashtrays. In the middle, an enclosed building housed a snack bar in warm weather. Rectangular, breaking the five-sided pattern, it sat like a cheerful, innocuous spider in the middle of the web.

Informally, we referred to the courtyard as "Ground Zero." It got its nickname supposedly because of a visit by Russian dignitaries after the USSR collapsed and the Cold War ended. When they were given a tour of the building and led into this inner courtyard, they discovered an area buzzing with uniformed and civilian personnel on breaks, smoking, relaxing on park benches, eating cones of gelato from a vendor's cart. Smells coming from the small building at the center would have been hamburgers and hot dogs on the grill. The Russians said something among themselves and laughed, then politely explained that they had been able to see the small building at the very center of the Pentagon from satellite photographs.

"But we did not know its function. We believed it was the heart of the war planning, where the most important people gathered to conduct war. So for years we aimed missiles precisely to take out this building. And now we find that all this time, we targeted a snack bar!"

The Americans laughed too. Everything about the Cold War seemed funny then, laughter springing from the relief of victory. The Evil Empire had imploded, and onetime enemies proved to be friendly fellows you could share a joke with. So the center courtyard became known as Ground Zero. At least that's the story I heard.

At that time, over twenty thousand people worked there, enough to populate a good-sized town. For the hoi polloi—of which I was one—office space consisted of a desk, a chair, a partition. In that first office, I was lucky enough to sit next to a grimy window looking down four floors to an alley that ran between C- and D-Rings. Not much of a view but it brought with it the blessing of natural light. It was in the wedge a plane would fly into five years later.

I worked Officer Plans in a small branch in the Headquarters Air Force Directorate of Personnel (DP). We dealt primarily with force structure, sculpting the active duty force—its size, its skill breakdown, its grade structure. We were still working on the 40 percent reduction Congress had mandated as the "peace dividend" after the Cold War. Fortunately, the most brutal cuts, requiring involuntary reductions-in-force of captains, had been taken already on the officer side. Now we primarily developed proposals to meet yearly strength requirements by enticing targeted groups with juicy early retirements and separation incentives. That is, until the day a civilian from the Force Structure office came rushing into a planning meeting with the unexpected news that we were now losing strength, hemorrhaging officers. Then DP coolly shifted gears and started working on retention programs.

Sounds dull, I know, though it wasn't boring for me at all. In fact, I loved the work. Mainly I loved the change: sitting in an office, writing papers and staff reports; responsible only for my own work; no people to counsel, no disciplinary actions to take, no one else's problems to solve. Dealing with personnel as numbers to be counted, grouped, and manipulated was refreshing after years of real people with all their problems. I was born to be a policy wonk.

Lynn's job had been moved to his agency's head office in nearby Rosslyn. Each morning around seven fifteen, he dropped me off a block from the Pentagon on his way to work. In those days, I could walk directly up to a side stairway, flash my badge at a bored civilian security officer, and be right in the concourse of the building, mingling with all the uniforms and suits as I made my way up the wide ramps and the stairs to the fifth floor. In the evenings I called him when I was ready to go, then walked outside and positioned myself on a corner where he barely needed to slow down to pick me up. It was a routine we got used to quickly and comfortably.

What I liked most about the Pentagon was that I finally had peers. Other women of my own rank and specialty worked in AF/DP. For the first time since Carswell, I began making friends, became one of a *Sex in the City*-type group of four women—except we talked more about work and less about sex. Eventually, we dubbed ourselves the Pentagang, our husbands honorary members. I thought of myself as Miranda, with a caustic wit and a load of insecurities.

Tina was our Charlotte, though petite and blonde rather than tall and brunette, a size zero. I'd had no idea such a size existed. I couldn't hate her for it, not even while I was struggling to fit into my size sixteen uniform pants before finally giving in and moving to a size eighteen. I could see that being so tiny could be a handicap in a culture as masculine as the military. No one ever made the mistake of underestimating Tina twice though. She was tough. I was a marshmallow compared to her (not just bodily).

When we first met, she was married to a pilot. After we'd been there a couple of weeks, Tina invited us to dinner. She and I talked about Villeroy and Boch china in the kitchen, while the men grilled salmon filets outside. Her husband barely spoke all evening, but Tina was cheerful and welcoming enough for both. After we left, he told her he wanted a divorce.

I didn't know Tina as well then as I would eventually, but I could tell the news had come to her as a shock. She was such a straightforward person herself that whatever she thought, she said; whatever she said, she meant. She took other people at face value. She had no understanding of secrecy and furtiveness. There must have been hints that something was wrong, but a person as open as Tina was incapable of reading them.

Not that she wasn't capable of subtlety. I bought a barely used exercise bike from her, as she prepared to move into a smaller townhouse. "You sure you don't want this?" I asked, wondering at the prime condition of the bike she was offering me at a fraction of its worth. "At least let me pay you what it's worth."

She smiled. "Oh, no. It's scummy hubby's. He asked me to sell some of his stuff for him while I was at it. So I am—*cheap*."

I bought the bike, took it home, set it up in front of the TV, and thought about exercising.

She'd been married so long that at first being single felt awkward. She didn't have a clue how attractive she was. As the word of her availability got out, the attentions she received from single men astonished her. "I was a plain Jane in high school," she said (which I doubted). "I barely even dated. I'm not used to this." But she learned to enjoy it. By spring, she was juggling dates. "Is it all right to go out for the afternoon with John, then have an evening date with Terry?" She worried about the rules. She read *The Rules*.

I luxuriated in Tina's stories and got a vicarious kick out of the flowers she occasionally received. "Who's it from?" I'd ask, because there were so many guys I could never be quite sure. Nor could she, till she'd read the card. Monday mornings began with my eager questions about her weekend—where she'd been, with whom, what she'd done? Even the boss hung around to get the newest installment of her adventures.

She rediscovered herself as a vibrant, sexy woman, and the confidence she'd always had on the job imbued her social life too. The Pentagon was a natural mating ground for her with plenty of men of equal or higher rank, almost all in top physical shape. One day the two of us came up from the food court, steaming lattes in hand. I was teasing her about a marine who'd kept staring at her. The boss joined in. "Haven't tapped the Marine Corps yet, have you?"

He was a clean-cut guy, a lieutenant colonel well on his way to the three stars he wears today. I felt sure he hadn't intended the double entendre. But when I started laughing, red began to spread across his face. Tina didn't seem to notice. She was modest, never one to take attention for granted. "Oh, I don't know that he was all that interested. Well, he did kind of look over our way a lot, didn't he?"

I pursed my lips and said in my most judicious voice, "Of course, we don't know who he was looking at." I thrust my chin and boobs up and out and stood, arms akimbo. "Perhaps his tastes run more toward the Rubenesque." The boss almost doubled over laughing. I pulled myself up, where I could literally look down on him, and said, "And what, sir, is so funny?"

"Oh nothing, nothing." I began laughing, but he found an excuse to scurry away.

Sue in the office next door was our Samantha as far as strength and confidence went. Sue was a slug—but not the kind I'd known at Spangdahlem.

As far as I know, the Washington, DC area is the only place in the country with "slugging" an authorized form of commuting. Because of congestion in the area, the interstates all have High Occupancy Vehicle lanes during rush hours; the largest even has a minimum of a three-person requirement. HOV lanes encourage car pools, but intense jobs make it difficult to keep regular hours. So slugging grew out of necessity, a formalized version of hitchhiking with parking lots set up off ramps along I-95 in Northern Virginia. Slugs were the extra bodies that enabled a driver to use the faster HOV lanes to get to the Pentagon or into the District. There were unwritten but widely known rules of conduct and etiquette, which enabled the informal system to work. You didn't jump line. You rode with whoever stopped next. The driver accepted whoever was next in line. The driver regulated heat, radio, and conversation. If the driver wanted to talk, the slug talked. If the driver was silent, the slug was silent.

There was a slugging station right outside the Pentagon. In the evenings, cars would pull in and the drivers would call out the number of passengers they could take. It was an efficient, orderly system, all these people in suits and uniforms, like Sue, hitching rides.

Sue got me into an exercise routine. Two or three days a week, we spent our lunch hours walking. There is no better place than Northern Virginia for walking, with paths everywhere. Most of the time, our walks took us along the Potomac or up into Arlington Cemetery, where we confided in one another. I even told her about my shameful stint on Weight Management. Sometimes we'd take the bridge into the District, circle around the side of the Lincoln Memorial, the reflecting pool, and back to the other side. We'd take extra time during cherry blossom season and slow our pace to wander under the pink and white canopy of blossoms along the Tidal Basin. I never stopped admiring the beauty of it all. It astounded me that what people took special vacations to see and do, was mine every day for the minimal effort of stepping outside my office.

When I'd been at the Pentagon only a month, I was already considered a seasoned pro, at least enough to orient a new major to the building, to the offices where she needed to check in, the people she needed to meet. As we wandered from place to place, me proudly showing her the tricks of getting around, we chatted politely, two female Air Force officers coming in from the field to push paper at the Pentagon. We ran into people I knew, walking briskly and purposefully to meetings, papers and folders in hand, the occasional briefcase. She ran into people she knew. The Pentagon was like that. It seemed that sooner or later, if your career lasted long enough, you'd end up here, and your past associates would be waiting to greet you.

I introduced her to a colonel I'd worked with at Ramstein. He stopped to chat. He was always a jokester and somewhere in his update of what he'd been doing, he came out with the chestnut: "So I won a week's vacation in Philadelphia. Second prize was two weeks." One of the things about the rank ladder is that you're expected to appreciate the humor of superior officers, so we tittered politely.

Eventually, he glanced at his watch, then went scooting away as flustered as the White Rabbit in Wonderland. (At the Pentagon, even full-bird colonels are outranked by a lot of people.) We continued on. I scrambled for something to say. "So, where are you from originally, Roxanne?"

"Pennsylvania."

"Ah." A pause while I considered the possibilities. "Not Philadelphia by any chance?"

She stopped, put her hand on my arm, lifted her face to the ceiling, opened her mouth and expelled the biggest laugh I'd ever heard. It boomed, bouncing against the staid walls, rolling down the hallway. Everyone in sight stopped whatever he or she was doing and looked up, smiling, as if the sun had made its way into the windowless hall.

"No, seriously," I said trying to pretend that I wasn't as funny as she made me feel.

"Bethlehem," she said and laughed again. I swear those laughs must have filled all seventeen miles of corridors and left fragments buried in the walls. I picture them leaving only after the plane crashed into the building and unescorted visitors were no longer welcome.

Roxanne was our Carrie, the heart and soul of our little group. Our boss used to say, "There's nice, and then there's Roxanne-nice." We all knew what he meant: not the bland passivity of ordinary niceness, but active, vital love for others. She scattered joy with huge, generous guffaws. Never a *sweet* person, with all the treacly associations that word implies, she was gritty, not afraid of the things of the earth, a warrior in her own right with a goodly store of righteous anger. Her being born in Bethlehem (albeit Pennsylvania) sometimes seemed to me like a cosmic wink.

Tina and I started the coffee thing as an afternoon break to sip what the boss jokingly referred to as our "foo-foo" coffee from the

Pentagon's coffee bar. Roxanne soon joined us. After Tina was reassigned to California, Roxanne and I began to switch our coffee to mornings before settling in to work. Gradually, the sometime thing became a morning ritual: coffee out in Ground Zero where I had my first cigarette (okay, first two) of the morning.

Roxanne didn't smoke, never had, but she only broached the subject with me once. "When are you going to quit?" she said.

"After I retire. I'm afraid I'll put on weight if I quit. The Air Force is much nastier to you if you're overweight than if you smoke." I spoke as casually as I could. She nodded and never mentioned it again. Slim and comfortable in her body, an inch or two shorter than me, she could see—anyone could—that I hovered close to being overweight. I never told her about the official struggle I'd had with my weight. I could have, I knew. She would not judge. But I was too ashamed.

Spring, summer, fall, all beautiful days with dry mornings, we took our coffee outside under the trees. Then one day in November, I arrived to work on a chilly, windy day. The kind of day in which only the diehard smokers (morbid pun intended) would brave the bluff outdoors, damning the Surgeon General the whole time. Glumly, I lingered in the office, feeling the beginnings of grief. Roxanne would show up in a few minutes for our coffee together. But without the cigarette breaks outside, there would be no reason not to head back to our separate offices. That is, for Roxanne to head back. I would still need that morning cigarette. I saw myself entering a long, gray, cold period of shivering by myself outside.

*It's natural*, I told myself. *To everything there is a season.* I resolved to be brave and cheerful about it. But when Roxanne walked into the office, she wore her heavy Air Force winter coat, buttoned up to the neck. She held the regulation white scarf and black gloves in her hand. All fall and winter, Roxanne shared smokers' exile with me, the two of us shivering outside in wind and sometimes snow, holding umbrellas in the rain.

Of everything I miss about those days, the three main things are coffee with Tina, walking with Sue, Ground Zero with Roxanne.

I could count my years in the Pentagon by the officers who worked as the DACOWITS liaison. It was a one-year position only. First Roxanne. Then Judy. Then Susan. Finally Bernadette. Established by Secretary of Defense George C. Marshall in 1951, DACOWITS stands for the Defense Advisory Committee on Women in the Services. It provides oversight on how the military services utilize and treat women in their forces.

DACOWITS has done and continues to do wonderful things to support women in the military. But in the late nineties, our office seemed to spend too much time responding to the demands of those few committee members who fell into one of two extreme categories: some were effectively hostile to women in the military; others so pro-woman their impact was often counterproductive. Too many failed to understand that the sensible regulations required to maintain a cohesive war-fighting machine couldn't be jettisoned to give women special treatment.

Out of all of them, I think we found most frustrating working with the committee members who were trying to make military life more comfortably feminine. They made our position as women in the Air Force more tenuous. With constant demands for data we didn't maintain (absurdities along the lines of how many women in the service had twin children and how did their career path track with those of men who had twins) or its outrageous recommendations, like having women automatically granted time off during their periods, sometimes it felt like some DACOWITS members were looking for ways to make us "other" again.

Not that, as individuals, women did not experience problems. Those of us in the support career fields at least felt firmly entrenched in our military branches, vital to the mission, equal members of the team, accepted and valued. But I knew that life could be more difficult in traditionally male career fields, like security police and aircrews. But by the late nineties there were few systemic discriminations, and women at approximately 20 percent of the active Air Force were a fact of life. At that time, even fighter aircraft were opened up to women.

The fighters were the sexy planes, the sleek sports cars of the air. Most pilots wanted a fighter. Normally weapon system choices were handed out by giving the highest scoring graduates from UPT (Undergraduate Pilot Training) first choices, but women had long been restricted to carriers, trainers, and tankers. Then bombers were opened up to them (the rationale being, I suppose, that bombers stay well above the conflict—and there's plenty of other crew on board if a woman should develop hysterics). Finally, in the late nineties fighter jets were opened to women.

That year, a woman graduated top of her UPT class and got first choice of weapon systems. She chose the fast, mean F-16 Falcon. The press slobbered all over the story, doing its best to generate conflict. They found plenty of whiny second-raters to complain about the women receiving what they confusedly seemed to consider preferential treatment.

Then I read an interview with one brand-new, male pilot who was asked by an eager reporter, "How do you feel about women taking fighter jets away from the men?"

He responded, "For years, men took the women's fighters away, and no one noticed. I congratulate this class of women pilots, who are finally receiving the aircraft they've earned."

I hope this young lieutenant is now rapidly working his way up to general officer.

Flying the fighters definitely put women in the role of combatants, still a controversial issue. As a squadron commander, I had to take a course on dealing with the media. During a fake TV interview with an Air Force public affairs officer pretending to be Diane Sawyer, she asked me, "Do you think your parents are prepared to see you come home in a body bag?"

I had no prepared answer, just a gut response. "No. But I don't think they're prepared to see my brothers come home in body bags either."

The instructor called out, "Cut! Good answer." The camera stopped. I stepped down from the dais and joined the other students. While the instructor talked about the power of a pithy sound bite, I thought about the question. It wasn't an unlikely one for a woman officer to be hit with. It had been the big concern since women were first integrated into the military services. The media had piously asked if the American public was prepared to have their daughters killed in wartime. They still ask it.

But the concern about women in body bags is specious. Women have participated in war for centuries. We've served as spies, as nurses and doctors, as instructors. We've cooked, ferried planes, provided support and entertainment. But whether active participants or not, women have always died in wars. Often we've been bystanders whose only crime has been an inability to get out of the way of armies. We've been raped, kidnapped, enslaved, massacred. We've been taken prisoner. We've been tortured. Woman as victim receives a grudging acceptance, just part of the natural order of things.

We often hear the pious precept about the willingness of military members to give up their lives for their country. Unspoken is the harsher truth: what makes the military unique is it exists solely to exert lethal force, and all its members must be willing to take the lives of others. To many it seems by definition "unwomanly." What truly makes the press, the politicians, society in general uncomfortable is the idea of woman with weapons. Woman as fighter. Woman as killer.

After a year at the Pentagon, I was promoted to lieutenant colonel. We held the pin-on ceremony in the large DP conference room. We'd kept a few chairs for guests of honor (primarily family members) but otherwise cleared out the space for coworkers and friends to stand in. The long conference table shoved toward the wall held refreshments, the standard cheese-and-vegetable trays, the ever-popular shrimp with cocktail sauce, punch, and wine. The thirty or so guests who had to stand shuffled back and forth, eager for the ceremony to be over and the snacking to begin.

I stood in front of them after most of the official, solemn parts were over. Silver oak leaves replaced the gold leaves I'd worn as a major. The floor was open for me to speak. Traditionally, this was the time for the promotee to humbly thank bosses, commanders, coworkers, staff, family, spouse for their assistance—all of which I did—before closing with a few pious unmemorable remarks about what a great country we live in. This I did not do. I never liked trivializing sentiments that should be deeply felt but seldom expressed.

I hadn't prepared a speech at all, but it wasn't in me to release a captive audience while I had the chance to talk uninterrupted. I looked around for inspiration. Lynn beamed at me. My stepsister Barb was there, glowing with the aura of our parents. Cathy and her husband sat directly in front of me, with baby TJ asleep in Cathy's arms and seven-year-old Stanzi looking around at the flags and uniforms with frank curiosity. She started when I called her name and took on that guilty kid look: *I must have done something wrong, but what is it?* I beckoned her to come forward, to stand next to me, and she did, slowly and warily. I stroked her long, blonde hair, then placed my arm around her shoulders. In the pictures, I'm pointing at her while she looks uneasy, a little frightened. We look like we're standing on an auction block, my mouth open as if I'm calling, "How much am I bid for this sturdy child?"

What I actually said was, "When I was Stanzi's age, my parents could never have pictured this event in my life. This—being in the Air Force, reaching the rank of lieutenant colonel—would have been inconceivable to them. It was so beyond their frame of reference." I talked about the changes that had brought the military to this point. I looked in front of me where men and women stood side by side in uniform and no one considered it unusual. All the while

I spoke, I shook in my highly polished plain black pumps, afraid they'd find out I was an imposter and run me out of the building. Shamelessly I held on to Stanzi, using the confused child as a prop (in more than one sense).

After the ceremony, Roxanne helped me wheel the leftover food and drink on a cart down to where Lynn and the others were waiting with the car. We loaded everything into the trunk. When we straightened up, Roxanne smiled and saluted me, her pride obvious at being the first major to offer me a salute. I remembered feeling the same way, saluting Mary in the parking lot at Carswell. I returned the salute and the smile. If Roxanne thought I was a real officer, who was I to deny it?

One early spring day in 1999, enjoying a solitary cigarette in Ground Zero, I saw a couple of officers I recognized from the Air Staff's Crisis Action Team (CAT). The CAT, windowless, underground and depressing, monitored our Air Force activities around the world. I'd only recently been released after a week of night-shift duties as the Personnel representative in the CAT. As part of NATO, the Air Force was performing bombing raids to convince the Serbs to leave the ethnic Albanians of Kosovo alone. It was a short campaign with few Air Force casualties. There'd been little work for me—which in the big picture was a good thing, but in my narrow, selfish little picture, sucked. Twelve hours with nothing to do but fight my body's desire for sleep made a night shift feel like eternity. And I'd just dragged myself through seven of those eternities back to back.

But now I'd returned to my normal daytime schedule. Out enjoying a spring morning on a cloudless day, I could almost forget the CAT if it hadn't been for the briefing I'd sat through two nights before. We'd received a lengthy update about the progress of the campaign, with a number of general officers and high-level civilians crowded into the darkened briefing room, looking at charts and graphs and grainy satellite imagery of the air strikes. One of these showed a blip travelling across a vague structure, apparently a bus crossing a bridge. Halfway across the bridge, a sudden flash, and the blip, the bus, was gone. "Now let's see that again," the colonel said. "Notice how—" Then he said something in Ops speak I neither understood nor had any interest in. He showed it again and then again, while some of the officers hooted and yelled "Bam!" or some such when the bus disappeared in the flash. As if it were all just a video game.

This disgusted me in a way that bombing the bus didn't. I'd come to terms with the notion that some things were worth fighting for, dying for, and even killing for. But death and destruction should be dealt out somberly, with sad dignity, like the American Indians apologizing to the prey they killed. Not this juvenile whooping and laughter.

In the bright sunlight of Ground Zero, I saw two of those officers again from the CAT briefing. They'd been among the worst of the offenders that night. Even now they carried on, loud and raucous, their conversation full of the "nuke 'em till they glow" talk I detested. I got up from my bench and started to leave, when a movement caught my eye.

From the edge of one of the tunnels that opened out into Ground Zero, a duck appeared. She moved out from dark shadow into the narrow sun-dappled lane that connected the tunnels. I waited to see if it was *the* duck. Every year she (or an identical duck—who can tell?) nested somewhere in the tunnels and eventually made an appearance, leading a brood of newly hatched ducklings.

Sure enough, this was it. She waddled out, disdainfully ignoring the military uniforms and suits milling about, and behind her came the babies. I counted eleven, wobbling on uncertain webbed feet and quacking nonstop. Everyone around me paused to watch the ducks. The babble of voices fell silent. Even the two raucous officers leaned quietly in their direction. I heard one say softly, "Aren't they cute?" The other murmured something in agreement. They remained quiet until the duck parade had passed. One glanced at his watch, and the two headed back into the building.

*I will never understand these military guys, brutal and tender both. I'm not like them—am I?*

Retirement stared up at me from the bottom of a long but rapid slope downhill. Lynn and I had agreed when we married that I'd retire once I had twenty years in and three years in grade. We were heading that way fast. There was no letup as far as work was concerned however—on the contrary. When my boss left, I replaced him as branch chief and got that Pentagon rarity—a private office. I didn't bother to move into it for a couple of months. It just seemed too much fuss and bother, when I already had enough to do without going through all my files and figuring out which ones to move. Carrying all my tchotchkes in, having my computer files transferred, etc. It was inertia, okay, laziness that kept me in my cubicle in the main office until another officer was assigned to us and needed my desk. But I found out later I'd been credited with modesty and teamsmanship and all the other things military folks admire.

Despite having retirement papers in, I still had to pass the annual aerobics test. It used to be you could pass a fitness test simply by walking three miles in forty-five minutes (for women over thirty like me). I had a naturally fast stride anyway, so I could stroll the course chatting with friends and still pass the test, barely breaking a sweat. I liked those days, but I doubt they did much to improve my physical fitness.

Then this skinny major at MPC came up with a stationary bike test, where you were hooked up to a machine monitoring your heartbeat. It didn't matter whether you could or couldn't complete your time on the bike—only what your heart did while you were performing the test. It was frustrating for everyone. Guys who ran and worked out at the gym every day failed it. You just couldn't control what your heart was doing.

Still, up to now I'd passed the test, mainly due to walking with Sue during the week and Lynn and Maisie on weekends. But a rough winter that last year got me out of the routine, and I failed what should have been my last bike test.

The sergeant who served as one of the DP's fitness monitors was a wiry man named Ben with solid upper arms and a razor-sharp mind. "Okay, you get another chance in a month, ma'am. Then if you don't pass, we have to put you on an exercise program."

I truly meant to exercise harder to prepare, but other things—opera, theater, restaurants, even work—got in the way. So a month later, I failed the test again. *Great, my last few months in the Air Force to be spent showing up in the wee hours for an exercise class.*

"We have to schedule you next week to get a good reading on your baseline," Ben said.

"Again! Why can't you just use this one?" The bike tests were a pain, the ever increasing breathlessness and pounding heart—okay, you can see how I failed it.

Ben shook his head. "No, it has to be a clean reading."

"What if I pass it next time?"

"Impossible." He explained that the test required bringing the heart rate up to a certain point and sustaining it. "We can't get your heart rate up to that point. You enter a dangerous level too soon so we have to abort the test early. It's a physical impossibility for you to pass next week."

I grumbled about it all week but at least there was no point in continuing my feeble attempts to use the exercise bike I'd bought so cheaply from Tina's ex. That last test was the worst, the hardest. It took longer and the pressure got harder and harder. But since I'd already failed, the pressure was only on my legs and lungs; my mind was stress free. I had nothing to lose.

Finally Ben began decelerating speed and releasing pressure for my cool-down. He called one of the other sergeants over. "Look at this."

The two men huddled over the findings on the machine.

"That's impossible," the second sergeant said.

"Yeah, but look!"

"Man. Never seen this before."

What was happening? Was I in imminent danger of a heart attack? It felt like it, my heart pounding like a hammer at my chest walls. Ben straightened up. "Ma'am, you passed."

"I thought that was impossible."

"Did you do anything special? Prepare for it differently in any way?"

I shrugged. "Since I couldn't pass anyway, I didn't prepare at all."

The other sergeant—a fitness expert—said, "That's probably it, ma'am. Stressing out about the test can drive the heart rate up. Just relaxing got you through it."

"I can't complain, but it does strike me as a pretty flawed system then."

He looked shocked. "Oh no, ma'am. It's a very accurate system. State of the art."

# B. COURAGE

Roxanne told me about the lump in her breast on a mild morning during my last few months at the Pentagon. A morning like any other except for the touch of early spring in the air. As we sipped our coffee, she discussed it casually, never one to dramatize things.

"The doctor says it doesn't appear cancerous but they need to do a biopsy just in case."

I wanted to believe it was nothing, so I shrugged. "Probably nothing to worry about then. A cyst or something. I've had those."

A few days later, Lynn and I took a week's leave to go to Florida. As usual Roxanne and her husband Jim took care of Maisie. I forgot about the innocent-seeming lump. When we went to pick up the dog, Roxanne was still at work. It was her husband who told us about the cancer.

She worked all that week, getting everything she could in order before her surgery and an uncertain period of absence. We still began each day in Ground Zero, where we talked casually about the cancer, the surgery. I was all cheer and optimism.

"You'll be fine. Most women recover and lead long healthy lives. My own mother-in-law—she's almost ninety now." I went on and on, determined not to allow for any darker prognosis. Roxanne smiled and agreed.

The last day before her surgery, we had our coffee as usual, but she left after my first cigarette, pleading a lot of work to do. I remained in Ground Zero, smoking, this horrible weight inside me. I was already missing her and resenting her horrible disease because it messed up my coffee mornings. I also felt guilty, as if my carelessness, my forgetting to keep focused on the lump inside her had somehow caused it to be cancerous. All about me.

Later, I closed myself in my tiny office. I stared at policy messages, barely taking in their meanings. I coordinated on plans proposals I didn't read and flipped through emails without answering them. I was thinking of my mother.

That last time I'd visited her while she was still conscious, she lay wearily on the living room sofa one morning, her face lined and thin. She began to talk about how it felt to know she was dying, to face her end.

I'd interrupted her, brusquely. "You don't know, Mom. We never know. I could leave here, get hit by a truck and die before you."

She bit her lip, silent for a moment, then said, "Yes, of course. Life is uncertain. So what would you like to do today?"

I knew I should have let her talk about how she felt, but I couldn't. Not true. I could have but I didn't. And now I was acting the same with Roxanne. I called her. "I know you're busy, but do you have time for lunch?"

We grabbed sandwiches at the food court and took them to my office. I closed the door so we could talk privately. Then I asked her how she felt about the cancer, the surgery, the future. If she was afraid or resentful or grieving. I gave her the opportunity I didn't give my mother.

I don't remember the specifics of our discussion, except one thing. Her sister had told Roxanne, "I wish I could have gotten the cancer instead of you."

"Wow, sisters are wonderful," I said. "Roxanne, I have to confess that, bad as I feel for you, such a thought has never once occurred to me."

I hadn't meant to call it forth, but there it was: Roxanne's laughter rang through my office like the sound of a summer morning. For those few seconds, the ragged regulations, the bulky desktop computer, the loaded inbox, the nasty shadow of cancer, all seemed to smile and wink. It was a measure of her extraordinary generosity that even at a time of fear and illness and stress, Roxanne could reach into her depths, pull out a laugh, and share it with me.

My last two months I had coffee and cigarettes in Ground Zero alone, exhausting myself with thoughts of the work that remained to be done before I could retire, then gradually slinking back into the office to stare at it. I seemed to live in silence those days, though Sue did her best to get me outside (and outside of myself) as spring warmed the afternoons up. With all the work there was right then, we were lucky to have enough time for a walk once or twice a week.

Over the winter, I'd gotten complacent in my eating habits; even portion control had flown right out the window. Pounds I'd lost crept back and brought friends. Oh well, I told myself, I just had to make it to June, when I'd retire. After that I could be fat and out of shape, and no one would care (except me, maybe Lynn, and a world full of thin people with pursed lips).

Six weeks before retirement I had the bad luck to be selected for a random weigh-in. This time there was no squeaking by. I failed it by several pounds. Fourteen years since I'd been on the Weight Management Program and now it loomed again. I couldn't,

I just couldn't. I'd toughened myself up at the idea of an exercise program, but my tough days were fading fast.

Since I was now a lieutenant colonel, no headquarters section commander had control over me, only a general up the chain of command. I went to see his executive officer. I loitered outside the general's office suite, till the outer office was empty of everyone but the exec himself, a colonel. He looked haggard and overworked behind a two-foot pile of folders.

I swallowed the tiny morsel of pride I had left and felt it squeeze its painful way down my gullet. "I failed the random weight check yesterday, sir."

"I know, Cheryl. I've got the paperwork right here." He flourished a sheet of paper, a cold, impersonal computer printout.

I took a deep breath. "I went through this, years ago, sir. Now you know and I know, that it will take at least a month, maybe more, of hospital tests and programs and interviews before I can actually start the program. I'll be retiring by then. Does it make sense for me to spend so much of the time I've got left doing the preliminaries for a program I'll barely even begin?"

He looked at me, looked at the paper in his hand. Then he opened his bottom drawer. "No, it doesn't." He dropped the paper into the drawer and closed it.

My sigh of relief was short-lived. The next DACOWITS conference would take place in Alexandria a few miles away, just weeks before I was to retire. The culmination would be a formal banquet on the last evening. I had planned to attend the conference but forgo the banquet itself till advised otherwise—strongly advised— by my division chief and her boss, a two-star general and one of the highest ranking women in the Air Force at the time. Formal dinner meant mess dress. I tried to remember the last time I'd worn mine but failed. I pulled it out: the long narrow, floor-length dark blue skirt (we called it "flight blue" not "navy"); the ruffled white shirt; satin cummerbund; bolero jacket. I tried the cummerbund first. I could squeeze it around my waist, but the Velcro gave under pressure. The blue band fell to my feet. Not a single piece of the mess dress fit me anymore.

I hated having to spend several hundred dollars to replace it for one last wear, but what must be, must be. With only two weeks till the banquet, I hunted for a mess dress in my size throughout the Washington, DC area, as far away as Langley Air Force Base in the Hampton Roads. The fourteen I was now wearing in civilian clothes translated to a twenty in military clothing—I wasn't surprised I couldn't find one.

I knew my bosses would be there among the bigwigs. They'd notice my absence. I thought of humbling myself before the colonel and explaining my problem, but the shame of it overwhelmed me. It was as much as I could do to tell Lynn that I wouldn't be going to the banquet for literally having nothing to wear, that I was going to have to come up with a last-minute excuse—by which I meant, as he well understood, that I would have to lie. I planned to come down sick the last afternoon of the conference, right before the big event. The colonel would suspect, but what could she do? I was retiring in a few weeks anyway.

I am not a casual liar, but when I choose to do so, I'm nervous enough to try to make my story foolproof. So the exposition of my great lie nibbled at my consciousness (though I confess, not particularly at my conscience) throughout the week of the conference. I felt like I was preparing for a daredevil, life-or-death feat. The last morning, however, when I walked into the ad hoc DACOWITS administrative office in the hotel, I could feel a flurry of panic in the air. Some bigwig had decided at the last minute to attend the banquet with a large entourage, and the staff was desperately trying to find space for them all.

"You can have my seat," I volunteered, not even bothering to make it sound like a sacrifice. They took it eagerly. So I was saved from the act of deception itself, despite having every intention to deceive.

When, a few days later, in a meeting with my division chief and the general, they made a point of talking about how fine the guest speaker at the banquet had been, I caught the curious looks they cast at me. We wouldn't have been seated together, and they might have wondered if it was possible they could have just missed me in the crowd.

"I wasn't there," I volunteered and explained how I'd been one of the people to give up her seat to accommodate the VIP's last-minute request. No lie but not the complete truth either. I could tell by the look on the colonel's face that she thought I'd put one over on her. And that's how I felt. The truth I told seemed like a lie, and an even bigger one for hiding beneath the veneer of fact.

As it turned out, there had been another reason I wouldn't have wanted to go to the banquet even if I could have fit into my mess dress. That last day of the conference, a major in Roxanne's office called me. Roxanne's mother was trying to track me down.

Apparently her follow-up visit to the oncologist had revealed that the first surgery hadn't removed all of Roxanne's cancer and she was back in the hospital for a second one. "Call her, Cheryl," her mother urged me. "Go see her."

Roxanne sounded weak and weary on the phone. "Do you need me?" I asked. "I can come and be there for you. Shall I come?"

She told me not to. Her husband was there. She didn't want a fuss to be made. At first I was hurt that she'd turn down my dramatic rush to stand loyally at her sickbed. But in truth it would have been more of a crawl than a rush, braving DC's Friday afternoon traffic to get from Alexandria, Virginia to Bethesda, Maryland. Roxanne would be conscious of that, and it was like her to spare me. She would tough it through. She was a warrior. Besides, she was exceptionally truthful (no fake illnesses for her) and knew what she needed. Other people's drama, she could do without.

I had seen the general at the conference after my call to Roxanne and thought it appropriate to pass the word on to her, since Roxanne also worked in her directorate. So when I blandly explained about giving up my banquet seat, she looked at me sympathetically. Of course, I wouldn't want to go to a formal dinner after such bad news about my friend. The truth I told seemed even more like a lie now, and one I had dragged Roxanne into.

The friendship that had grown between us in Ground Zero I liked to think had become a legend in the DP community, like a female version of Damon and Pythias without the ultimate sacrifice. Even our bosses used to leave messages like, "Tell Cheryl [Roxanne] to come see me after her coffee with Roxanne [Cheryl]," with no hint of sarcasm.

The weeks that Roxanne was gone, I walked around within a cloud of anxiety and disorientation. I could stop here and imply it was all about Roxanne's health, but truly I felt it wasn't fair to *me*. My last three months at the Pentagon, in the Air Force, everything had changed. Though Lynn and I drove out to see Roxanne once or twice a week, it wasn't the same. That twenty minutes with her every morning at work had fueled me, sent me to work with something like a charge. Now I was finishing my time at the Pentagon without it. If I had known and could have prayed to the cancer gods beforehand, of course I would have prayed that Roxanne not be stricken. But if that were denied, the shameful, selfish truth is that I would have prayed next that the cancer be delayed a few months—till after I was gone.

There were still those who suspected that women were in the military either to catch a man or to catch another woman. They categorized us as one or the other based on size and perkiness. My abundance of one and lack of the other probably put me into the lesbian column, despite my obviously happy marriage. After several weeks of my solitary morning coffees, I noticed a few of the guys in the office eyeing me curiously, even a little eagerly, as if they sensed a luscious, tasty scandal. I imagined them thinking, *So, you and your girlfriend had a spat. Split up, did you?*

Finally one of them asked me as I was heading out the door one morning, "What happened to your coffee buddy? Haven't seen her in awhile?" Beneath the studied casual tone, I heard drooling anticipation. All the men leaned forward, listening intently.

I raised my eyebrows as if surprised. "Roxanne's still on convalescent leave."

The sly look on his face vanished, replaced by shock. "Convalescent leave? What's wrong?"

"Breast cancer. I thought everyone knew."

I heard him stammering something as I walked away. I couldn't resist an internal giggle when I heard Bernadette berate him and the other men. "I can't believe you didn't know that. Everyone in DP knows about Roxanne. Don't you guys pay any attention?"

So I had a slight moment of satisfaction, but it didn't change a thing. Roxanne, still weak, still home or in the hospital, still not here. And with the second surgery, unlikely to return any time soon. The last few weeks passed wearily.

Just two more days in the Air Force. I dragged myself into the office that morning. Each day over the last week, I'd taken stuff home, standing on the street corner waiting for Lynn, while I balanced a box full of pictures in frames, my personal reference books, my calculator, my mug, the paltry personal belongings of a public career. Noon on Friday this would all be over. Two interminable days to handle all the last-minute crises when unfortunately I'd already stuck my give-a-damn mechanism into one of the boxes and shoved it into a closet at home. I looked over the list of things I still needed to complete. Oh well, nothing got done without a hit of coffee and nicotine first. I grabbed my purse and stepped out into the main office.

"Earl, can you check on the status of the chaplains' package this morning? And Vic, don't forget—" The sudden change in Vic's face stopped me; his eyes shifted to something behind me and lit up. I turned.

Roxanne stood there in uniform, wan and thin but smiling, a look that said, *Did you think I wouldn't do everything I could to be back before you left?*

"Go get your coffee," Vic said. "Take your time. We can handle things here."

For fifteen years Lynn and I had been doing things together, and now we retired in a joint ceremony at WIMSA (Women in Military Service to America, a monument at the edge of Arlington Cemetery). We sat on the stage with our individual officiants. My general would retire me first; then an SES-god (as we referred to civilians high in the senior executive service) would retire Lynn.

While the general talked about what sounded like an extremely illustrious career, the things I'd accomplished taken from grossly exaggerated evaluation reports, I tried to figure out what to say when it came my turn to talk. I had plenty of time to look over the people who sat in the auditorium, both civilian and military. Stanzi was there, ten years old now—probably wouldn't work to use her as a prop again. I struggled with how to tell what the Air Force had done for me, how it had shaped me, molded me into someone who belonged in the uniform, even if it wasn't always the most comfortable fit.

*People like stories. Tell them stories.* The thought came to me with startling clarity.

So when the general introduced me and handed the mike over, I began talking about two arrogant lieutenants at Squadron Officer School who taught me about teams. I drew laughter when I concluded, "We never learned to like each other." Then again, when I added with a moue of self-deprecation, "Both of those young men have long since outranked me." They were already full-bird colonels from below-the-primary-zone promotions.

Heartened by audience response, I shifted gears and told them a melancholy story about a young man on a streetcar in Zagreb rendering his strange salute. I talked about what I learned about military service from the look in his eyes. As I spoke, I looked around the audience seated before me and saw people I'd known from almost every stage of my career.

Roxanne sat smiling in the audience, pale and tired from her two cancer surgeries, her husband watching her solicitously. Tina had flown in from California with her new husband, who wore the only Navy uniform in the room. Sue grinned at me; her strength and good sense had kept me going over many a hard day, but now I thought I saw tears in her eyes.

My division chief had delayed her drive to Colorado for a new assignment just so she could be there. Her car was packed; she would leave as soon as the ceremony concluded. Bernadette and the others I'd worked with were there, a good selection from DP.

I saw friends from Croatia, not least of whom were Christine and the U.S. Air Force captain she'd met in C-SPT and later married. My Army boss was there. I'd learned after the deployment that he had delayed a double hip-replacement surgery, in order to do a job in Zagreb he was uniquely qualified for. He'd survived on pain medication, but no one could have told.

I saw Colonel Collins, my support group commander from Ramstein, now a contractor, a "beltway bandit," as we so callously called these necessary people. Why did I never tell him that every day working with him, he'd modeled for me the integrity the military so prided itself on, but which too often seemed like nothing more than a tagline?

Right in front of me sat Linda. Ever since our meeting over dinner at my parents' house, we'd been following each other from base to base, location to location. I thought of the systemic bias in the Air Force when she'd first enlisted and how she and women like her had created the opportunities I had taken advantage of. Twenty-one years ago, I'd visited her in the hospital the day after she gave birth to a daughter. Her law books were stacked high on the table beside her. She had to take her bar exam the following week, and she knew the Air Force wouldn't consider having a baby reason to delay it. Now she smiled and winked at me; her lopsided dimple belied the fact she was now a full-bird colonel and circuit judge for the Air Force.

Next to her, her husband, a Personnelist like me, sat as seriously as the ceremony demanded, but I thought I saw a smile. Near him I saw another Personnel officer I'd worked with when he was accused of a hideous act. He'd refused to take the easy way out by resigning, but had spent every drop of strength he had in a year of messy legal battles. Now vindicated, he sat proudly, displaying his new rank from the promotion that seemed impossible at one time.

At least two friends there battled alcoholism, the bane of the military brought on by stress and cultural acceptance. Each continued to fight and win that battle every day. I knew one of them occasionally lost, then climbed right back on the wagon dazed but determined.

I wished Mary could have been there, but she was far away in Germany, a civilian now working for NATO. She spent months at a time, not in comfortable Zagreb but in battle-weary Sarajevo. I longed for Captain Peck and Lee and Stacie and Major Cantore, Colonel Starr and Colonel Boston, all the people who had helped me reach this day. The most important person sat there on the stage: Lynn looked proudly up at me from his chair, so dignified in his dark suit, his face still so youthful and unlined. I smiled and began wrapping my speech up with thanks to Lynn for the incredible support he'd given me. But he and I would be moving on together, so I saved my last tribute for all those people in uniform.

"Finally, for you, my fellow members of the United States military, I salute you." I slowly but precisely brought my right hand up in one unhesitant line from the elbow, fingers pressed together. I rendered my sharpest salute, while my eyes slowly filled with tears.

How awed I was by them all, by their courage—that quintessential military virtue I had seen them demonstrate day after day. As I dropped my salute, I thought, *I will never again be surrounded by so many brave men and women.* I felt so fortunate to have been part of this company. It occurred to me suddenly that perhaps God doesn't always speak in a clear, booming voice, but in the low nagging buzz of an insect.

Later, leaving the building, I put on my hat for the last time—by now a narrow flight cap. The silver oak leaf on the front left side was attached by pins pushed through the stiff fabric and held in place underneath by two metal frogs that chafed my temple. I smiled to remember one time when I'd put my hat on backward as a second lieutenant, how embarrassed I'd been.

It was midafternoon when we got home, a hot June day. I quickly changed into shorts. Then I considered the uniform items I'd hastily doffed, which lay strewn across the room. I put the plain, sensible black pumps in the closet with my other shoes. I picked up the light blue blouse and removed the dark neck tab attached with Velcro beneath the collar. I began to unbutton the epaulets at the shoulder so I could slide off the blue covers with their fabric rank insignia. Then I hesitated. My hand hovered over the epaulets for a moment, then I rebuttoned them with the rank still on.

I placed the blouse on a sturdy hanger. I buttoned it and attached the neck tab. I left on my plastic nametag, neatly centered between the shoulder seam and the button holes. I picked up the blue skirt lying crumpled on the floor. I clothespinned it to the hanger and tucked the shirt bottom into it. I threaded the dark blue web belt through the belt loops and tightened it to provide the hint of a waist. I fastened the shiny metal belt buckle. I found my discarded flight cap and tucked it beneath the belt.

Over the blouse and the skirt, I draped the dark blue suit jacket I'd removed in the hot car coming home. Pieces of metal shone from it: rank, the Air Force insignia, the simple letters U.S. Four proud rows of ribbons brightened the left breast of the jacket. The new Meritorious Service Medal I received at the ceremony hung above them, a bronze-covered medal dangling from a magenta-and-white striped ribbon. I encased it all in plastic and hung it away in the guest room closet.

Since I retired, my mind has gradually forgotten details it collected over my career. My body remembers though. I still carry my purse over my left shoulder and lug shopping bags in my left hand, even though my right hand no longer has to be free. My body remembers how to walk, which foot to step out on, the swing of the arms; the stance of attention as the flag passes; the smooth arc of the salute.

I still dream about the Air Force. I dream that I've been called back from retirement to perform duties I no longer understand. Always in my dreams the uniform refuses to fit (which is nothing more than realism now) or I forget to wear it. I show up in jeans or pajamas or underwear, or nothing at all. Most commonly what I forget is my hat.

# EPILOGUE

September 12, 2001, I drove past the Pentagon on my way into Washington. Smoke still billowed from the crash site. Through it I could see the glint of the plane and figures in bulky coveralls fighting stubborn outbursts of flame. I didn't expect the sudden sensation of being kicked in the chest. I gasped for air, then began to cry.

I hadn't worked there for over a year, and I'd already determined that everyone I knew was safe. So I wasn't crying for friends, or for the unknown victims, or even for my country—not yet. I cried for the building, its concrete and mortar and glass, its perfect beauty maimed with that great gaping wound. The trees and benches in Ground Zero. The ducklings. Even the CAT. I cried for the Pentagon itself.

Roxanne and I, drinking coffee in Ground Zero, had frequently seen planes passing overhead and once or twice spoke of the possibility of a crazed pilot suddenly diving into the building. Just casual chitchat. It never occurred to us that someone would actually do such a thing, especially that it would be part of a conspiracy of terror. So it also didn't occur to us that if it ever happened, this country would change dramatically. That, from being secure and welcoming, we would adopt distrust, fear, and exclusion. That we would begin to fight wars so different from the Cold War Roxanne and I had known, different even from Just Cause and Desert Storm and all the other nicknamed skirmishes of the past few years. That the Pentagon I loved would stop welcoming me and would barricade itself behind suspicion and security.

My last year in the Air Force, a letter to some newspaper's editor had made the rounds of the Pentagon, passed around like a virus. In it, a civilian woman inveighed against the military, the drain of the nation's resources it represented to her, the evil it devised. I couldn't entirely disagree with her letter, no rabid rant but well expressed, calmly reasoned. She made some good points. The military in tandem with the political structure can do really awful things; wreaking havoc is part of the job description. So if this woman wanted to lambaste the military for the atrocities in which we have all played our parts, I for one wouldn't have blamed her. But I probably wouldn't have taken much notice either. Such letters frequented the editorial pages.

What made this one so shocking was the calm decisiveness of its conclusion: *I would rather see this country overrun and conquered by an enemy force, subjugated to an enemy power, than see my son or daughter in uniform.*

After I read it, I passed the letter on to the major next to me with no comment. I didn't have the heart to say anything. He read it and handed it to the next person. It traveled around the office, shocking everyone into silence. There were a few attempts at discussion but our sentences went unfinished, our indignation fading into bleak discouragement.

It's been over ten years since the terrorist attacks, and I think sometimes of that letter to the editor and the woman who wrote it. I wonder if she joined the other American voices eager for war after 9/11. We have been constantly at war since then, easy wars, the kind other people's children fight. A different 1 percent of the population.

In Gilbert and Sullivan's *Pirates of Penzance*, cheerful young women perform a rousing number addressed to a force of terrified constables going off to battle the pirates. It's sung to a martial beat, meant to send the quaking men off eager to fight. The lyrics include verses like:

*Go to death and go to slaughter.*
*Die, and every Cornish daughter*

*With her tears your graves will water.*
*Go, ye heroes, go and die.*

*Go, ye heroes* . . . We send them off with rousing songs and promise them glory and gratitude. We now, as the popular saying goes, "honor our men and women in uniform": the others who fight our enemies at a distance, while we shop and kvetch about politics and forget for weeks at a time that we're at war.

Out of the Air Force for twelve years now, I count myself among those "We." I live in a community that, in spite of a large regional VA hospital, has little involvement with or awareness of the military. At one time, so caught up in the fascinating retirement hobby of redefining myself, I felt at risk of forgetting who I was, who I had been. So I began to write. I wrote to rediscover myself as an Air Force officer—or maybe just a civilian who disguised herself as an Air Force officer for twenty years, with varying degrees of success.

To most of the people I know here, the Air Force is less an organization or even career than it is a place. An exotic, foreign country with its own language, outlandish customs, peculiar inhabitants. They respond to my tales of the Air Force with the curiosity of people watching a documentary about isolated, primitive tribes. *Couldn't you just tell your boss no? You had to work while you were in a gas mask? But at least you got paid overtime, right? So, what's with all that saluting?*

In a writing class, when I wrote about how the Air Force reminded me of a Bruce Springsteen quote ("This is the land of peace, love, justice . . . and no mercy"), one of the other students circled the word "love" in heavy, black ink. In the margin, she wrote, *LOVE????!!!!* Big and bold and to me, obscene. I might have understood if she had questioned the word, "peace," but her certainty that love and the military couldn't coexist shocked me.

The Air Force taught me to love, gave me the courage it takes to love family, friends, spouse, and all those important others: the person working next to me when the pressure was on; the face blurred behind the gas mask; the flyer whose dreams were haunted by innocent victims; the guy at the desk across from me; the gal at the noisy rock concert; the jerks who gave me a hard time but also a hand when I was ready to give up; the strangers I met for a few minutes in a streetcar.

And so I wrote this book. A love story.